COWBOYS, GENTLEMEN, AND CATTLE THIEVES

COWBOYS GENTLEMEN & CATTLE THIEVES

Ranching on the Western Frontier

WARREN M. ELOFSON

McGILL-QUEEN'S UNIVERSITY PRESS
Montreal & Kingston • London • Ithaca

ISBN 978-0-7735-2100-1 (cloth)
ISBN 978-0-7735-3252-6 (paper)
Legal deposit fourth quarter 2000
Bibliothèque nationale du Québec

Printed in Canada on acid-free paper
First paperback edition 2007

This book was first published with the help of a grant from the Humanities and Social Sciences Federation of Canada, using funds provided by the Social Sciences and Humanities Research Council of Canada.

McGill-Queen's University Press acknowledges the financial support of the Government of Canada through the Book Publishing Industry Development Program (BPIDP) for its activities. It also acknowledges the support of the Canada Council for the Arts for its publishing program.

Canadian Cataloguing in Publication Data

Elofson, W.M.
Cowboys, gentlemen and cattle thieves: ranching on the Western frontier
Includes bibliographical references and index.
ISBN 978-0-7735-2100-1 (bnd)
ISBN 978-0-7735-3252-6 (pbk)
1. Ranching – Canada, Western – History. 2. Frontier and pioneer life – Canada, Western. 3. Canada, Western – History. I. Title.
FC3218.9.R3E46 2000 971.2'02 C00-900350-9
F1060.9.E46 2000

Typeset in Palatino 10/12
by Caractéra inc., Quebec City

For Betty Lou, Shane, Brett, and Wade

Contents

Illustrations

PHOTOGRAPHS

(All photographs are from the Glenbow Archives and are published with permission.)

Preface

The completion of this book has fulfilled two basic needs for me. The most obvious is the academic one. I have sought here, like so many other scholars in so many other works, to bring to fruition the training and the craft of the historian. I have enjoyed immensely making my way through all the secondary materials relevant to ranching in western Canada, and I have taken pleasure in exploring the valuable manuscripts and other primary resources in the archives. The second need, however, is probably the more important one. This project has enabled me to draw on the practical experiences of a good portion of my own life and to apply them in a positive way to historical analysis. I have ranched and farmed in Alberta since I was a child and in doing so have gained insights, sometimes at considerable emotional and economic pain, that I think are priceless. It is my sincere hope that I will be able to pass some of these insights on to readers interested in Canadian agricultural development.

In the process of compiling the information base and preparing the groundwork for this study I incurred many debts of gratitude. I should like first to thank the staffs of the Glenbow Archives in Calgary and the Provincial Archives of Alberta. I should also like to acknowledge the assistance of students at the University of Calgary who in classes, discussion groups, and one-on-one sessions in my office or over coffee, helped to shape and hone my own ideas about the ranching frontier. I am particularly indebted to John Feldberg, Joel Bulger, Donald Petker, and Roderick Martin. Among the experts in the field of ranching history Richard Slatta, Terry Jordan, Sherm Ewing, David Breen, and Simon Evans have all had a profound impact on my interpretations through their own published works but also in discussions and papers at various conferences over the years.

A special thanks goes to Joan McGilvray at McGill-Queen's University Press for crucial editorial assistance and endless patience. Whatever the merits of my work, her input made it far better than it would otherwise have been. Lastly, my wife, Betty-Lou, read various drafts of the manuscript and consistently offered advice on practical and strategic matters.

Introduction

This study focuses on the ranching industry in western prairie Canada from the early 1870s until just before World War I. Western prairie Canada refers to the region that stretches from the Bow River near Calgary on the northern extremity to the American border on the south and from the foothills of the Rockies on the western side, to the Cypress Hills and Wood Mountain districts on the east. Before 1905, of course, this entire region was part of the North-West Territories. The Cypress Hills and Wood Mountains were in southwestern Assiniboia, but the rest was in southern Alberta. The ranching industry was serviced principally by the four urban centres of Calgary, Fort Macleod, Lethbridge, and Maple Creek.

My main purpose is to offer serious resistance to views about the ranching frontier that have gained currency amongst academics and been disseminated to the general reading public. Essentially there are two views of concern. The first is that the frontier environment itself made a comparatively minor impact on the society that participated in the ranching industry. This argument did not originate from, but it has, at least inadvertently, been bolstered in recent years by two major ranching authorities.[1] First, it is implied in L.G. Thomas's seminal work *Rancher's Legacy*. Thomas depicts the families in the High River area as British and eastern members of polite society who looked after their lands with minimal physical effort and spent their leisure hours attending polo matches, grand European balls, and turf club gatherings.[2] Substantial support for his depiction has come from the prodigious research of David Breen. In *The Canadian Prairie West and the Ranching Frontier, 1874–1924*, Breen concentrates on the great ranches that were established on the very large twenty-one year leases provided by the Conservative government in 1881. He tells his readers that "a majority of those who came to the southwest corner of the Canadian prairie … were collectively very different from the American ranch community." They were also "distinct from the larger western farm population with whom they are usually included." These "uniquely Canadian"[3] people were not "frontiersmen" but "representatives of the metropolitan culture of the East and of the stratified society of rural Britain."[4] Their presence rendered frontier forces in general "much less effective" here than in the United States because they "did not seek their "identity in the land." Their "spiritual home was elsewhere and existent technology facilitated continued nourishment from distant quarters."[5]

What thus supposedly developed in western Canada was a high culture transplanted essentially intact from England and the East which, because of its Old World links and its wealth, did not need to adapt to the crude, unsophisticated conditions on the frontier. This picture is painted in present day newspapers along with the other view that will be contested, which is encapsulated in a 1988 *Calgary* magazine article whose central argument is succinctly enunciated in its title – the "Tame West." "Calgary," the article declares, "was hardly the 'rootin' tootin' rodeo that some would have us believe in." Upon the advice of western Canadian ranching historians, the author insists that the city was genteel and refined at the top and law-abiding at every level.[6]

The basic British character that so many of the early ranchers from both eastern Canada and overseas carried with them was crucial to this picture. On this view, it overcame the normally pervasive influence of the environment and relegated it to a secondary role in shaping the new society. "The Canadian frontier was peopled by peaceful, law abiding ranchers, families and government-encouraged colonists ... In this instance it does appear that the inherent British respect for legal authority and desire to perpetuate tradition survived its period of exposure to the destructive influence of the frontier."[7] While this argument had its origins well before the writings of Thomas and Breen, their works have influenced readers to continue to picture a social hierarchy on the frontier dominated by its elite and sustained in a traditional and orderly fashion.

The "tame" image is also a reflection of a widespread belief that certain forces of law and order were at work in western Canada that were missing on most frontiers, in particular those south of the forty-ninth parallel. The most important of these forces was of course the North-West Mounted Police, who moved west in 1874. The Mounties took control of the ranchers and their Indian contemporaries and offered a measure of security and respect for the law never achieved below the border. The police symbolized the government's full commitment to the western hinterland. They spearheaded an extensive, determined, and unrelenting metropolitan influence. As a result, Canadian cattlemen did not have to fight for possession of their land. Moreover, they had to worry very little about the depredations of would-be rustlers. The "single most important function" of the Mounties "after the maintenance of peace and order," says Breen, "was to prevent the killing and stealing of livestock ... on no other frontier was the cattleman afforded such protection."[8]

The fact that the Mounties secured property, this view maintains, did much to create the peaceful environment upon which the ranching industry in western Canada could rise and prosper. Besides preventing theft, it made the blight of vigilantism both unnecessary and inappropriate and also averted range wars between squatters and bona fide cattlemen.[9] In general people learned quickly to look to the law and its enforcement agencies to solve their differences, and violence was "most uncommon."[10] The lease system also receives credit: initially it facilitated a peaceful occupation of the land, and it afforded the dominion government a strong source of control over a fledgling society. After the turn of the twentieth century the lease system also became a vehicle of transition, as authorities in central Canada were able to amend and dismantle it to move into the settlement phase.

The intention in the pages that follow is not to cast doubt on the immense value of the work of Thomas and Breen. They have used the best of modern historical research and technique to break new ground in elucidating a part of Canadian history about which formerly too little was known. A substantial segment of southern Alberta's ranching society is portrayed in Thomas's *Rancher's Legacy*; and its political and economic connections and the network of government policies that helped to stimulate its rise and decline come to life in the pages of Breen's *The Canadian Prairie West and the Ranching Frontier*. Moreover, both historians' conclusions are in some respects well founded. The Canadian version of ranching was somewhat less chaotic and a little more closely watched and controlled by the metropoles of the East and the dominion government than that of the American West. And Breen's central conclusion that the Canadian ranching industry did not merely flow into the North-West Territories as an extension of that to the south is beyond dispute.

The problem is not that these two historians are wrong but that their conclusions have been pushed too far. Because they demonstrate that Old World cultural, legal, and political influences were stronger on the Canadian than the American side, other scholars have deduced that the power of the frontier environment was weak and that western Canadian ranching society had an extraordinarily deep respect for the law. It is those points alone that are contested here through two basic arguments. The first is that while the frontier may have made a less substantive mark in some respects on Canadian than on American ranching, its impact was nonetheless profound.

The second is that while many Canadians may have shown more regard for authority than their American counterparts, they at times behaved in astonishingly undisciplined and intemperate ways. After investigating certain aspects of their lives it is hard to imagine how they could have been less deferential to both legislation from Ottawa and the North-West Mounted Police.

If overall the gulf between the interpretations of current scholars and that presented in this work is not enormous, it is extremely important that it should be bridged. Indeed, until it is bridged modern historiography will not be able to claim to have offered a sophisticated portrayal of early ranching society in the Canadian West nor to have precisely outlined what was in fact "uniquely Canadian" about it. It is time to stop insisting on the absence of factors such as the frontier environment and lawlessness in western heritage. The frontier not only determined to a considerable extent the day to day practices utilized by the ranchers to run, protect, and nurture their livestock but did much to fashion their entire way of life, or culture, in the broadest sense. A tendency towards extra-legal and even illegal modes and measures was part of that culture.

To accomplish the objectives outlined above it is necessary to take a new approach. The mode employed by most historians to date in elucidating the rise and decline of ranching in southern Alberta and Assiniboia/Saskatchewan is what might be labelled "top down." It focuses on the owners and managers of the big ranches on the original closed leases, elucidates their social and political lives, and demonstrates their managerial conventions at the highest level. It also concentrates heavily on federal government policies. This is certainly useful but it leaves out a considerable portion of the story. It neglects the grass-roots of society.

It fails to depict the lives of the cowboys who provided the manpower for the larger spreads, worked the cattle, and were forced regularly to deal, as the elite did not have to, with the natural environment and the frontier. All the big ranches employed a number of cowboys. Initially, as will be seen, many of them had to be brought in from the cattle frontier in the mid-northwestern United States. As time went on Canadian and British workers learned the trade from them.[11] Whatever their backgrounds, it is clear that on many of the bigger spreads where the herds numbered from a few thousands to many, the workers who lived "on the cow trail" and whose job it was to "ride and handle stock" far out-numbered the owners and the managers.[12]

The top down approach also neglects the vast majority of the men and women who took up land on a much less grand scale than the lessee and, because they could afford to hire little or no help, rode

Cowboy at the Canadian Pacific Colonization Company ranch at Queenstown, Alberta (ca. 1900–03)

the herds themselves, and encountered the frontier first hand. There were a good many of these also. A considerable portion moved onto the closed leases at an early date as "squatters," in some cases with the leaseholder's blessing. In 1884 the wife of one leaseholder told relatives in Ontario that "a lot of young men" had got permission from her husband and "fenced in a few acres of land" on his holdings. "It seems a hard life for very little return," she commented, "except that it suits the nomadic nature of the men."[13] It is well known that there were squatters who settled on leased lands without the blessing of the leaseholder and that conflict, and in one or two cases violence, occurred. In 1887 a Conservative spokesman, ostensibly at the behest of the Cochrane interest, publicly announced that "squatting to some extent is being done on the lands under lease to the British American Ranch[14] Company, situated on both sides of the Bow River west of Calgary." The announcement stated emphatically that "the Government will in no way recognize such squatting."[15]

From the mid-1880s, however, government policy increasingly supported the establishment of dense population in the West and, often at the expense of the great ranches, more and more land was turned over to homesteaders.[16] Leases granted after 1884 were not closed to settlement, and squatters other than those on the lands of the first ranches were allowed to become bona fide homesteaders.[17] Moreover, new settlers poured onto the frontier to establish operations virtually everywhere that seemed suitable to agriculture. They arrived in two major waves. First, starting in the early 1890s came what Simon Evans has called "rancher/farmers," who took up holdings that combined 160-acre homesteads with grazing leases that were considerably smaller than those issued in the earlier period.[18] Then began, a few years after the turn of the century, the influx of the homesteaders proper, most of whom initially settled on the 160-acre free grant without lease. Many of the settlers, particularly in the second wave, intended eventually to become farmers. However, in their earliest years when they were preoccupied with building shelter for themselves and their families, they, like the leaseholders before them, allowed their livestock to roam the wilds, fending for themselves most of the time, and they did little or no soil cultivation or plant husbandry.[19] In short, they were ranchers too, and, as will be seen, their significance in the agricultural history of the West is no less noteworthy than that of the lessees.

Presumably, historians have tended to overlook ordinary people in the early history of western ranching, in part because records of them are sparse. Unlike the elite, small owners and hired hands tended not to correspond with government officials in the Department of the Interior in an attempt to influence agricultural policy. They also were not on boards of directors and therefore do not appear in the records of organizations such as the Ranchmen's Club and the Western Stockgrowers Association. And, except for a few like Monica Hopkins near Millarville and Claude Gardiner in the Porcupine Hills northwest of Fort Macleod, ordinary people did not preserve copies of the letters they sent home describing the conditions they were living under.[20] Many of the heads of the great ranches did preserve their correspondence, and consequently in archives such as the Glenbow in Calgary it is the attitudes and assumptions of the Cochranes, the Crosses, and the H.M. Hatfields that are most easily grasped.

There are, however, ways to get at the lives of ordinary people. The diligent historian can uncover events that concerned many of them in the newspapers of Calgary, Fort Macleod, Pincher Creek, Lethbridge, and Maple Creek. The annual reports of the North-West Mounted Police give invaluable glimpses through their accounts of indictments, court cases, and general descriptions of conditions under which it was necessary to enforce the law. Also, L.V. Kelly's 1912 work, *The Range Men*, is a marvellous contemporary compendium of information about ranchers and cowboys of all sorts. Kelly did not

Riders on southern Alberta round-up, 1901

document his sources but, as any scholar who has done an in-depth study of early ranching will attest, nearly everything he has said can be verified in the *Macleod Gazette*, the *Calgary Herald*, and the police reports. Moreover, since the early 1960s, local history societies, historical journals like *Alberta History*, and publications like the *Canadian Cattleman* have been printing recollections and accounts from the past of cowboys, ranchers, and a rich variety of individuals who witnessed the ranching era.

Having said so much about the smaller operators it is perhaps appropriate to close by stating that no attempt is made here to denigrate the elite members of ranching society. Nor are they ignored. No study that purports to elucidate early western Canadian history could possibly overlook the large leaseholders. What I hope is achieved is a balanced account, which provides at least a reasonable glimpse of life from a variety of perspectives. As will be demonstrated, there were "good" and "bad," constructive and destructive, aggressive and passive individuals at every level. The intention here is to present a picture that gives the majority their proper place. Most people did not occupy the stately homes described by L.G. Thomas nor hobnob with powerful politicians who were instrumental in running this and the Mother Country. Many lived with other hired hands in bunkhouses or by themselves in crude shacks with earth floors.[21] When life is seen through their eyes, as well as those of their social superiors, what emerges is something much more clearly moulded by the frontier environment and much less controlled, orderly, law-abiding, and insulated from death and violence than has traditionally been suggested.

COWBOYS, GENTLEMEN, AND CATTLE THIEVES

1
The Ranching Industry: An Overview

The first ranchers in the Canadian prairie West were grazers pure and simple. As in the southwestern American states, including Texas and California, and in Mexico, they ran herds of cattle or horses, or both, which they grazed summer and winter on the open range. They did the bulk of their work from the saddle, watching over their animals and rounding them up at certain times of the year for branding, vaccinating, sorting, and marketing. They did not till the soil, plant crops, hand feed any livestock, or milk any cows. In other words, they were not farmers.[1]

Starting in the early 1870s, a number of men in the southern North-West Territories of Canada kept a few head of cattle for their own meat and dairy supplies and, from 1874, for trade with the North-West Mounted Police and the Native population. The missionary brothers John and David MacDougall began to maintain a small dairy herd near Morley in 1870, which they augmented with beef steers the next year.[2] They seem to have grazed their animals only in the summertime and in winter penned them up and fed them supplies of wild hay, which they had mowed, raked, and stacked the previous summer. A man named Olsen apparently had a "small bunch" of cattle in the mid-1870s which "practically wintered out."[3] However, the first person to attempt to adhere strictly to the traditional ranching approach seems to have been H.A. (Fred) Kanouse. Kanouse originally came to the southern frontier in the early 1870s as part of the whiskey trade.[4] He smuggled in his brew from Fort Benton to trade with the Blackfoot Indians near Fort Whoop-Up, which later became known as Lethbridge. Kanouse soon found his chosen profession a bit too risky for his liking. His clients proved dangerous and sometimes violent, and it became increasingly difficult for him to hide his illegal activities from the Mounties.

Therefore he decided to look for a new profession. He first tried buffalo hunting, apparently hoping to supply the police themselves, and then he went into the cattle business. In 1877 he imported cattle from the American West and in the autumn he turned twenty-one cows and a bull loose on the open range near Fort Macleod. He was joined by John Miller, who came from Montana with a small herd which "he too put out to rustle for themselves."[5] That winter was mild, and both men's cows not only survived but also produced a full contingent of calves in the spring. This was fortunate for them, but it may well be argued that it ultimately led to serious problems. It almost certainly helped to create the impression that even in this northern environment cattle could regularly survive and even prosper without human assistance in winter. This was one of the principal mistakes of many ranchers, and it resulted in huge losses of stock.[6]

Others soon followed Kanouse's example. During the spring of 1878 two traders named George Emerson and Tom Lynch, along with a number of less well-known cowboys and small businessmen, drove hundreds of horses and cattle from Montana into what is now southern Alberta.[7] These were sold to men already on the frontier, the majority of them police officers who had attained discharges from the force to take up ranching, believing they too could successfully graze cattle year round. In 1879 Emerson and Lynch drove a thousand head up from Montana to establish their own ranch near present-day High River where they eventually grazed both cattle and horses. When they dissolved their partnership a few years later, they arrived at a simple but apparently amicable deal: "Lynch took the horses and Emerson the cattle."[8] Emerson then started up the Rocking P outfit which today has become part of the eminently successful Macleay/Blades/Chattaway aggregation.[9] Lynch took the T over L brand for his ranch in the High River district.[10]

At about the same time that Lynch and Emerson moved into the foothills of the Rockies, an unsuccessful attempt was also made at ranching in the high country just north of the American border. George Maunsell, who had taken a discharge from the North-West Mounted Police in 1879, with his brother, Edward, put 103 cattle on the range on the Milk River Ridge. A half dozen or so others followed suit.[11] However, within thirty days all but fifty-six of the Maunsells' animals had disappeared, along with a large percentage of his neighbours' herds. This was blamed on the Indians, who at that point were threatened with starvation as a result of the decline the buffalo, their traditional food supply.[12] As soon as they became aware of their losses, the ranchers went to the local police.

Indian Commissioner E. Dewdney, backed by Colonel Macleod, the commanding officer in the police post that now bore his name, told them in no uncertain terms that attacks by ranchers on Indians would not be tolerated. Much of the "death loss," Dewdney informed a delegation of the ranchers, was undoubtedly the result of cattle wandering back to Montana and of rustling by whites. "If we corral

Cowboys on horseback, southern Alberta, 1910

our stock every night, can we shoot any Indians we find killing them?" the ranchers asked Macleod. "If you do you'll probably hang," they were told. The Maunsells and six of their neighbours drove what was left of their herds across the line to Montana where they felt they would be safer.[13]

The Maunsells returned to ranching in the Canadian West a few years later with a third brother, Harry. Over time Edward was to become "the only absolutely independent 'big' cattleman, who owns his herds with no associates."[14] In 1884 he would take a small lease on the Peigan Indian Reserve northwest of Macleod and then much larger leases in the Grassy Lake and Pot Hole districts. In the meantime the Mounties established herds near Macleod and Calgary to enable the government to supply beef to Native people faced with starvation. By 1880 some two hundred small herds were grazing on the free grass between the United States boundary and the Bow River.

In 1881 the history of the Canadian West altered dramatically with the beginning of the era of the so-called "great ranches." The owners of these operations came intending to set up on a grand scale and to garner what they believed would be immense rewards in this former wilderness. And they expected to do it with as little effort and financial layout as possible. Their objective was to bring in cattle by the thousands, allow them to breed, multiply, grow, mature, and fatten on the open range, and then to market their beef with profitable margins. In their quest to keep costs down to a bare minimum, they intended to do little or no farming because that entailed the purchase of machinery and the hiring of labourers to cultivate, sow, weed, and harvest.[15] They kept telling the government that this land was insufficient in terms of soil and climate to make intensive agriculture, with its large investments in both labour and equipment, economic.[16] Even the numbers of cowboys they hired to drive and tend the cattle on their spreads were kept as low as possible. In the summer when the herds had to be rounded up, treated, and sorted two or three times, one man for a thousand head or even slightly more was deemed to be sufficient.[17] In the winter when the animals were expected to survive largely on their own and unattended, a number of the ranch hands were laid off and the manager, one or two foremen, and a few others looked after the entire operation.[18]

In retrospect it seems amazing that the big ranchers should have thought it appropriate to operate this way. In a land that to them was new and relatively unknown, they turned out hundreds of thousands of dollars worth of livestock to roam wild country with very limited supervision. This, they must have understood, subjected them to much greater risks than operations with only a few cattle to watch and nurture. They seem to have felt, however, that they had some distinct advantages over their smaller counterparts. One of the most substantial of these was the land they selected. With the exception of Emerson, Lynch, and a few others, most ranchers who had come to the frontier before them had established their operations on the lower plains. There the cattle had access to the much sought after "prairie wool," a hard, dry, short native grass that was thought to be excellent for putting weight on stock as quickly as possible.[19] The main drawback of this grass to the big operators was that while its food value was high, its quantity tended to be low. It was adequate to supply the needs of small herds that could graze over large acreages, but it could not produce nearly enough volume for the immense numbers of cattle the big ranchers wanted to run. To attain that volume, they turned to the high country of the foothills, the Milk River Ridge and the Cypress Hills, where the climate was wetter and where taller, more plentiful grasses grew in abundance. These areas, they seem to have understood, were also well endowed with drinking water for stock in a plethora of rivers, streams, sloughs, and lakes and with much better natural protection from severe winter weather. The great ranchers were undoubtedly aware that prairie winters were capable of wreaking havoc on unattended cattle. Some of them had probably heard stories about an experiment with year-round grazing in Manitoba that had seen hundreds of animals freeze and starve to death in two successive winters in the 1830s. They must also have known that in early 1879 blizzards had destroyed a large percentage of the cattle grazing on the prairie near Fort Macleod.[20] The owners of the big spreads understood that the high country had forests, hills, and valleys to shelter livestock from freezing winds that blew across the land at the coldest time of year.[21] They seem to have reasoned as well that the taller stands of grass would normally stick through the snow so that the animals could continue to graze and maintain the energy levels their bodies required during prolonged cold spells.[22] On rare occasions when so much snow fell that it covered the grass completely, the warm chinook winds that were known to be characteristic of the prairie West could be relied upon to melt much or all of it away in time to prevent starvation.[23]

The great ranchers' experiences on the cattle frontier were to fall far short of their expectations. In the years after they became established they saw their roaming herds devastated not only by severe winter weather but by other ills as well, including fire, wolves, disease, and the constant depredations of rustlers. The cattle barons have been viewed as shrewd businessmen with foresight and vision. They have been credited with seeing the immense potential of the frontier and recognizing that there was money to be made. If the government had not decided to turn the grazing lands into farm country, this view asserts, they would have stayed, and their methods of beef production would now be a tradition rather than a mere cultural vestige of the past.[24] On the contrary, large scale ranching was doomed before it got started because the environment it was founded in was patently unsuited to it. The principal enemy of the cattle baron was not the government or the homesteader but a climate, terrain, and social setting that were harsher and more destructive than they ever dreamed. This enemy was almost impossible to tame given the magnitude of their ambitions and the extensive (or unsophisticated) nature of their approach.

The history of the great ranches stands as solid evidence that in an environment such as existed in the southern North-West Territories, big was anything but better. Too much livestock roaming over enormous areas where it could not adequately be protected from numerous perils for the most part consigned the big operations to a short and eventful life span. The rise and demise of the cattle barons occurred with almost dizzying velocity.

The story begins with Captain William Winder, a Mountie who took leave from Fort Macleod in 1879 to return to his home in Lennoxville, Quebec, with grand visions of building an immense cattle empire on the western frontier.[25] Winder's idea was to undertake an ambitious grazing operation by raising capital through a syndicate of wealthy English-speaking breeders in Quebec's Eastern Townships.[26] His enthusiasm must have been infectious as he managed to raise money with little effort. Initially his main setback was political – he was stymied by his inability to secure a large tract suitable for such an enterprise. The Macdonald government was seriously contemplating dense western settlement at this stage but had not considered selling or leasing big blocks of crown land to individuals or corporations. Therefore the legal instruments for securing the land he needed did not exist. To create them required someone with Winder's ardour but somewhat more political clout.

Such a person did come forward. Senator Matthew H. Cochrane owned a leather factory in Montreal that employed some three hundred people and grossed more than $500,000 a year.[27] Cochrane's fortune had been made in leather, but his heart was in the cattle business. At his Hillhurst Farm east of Montreal he had established a herd of high quality purebred Shorthorns, and when he heard Winder's stories of unending, untapped grazing lands in the West, he decided to put together a sizeable operation of his own. His ideas, however, grew more and more grand with time. There is every reason to believe that even at this early date he was feeling the effects of the frontier.

Frontiers, and the seemingly unlimited possibilities they offer to people who want to start over again or begin a new venture of one sort or another, stimulate the human imagination tremendously. Historians have demonstrated this in numerous ways with respect to the Canadian West. Anthony Rasporich, for instance, has shown that various ethnic and/or religious groups have set out to build utopian communities on the prairies.[28] Douglas Francis has pointed out that a host of artists, poets, and writers became so enthusiastic about the West that they constructed a myth about a great new land destined to be more prosperous, more morally sound, and more free than any that had existed in the past.[29] John Feldberg and I have argued that prior to World War I this kind of reasoning helped to draw British and other European financial capital to the wheat fields of the prairies in such large amounts that it brought to ruin thousands of settlers and resulted in substantial losses to a great array of banking and mortgage institutions that perhaps might have been expected to know better.[30]

Senator Cochrane seems to have been subject to the same sort of frontier virus. In the Eastern Townships the largest holdings would have had three hundred head of cattle on perhaps a thousand acres of land.[31] Cochrane eventually decided that he should construct an operation with forty times as many cattle as the biggest farmers in the townships and a hundred times more land.[32] He took a plan to his friend and neighbour, Minister of Agriculture John Pope, that would allow him to lease an enormous tract in the foothills of the Rockies. This plan was laid before Colonel James S. Dennis of the Department of the Interior and then before Sir John A. Macdonald himself.[33] This lobbying brought about an act of Parliament in 1881 that allowed applicants to secure twenty-one-year closed leases of up to 100,000 acres of crown land for a cent an acre per year. It also gave them the right to purchase some of the lease for "a home farm and corral," at two dollars an acre.[34] The leaseholders were to stock their lands with one animal for every ten acres.

Cochrane immediately leased 134,000 acres west of the present city of Calgary and set out to find the more than ten thousand cattle he needed to fulfil his side of the bargain. Eventually, by taking on a total of five leases in two company names, he controlled over 300,000 acres.[35] After Cochrane had paved the way, Captain Winder was able to secure a lease of 50,000 acres of his own,[36] and in 1883 he and his fellow shareholders began operations with 1,200 head of cattle and seventy-five purebred Percheron horses.[37] In 1885 Winder died, and seven years later the ranch was dissolved and its three thousand cattle and seven hundred horses were sold to John Nelson of the Quarter Circle Ranch.

Cochrane purchased his first herd – 6,634 head – in Montana for about $125,000, at the same time arranging for men to drive the cattle north.[38] The drive, bigger by far than any that had previously brought stock to Alberta, took the cattle to his lease on the Bow River. This first lease soon proved disastrous. Severe winter storms and human error wiped out thousands of cattle during and in the aftermath of both the first and the second cattle drives. Cochrane decided to relocate. In 1883 the senator acquired a further lease well to the south, along the Oldman and Waterton Rivers near present-day Cardston. Here it was hoped the winters would be milder. The Waterton ranch, which was given the family name, eventually ran over twelve thousand cattle.[39]

The Bow River lease was transferred to a newly formed Cochrane subsidiary, the British American Ranch Company. Cochrane used his

Cochrane Ranch riders near Cardston, Alberta, 1904

special relationship with the Macdonald government to gain permission to place sheep there,[40] and in 1884 brought in over seven thousand head of sheep from Wyoming and Montana. The winter was mild but hundreds of the animals died, from lambing, prairie fires, and one particularly severe blizzard. Then, to make matters worse, a substantial drop in prices for lamb occurred due to an oversupply in Australia. In 1887 the British American sold its sheep in Alberta for considerably less than they had cost.[41] The lands of the Bow River lease reverted to the crown and over the next two decades were settled by homesteaders or purchased by individual livestock producers.

Senator Cochrane seldom visited the Waterton ranch personally, perhaps because he was preoccupied with his business interests in Quebec.[42] He chose instead to operate through a succession of ranch managers. He also got his sons involved. His eldest son, James Arthur, was a director and shareholder of the Cochrane Ranch and made regular visits.[43] William F. Cochrane, his second son, was made manager of the Waterton ranch in 1887 and ran the operation for eighteen years.[44] About 1900 the third son, Ernest, came out. In 1903 Senator Cochrane died, and two years later the ranch lands were sold to a group of Mormons who had moved into the area and began building the town of Cardston.[45]

Cochrane and Winder were not the only ones unable to restrain their imaginations when contemplating the new frontier. In 1882 three more great ranches were started. These were the Oxley Ranch Company and the Walrond, with 253,934 and 216,640 acres respectively, and the Northwest Cattle Company, better known as the Bar U, which started with 157,960 acres.[46] These three, along with the Cochrane, were what David Breen has labelled the "patriarchs" of the early ranching frontier. At their peak they controlled 40 per cent of the leased land in southern Alberta and owned about the same proportion of the cattle.[47]

The Oxley Ranch syndicate, formed in March 1882, included some very highly placed and well-heeled individuals from England. Its prime mover, however, was a Canadian named John Craig, a veteran livestock breeder from Ontario who was reputed to be one of the finest cattle judges in the country.[48] Craig too caught the frontier fever. He raised some $200,000 for a western ranch from a group of his Canadian friends. He then journeyed to London in search of more capital and met Alexander Staveley Hill, QC, PC, DLC, JP, recorder of Banbury, deputy high steward of Oxford University, judge advocate of the Fleet, and member of Parliament for Staffordshire West. Stavely Hill persuaded Craig to drop his Canadian investors in favour of English gentlemen whom he claimed could come up with a great deal more money. A syndicate was formed in which Stavely Hill became the largest shareholder. Craig also enlisted Lord Lathom, earl of Lathom and head of a family called Wilburgham or Wilbraham in Lancashire and Cheshire that was able to trace its origin to the sheriff of County Cheshire in the reign of Henry III (1216–72). Lathom owned what was a gigantic amount of land for Britain, some eleven thousand acres, and he was also an avid cattle breeder. Like Cochrane, he was quick to seize the opportunity to be a major shareholder in a frontier operation that dwarfed his existing holdings.[49]

Despite the social standing of its main investors, the Oxley's history was coloured by faulty management and half-hearted financial commitment. Much of the problem seems to have been Stavely Hill, although it is difficult to get an unbiased account.[50] He initially travelled to the West with Craig, acquiring one lease near present-day Stavely and further tracts of excellent grazing land in the foothills to the northwest of the original lease along Willow Creek. As the principal shareholder, Stavely Hill was supposed to ensure that the ranch had sufficient working capital. However, he seems to have failed to understand how much money such a large undertaking required and must have been hampered by the impossibility of regular communication with Craig, who was in charge of day-to-day operations. In the first few years the cattle numbers rose to something like eleven thousand head, but many of them had never been paid for. Twice animals the Oxley had acquired on agreements of sale in Montana were seized before they could be moved north, and in one

Walrond Ranch round-up riders, 1903. Dr Duncan McEachran on far left

case some of them were sold to cover unpaid debts in the state.[51] On another occasion proceedings were started to seize the Oxley property in Canada. Only a last minute infusion of cash from the directors stopped them.[52] In 1885 a young American rancher named Frank Farmer, who was owed a great deal of money for cattle he had sold to the Oxley, froze to death during a snowstorm while travelling north to collect.[53] Craig conducted a bitter feud with Stavely Hill in an attempt to get sufficient capital sent from England to operate properly. At one point Lord Lathom reprimanded Stavely Hill. Craig "severed his connection" with the Oxley in 1885 and was replaced with Stavely Hill's Australian nephew, Stanley Pinhorne.[54] Pinhorne was a respected cattleman but he had little more success than Craig, which may have contributed to his untimely death. He became a heavy drinker and seems to have suffered from depression. In 1892 his lifeless body was found in his bed at the ranch. There was a bullet hole in his head and his gun was still in his hand.[55]

After Craig left the Oxley he took out his own lease in the Macleod area. In 1903 he published a book about his experiences with the Oxley in which he blamed his elite English colleagues for all the ranch's difficulties.[56] Later the same year the Oxley was sold to stock dealer William Roper Hull.

The Walrond Ranch was organized in 1883 by Duncan McEachran, then the Dominion veterinary director-general.[57] McEachran came west as the general manager of the operation. Most of the capital came initially from Sir John Walrond and other British investors. The company leases were situated along the Oldman River and into the Porcupine Hills to the northwest of Fort Macleod. The first foreman was an American named James Patterson who was experienced with ranching in a frontier setting,[58] and the company at one point claimed to have over ten thousand cattle and five hundred horses.[59] It is reputed to have made money at least in the early years. Between 1883 and 1895 it "paid eight dividends of 5 percent and one of 7 percent."[60]

These dividends, however, appear to have been the result of unrealistic accounting by the directors. On a cattle operation, profits (and therefore dividends) depend on the value of the livestock. Because in the early years cattle were left to wander on the open range, it was extremely difficult for owners, managers, and cowhands to get a clear estimate of the number, quality, and weight of their herds. It seems astounding to the modern rancher that the Walrond went for years without ever taking a thorough count of the livestock. Dividends were paid on estimated rather than actual values which were often inaccurate. For instance, in the 1890s the management estimated death losses at 5 per cent per year. As it turned out, this was far too low.[61] Disasters such as bush fires, harsh winters, and disease cut deeply into the Walrond's inventory in the 1890s and early in the twentieth century.[62] In 1895 one of its leaders announced that the English shareholders "have determined to quit the business ... the affairs of the company will ... be wound up as quickly as possible ... the returns for the years past not having been what was expected."[63]

McEachran and some of the other shareholders bought out a number of the original shareholders in 1898, but their luck did not improve. In the terrible winter of 1906–07 the Walrond lost more than five thousand head of cattle, and in 1908 its directors sold the ones that were left to Patrick Burns. Much of the Walrond's land then passed, like that of the Oxley, to cattle dealer William Roper Hull.[64] Later it too was leased to Burns.

The Bar U or Northwest Cattle Company was reputed to be the most efficient of the great ranches. Its manager was Fred Stimson, Captain Winder's brother-in-law. He started the ranch and then brought in the steamship magnates Sir Hugh Allan and Andrew Allan of Montreal for financial backing. Sir Hugh Allan, like so many others involved in these big operations, was a man not just of considerable wealth but also of high political standing. He had used his influence to achieve lucrative contracts for his steamship company from the British government to transport emigrants to Montreal. In the early 1870s he had helped spark the celebrated "Pacific scandal" by passing influence capital into the coffers of Sir John A. Macdonald's Conservatives in an attempt to gain the contract to build the Canadian Pacific Railway.

Bar U cowboys on round-up, 31 May 1901

The Bar U's reputation for efficient operation probably began with its very first cattle drive. After selecting his home ranch site at Spitzie Crossing on the Highwood River southwest of Calgary,[65] Stimson began importing his first herds. He brought twenty-one purebred bulls from Chicago and then trailed some three thousand cattle in from Lost River, Idaho, in what was apparently a model drive.[66] The cowboys, led by High River rancher and cattle dealer Tom Lynch and the celebrated black American cowboy John Ware, moved the cattle at just the right speed, coaxing rather than pushing them at a pace that both older cows and newborn calves were able to withstand. As will be seen, losses were negligible, a stark contrast to the disasters the Cochrane outfit suffered from its first drives.

Stimson's good management continued once the cattle arrived on the Bar U lease in September when the trail-weary animals were subjected to eight days of heavy snowfall. Temperatures dropped, and the grass that the animals badly needed to recuperate was covered. As it happened, the Cochrane outfit was undertaking its second major drive and found itself in exactly the same predicament. Stimson, who had years of experience in handling cattle, was prepared to take the advice of his cowboys and allowed the animals to wander south to lower elevations around Fort Macleod where the storm was less severe and where the snow melted as fast as it hit the ground. As a result the Bar U animals managed to find an adequate supply of natural grasses, and only a handful died. At the Cochrane, on the other hand, the unseasoned manager, Major James Walker, listening to the orders of his directorship in the East, ignored the warnings of the cowboys and attempted to keep the animals boxed up on the high country lease. The cattle soon exhausted their food supply and perished in droves.[67]

In the next few years the Bar U built up a herd of over ten thousand cattle and eight hundred horses.[68] George Lane, another veteran cowboy from the United States, arrived in 1884 to be the first foreman. He eventually started ranching and became a cattle merchant in his own right. In 1902 he formed a syndicate with a cattle-buying company known as Gordon, Ironsides and Fares and purchased the Bar U for $220,000 – the biggest sale in western Canadian ranching up to that time.[69] The fact that the Bar U survived as a single unit longer than the other great ranches should not necessarily be seen as evidence of superb financial fortunes. On Lane's death in 1926 all his land and livestock were mortgaged to their full value. Pat Burns stepped in and bought this ranch too.

The history of the original great ranches does not suggest that the secret to success in the Canadian West was bigness. In just over two decades the four "patriarchs" had come into existence, become gigantic in terms of numbers of cattle and total acreages, and then had sold out. They were all taken over by companies involved in aspects of the business other than ranching. Hull, Burns, and Gordon, Ironsides and Fares marketed western beef in eastern Canada and Great Britain. They were middlemen in a frontier where competition was almost totally lacking. Their companies skimmed off a commission on every head of cattle they shipped to the East whether the original owner was making money or not. It may have been useful for them to have access to ranches that kept them attuned to the grass-roots, so to speak, of the industry. The cattle buyers do not appear to have considered the ranches of much direct financial benefit. In 1920 Gordon, Ironsides and Fares agreed with little apparent hesitation to sell all their shares to Lane. It is probably the obligations that Lane incurred in that transaction that put him under the financial burdens from which he would never recover. Hull got out of ranching altogether in the 1920s. Burns stayed in the business until his death in 1950, but he was able to continue to amass his immense fortune primarily as a dealer and through his giant meat-packing firm, Burns Foods.[70]

The same pattern of rapid rise and fall describes the history of numerous other leased operations (as distinct from those of squatters and settlers) on the ranching frontier. In 1888 there were 111 leases covering several million acres. The majority of these, including the big four, ran in a north/south direction along the foothills of the Rockies from the international border to the Bow River valley. There were the Cochrane, the Glengary (or 44) Ranch, the Alberta Ranch, the Circle Ranch, and the Quorn. A smaller block that included the Spencer Brothers from Montana ran east/west along the Milk River Ridge north of Coutts and southwest of Medicine Hat;[71] a third that included the Stair Ranch was situated in the Cypress Hills country centring on Maple Creek.[72] The remarkable vitality with which the industry sprang to life can be seen in the livestock numbers. In 1883 some 25,000 cattle roamed the West. Three years later the cattle population had more than quadrupled and there were 11,000 horses. The leases varied considerably in size but clearly many of the men who took them up shared grandiose visions. In 1884 two-thirds of all the stocked land in southwestern Alberta was in the hands of ten companies and almost 50 per cent of that was in those of the big four. Of the 111 ranches that were leasing land in 1888, some thirty held between 1,280 and 10,000 acres with the rest holding between 11,000 and over 200,000 acres.[73] Today a ranch of 10,000 acres is thought to be big indeed. By modern standards the wide majority of the leased operations in the 1880s were somewhere between big and absolutely enormous.

Nearly all the big operations that sprang to life about this time accompanied the four patriarchs into obscurity. The few that had not been terminated by the end of the first decade of the new century operated under special advantages. Thus the Copithornes, who still maintain their livestock, pastures, and fields west of Calgary, had started not as an enormous mega-ranch but as small squatters on the first Cochrane lease. They became homesteaders and built up their spread slowly. It took generations for the family to accumulate the immense holdings it now maintains near the town of Cochrane.[74] The McIntyres, far to the south on the Milk River Ridge, started in 1894. They had the benefit of years of experience on the American ranching frontier and extensive family financial resources.[75]

A.E. Cross, who got his start in 1883 as a bookkeeper and veterinarian for the British American Company before striking out with his own A7 Ranch at Nanton, continued operations throughout his

Sam Copithorne, Irish cowboy, 1912

life and then passed his holdings on to future generations. However, to Cross ranching was a hobby as much as a business. His money came from a substantial family fortune and from the sale of liquor through the Calgary Brewing and Malting Company, which he had started when prohibition ended in the West in 1892.[76] Furthermore, in the early 1900s Cross abandoned the idea of seeking great ranch status. He kept his holdings and his cattle numbers at manageable levels and in reality became an intensive mixed-farmer rather than a rancher in the traditional sense.[77] Before World War I he ran two thousand cattle on eighteen thousand acres which he isolated from the open range with fences and cross-fences, and he cultivated the land to put up roughage to feed his cattle through the winter. This approach has tended to be much more successful than large scale, year-round grazing in the foothills of Alberta.

In accounting for the demise of the great ranches historians have been inclined to stress political factors. By the 1890s, government policy in Ottawa had shifted away from size of acreage and towards numbers of people and thus towards settlement rather than huge leases. The ranges were then turned over to homesteaders, who criss-crossed them with fences and crowded out the big operations. Notes Simon Evans,

> The [1881] legislation had involved a departure from the ideal of the family farm and was justified by the belief that the "grazing country" was unsuitable for agriculture. This tenet became less and less easy to accept as farms were developed and homesteaders flourished …
>
> The political costs of supporting the ranchers rose as the Conservative government was assailed with increasingly vocal and intense criticism of its range policy. On the one hand, a flourishing industry had been established, which was represented in Ottawa by a powerful lobby; on the other hand, the lease regulations were presented by the Opposition in Parliament, the Territorial Assembly, and by local interests led by C.E.D. Wood, the editor of the *Macleod Gazette*, as an obstacle to settlement.
>
> The government sought to diffuse the opposition by removing the most glaring abuses of the system. Unstocked leases were cancelled, and new leases were to be open to homestead and pre-emption entry. Rental for leased land was doubled, and those who held the original closed leases were urged to accept homesteads and to purchase deeded land at favourable rates …
>
> The situation was brought to the attention of Parliament in 1889 and again in 1891. At this time a start was made on the railway to link Calgary to Fort Macleod. This line ran through the heart of the closed leases and would naturally become the axis for rapid homestead settlement. The government gave notice that the leases would be cancelled at the end of 1896.[78]

This line of reasoning is sound enough in pointing to a major policy shift with respect to the frontier that was necessary for the era of heavy settlement to begin. It makes the transition look a little too straightforward, however, in that it assumes that dense settlement of the West was incompatible with large scale ranching. It is true that from the early 1890s settlers were allowed to take up and fence off homesteads where cattle had once roamed free. But contrary to popular opinion, fences are not the enemy of ranching. Indeed, as will be seen, the big leaseholders themselves had for years been fencing off major portions of the open range in order to attain greater control over their herds. The settlers' fences could have hurt them only if they had taken away pastures and watering holes that were crucial to their existence, and this was simply not the case. And as Evans recognizes in the above quotation, the lessees were all given plenty of opportunity to protect their holdings through purchase. The original lease legislation as well as that in 1892 and in 1896 allowed them to purchase substantial amounts of their lands at favourable rates. After the Calgary Edmonton Railway came into existence in the 1890s, it sold them sizeable pieces of the land that the crown had granted it in the foothills of Alberta in order to finance construction.[79] Also, between 1906 and 1911 the ranchers were given the right to bid on the precious water reserves that had been protected for them over the years by successive federal governments.[80]

The directors of three of the four big ranches, as well as a host of others, took advantage of these opportunities, and by early in the new century their spreads, though considerably reduced in size, were still very large by industry standards. And the owners were more secure and better insulated from political interference than they had ever been. The Bar U held close to 19,000 acres of deeded land, the Cochrane 63,000 acres, and the Walrond, 37,500.[81] As these were based more on freehold tenure and private ownership than lease, the ranchers had little to fear from future government legislation.

There is reason, however, to argue that there was much more at work than mere politics.[82] Breen believes that ranchers sold out when they were able to make a profit on the price of their land resulting from the increased demand provided by hordes of new homesteaders.[83] It could be inferred from this that the ranchers were enticed to forgo the high profits they were making in the cattle industry in order to take advantage of the colossal ones they were able to secure by liquidating their initial investments. But evidence of the litany of disasters that the big ranches suffered makes the possibility of regular profits of any sort for them look remote indeed.

As much as anything else their difficulties derived from their own unrealistic expectations. The rise and survival of small-scale husbandry seems to corroborate this. In the last decade of the nineteenth century there were two clearly discernible developments. First, the livestock man disappeared altogether on the lower plains except from the major river valleys where wind protection and water were available and deeper sedimentary soils produced relatively thick growths of both grass and hay. He was replaced by the wheat farmer.[84] Secondly, and more pertinent to this study, the mega-operations in the hills were replaced by numerous small ranches and mixed farms.

Starting in the 1890s the average livestock operation began to decline substantially in size.[85] This decline is reflected in the available statistics. In the period of 1884 to 1896 which signalled the arrival of the rancher/farmer, the leased area held by the average cattle operation fell from over 30,000 to just under 1,100 acres.[86] From time to time the North-West Mounted Police gave overall accounts of ranches and cattle numbers in specific districts. They indicate that in the Calgary area in 1892, well ahead of the final wave of settlement, there were only five ranches with one thousand or more animals. The Quorn had 7,800, the John Quirk 1,025, McHugh Brothers one thousand, the Northwest Cattle Company eight thousand, and the Samson Ranch three thousand. At the same time there were over 130 ranchers with between nine and eight hundred head.[87] In the Macleod district in 1893 had only four big ranches: Conrad Brothers' Circle Ranch with 11,500 animals, Cypress Cattle Company with 1,900, James Pearce with 1,100, and Browning and Maunsell with two thousand. In that year eighteen Macleod outfits were running between nine and 650 head.[88] In these two districts therefore, there were between three and a half and twenty-six times as many small to medium ranches as large.

That contraction continued as the second wave of homesteaders moved in to take up land based on the 160-acre grant normally without lease.[89] In 1901 Walter Skrine was already feeling threatened by in-migration. He told A.E. Cross that the "prospect of too much settlement makes me think of ... [salvaging] what I have got & pulling out... I have no intention of sacrificing any thing... but this may be the best time to sell."[90] The census reports for individual districts indicate that the country was still sparsely settled compared to what would soon be the case. The number of small outfits continued to increase steadily for two or three years and then began to rise at a much faster pace. In 1901 there were 1,091 rural dwellers surrounding Maple Creek; by 1906 the number had almost tripled to 2,801, and by 1911, it had risen to 18,098. The Macleod area had 4,358 residents in 1901, 13,885 in 1906, and 18,312 in 1911. The numbers for the two Calgary rural districts rose from 3,844 to 14,070 to 15,139 in the same period.[91] A considerable portion of the homesteaders acquired a second 160-acre parcel as soon as they were able.[92] Still their acreages were obviously tiny in comparison to those of the big ranchers, and their cattle herds were also much smaller. Most settlers started with as few as a dozen and as many as several hundred animals. As they became familiar with their surroundings, they adjusted to what the "owned land could support,"[93] and within a few years the average outfit seems to have been keeping around forty or fifty head.[94]

By World War I scores of these small units were family operations. Initially, as with most North American frontiers, young single males arrived in much greater numbers than married men or women.[95] In 1901, 207 of 296 adult men in the Macleod rural district were unmarried, and single males outnumbered single females by nearly two to one. Around Pincher Creek, 168 of 235 men were unmarried and

Woman mowing oats for greenfeed on Springfield Ranch, Beynon, Alberta (ca. 1901)

there were only 83 single women. Near Millarville 209 of 311 men were single compared to 139 of 233 women.[96] Gender balance was not achieved before the war but it steadily improved after about 1906. This suggests that many men took wives and started families.[97]

The movement to smaller scale derived in part from political factors. However, it was also an expression of the ranchers' realization that given the western environment, they were much better able to care for their livestock, improve breed selection, and generally extract a living from the land if they operated on a smaller scale. They moved slowly away from what might be called pure ranching and towards something that would more realistically be described as ranching and mixed farming. Fencing off the open range, they built corrals and small pastures, began putting up hay, greenfeed, and crops of oats, barley, and wheat. They also branched into dairying, chickens, and hogs in quest of the most efficient means of dealing with their surroundings.

As this process proceeded, the West became not only more densely populated but also more complex. Just about the time of the formation of the provinces of Alberta and Saskatchewan, contemporaries were already regularly commenting on the transformation that had taken place.[98] When the Cochrane Ranch sold out, a reporter noted that it was "one of the oldest and best known of the big cattle ranches of Alberta, and its division into small holdings is one of the signs of the times, with the settler and the small farmer forcing the cattle men and the wide open range out of existence."[99] This change altered the complexion of the frontier dramatically and manifested itself not just in the countryside but in urban centres; services and culture began to reflect a larger population base and a more heterogeneous society, both producing and requiring a much greater variety of resources. In 1905 the *Pincher Creek Echo* observed about the town of Pincher Creek on the edge of the foothills to the west of Fort Macleod,

> If [it]... could have been maintained as the residential centre of a ranching community nothing could have been more in keeping ... than the original mismanagement of all sorts and conditions of houses and small shops. But that interesting dream of the Old Timer has had a rude awakening with the disappearance of the ranch and the advent of the farm. We are now making an effort to accommodate ourselves to the change. The shops are being enlarged to meet the increased demands of trade, the houses rebuilt in accordance with the more conventional mode of the inhabitants; attempts ... are being made to decorate residential grounds by means of lawns and trees and flowers.[100]

It is this transformation which the pages that follow describe.

2
The Old World and the New

The western ranching community of the late nineteenth and the early twentieth centuries was to a considerable extent a product of the frontier environment. In recent years historians have increasingly propagated the conflicting view, insisting that the early ranching industry north of the forty-ninth parallel differed from that on the American side largely because its development was more profoundly controlled and influenced by legal, technical, and cultural forces from the East.

It is certainly true that the Canadian West was never as free of Old World institutions as the American. In Canada there were surveyors to provide for a uniform distribution of land, the North-West Mounted Police to impose at least a modicum of law enforcement, and concerted efforts by many landowners to establish and maintain a British and eastern way of life. Accounts of hunters on thoroughbred horses chasing baying hounds across the prairie in pursuit of prey help to illustrate that Old World customs made a significant impression on this early ranching society.[1] In painting such images, however, historians have gone too far. They have forgotten that, in the struggle for economic survival, all the ranchers who actually came out to the West and participated in the day-to-day operations regularly came to grips with the environment and were forced to develop practices and conventions appropriate to it.[2] Because the older societies of Britain and eastern Canada could not equip them for that task, they were forced to utilize a plethora of new skills and techniques. Some of these they devised themselves, but many others they imported from the American West where the ranching frontier had only recently been established and where stockmen were grappling with similar conditions. Either way, Canadian ranchers became frontiersmen, simply because they had no other choice.

Both the conditions of the frontier and the forces of nature shaped the environment to a considerable extent. The forces of nature were, of course, those emanating from the climate, terrain, and ecology. Frontier conditions refer to the circumstances arising from the fact that a new society and economy were being established where they had not existed before.[3] This implies a sparse population base in comparison to what would later be the case, and a stage when single young men predominated numerically over married couples and families. Throughout this period in-migration was still of necessity more important to population growth than natural increase. There was also a relative dearth of almost any kind of facilities. The cattlemen had to build their industry without the advantage of an adequate supply of barns, corrals, chutes, and fences to protect and control their livestock, and also, in many cases, without proper buildings and roads to service their own personal needs.[4] This subjected them and the herds more deeply than at any other time to climatic conditions such as winter storms and drought, to predators such as wolves, and to outbreaks of diseases like the mange. It took a special technique to operate under these conditions. The frontier environment also refers to a time when legal foundations such as the police themselves were somewhat weak and the jails inadequate for establishing and maintaining control over crime. Moreover, conventions such as branding livestock to determine ownership on the open range had not yet been sufficiently sanctioned and/or refined either in law or in custom.

The frontier was also a period of experimentation. Because the society was in its earliest phase, its members were still relatively poorly informed about their new environment. It was necessary for them to experience their surroundings in order to learn what kinds of practices and ways of life were appropriate. This meant that they would make mistakes. In operating their ranches, trial and error told the cattlemen as much about what did not work as what did. The learning process was at times both costly and painful. However, it eventually played an important part in constructing the modern agricultural industry in western Canada.

The power of the frontier was not, of course, consistent. It declined over time as homesteaders and more families arrived, as the ranchers worked at developing the infrastructure they lacked, and as new businesses were established to service human wants and needs. Thus when writing about the condition of the frontier, the historian is describing a period of transition when the crude and unsophisticated circumstances of a new society were being changed and participants inched their way towards something more complex and almost certainly more practical. It was many years, though, before the influence of the frontier was eradicated. Ranchers began building facilities for themselves and their livestock from the beginning, and they soon formed livestock associations – in part to work out all the rules of the industry and get them reinforced in law. However, it was not

Branding cattle, Milk River area, 1912

until about 1910 that this job was anything like complete. Consequently, the period of the frontier can be considered to have continued until just before World War I.

If the power of the frontier in western Canada was not uniform over time, it and nature also were not the only elements establishing and moulding the ranching community. Clearly, Old World political and legal forces played their part in providing the legislation for the initial rise of the cattle kingdom, as well as its decline in the first decade of the twentieth century.[5] British and eastern capital was also crucial as it not only paid for the initial leases but provided the funding necessary to stock the ranches and purchase equipment and construction materials to get started. A traditional culture also made its effects felt on many ranches. On their home site at Waterton, for instance, the Cochranes eventually erected a "fine stone mansion … with green lawns, beautiful flower beds … vines and rose bushes." The family home was furnished "with all the refinement that wealth and taste can suggest." It had a handsome reception hall, open fireplaces, elegant pictures, and trained servants from the Old Country. It was also known to feature a "pianola interpreting Chopin's music with the skill of a virtuoso and even a mocking bird in the conservatory."[6]

This kind of elegance was not attained on most of the ranches. The first homes were usually quickly built in makeshift fashion out of logs and furnished with packing cases for washstands and tables and homemade cupboards and chairs. In due course, however, more stately houses were erected on the wealthier operations, usually in a two-storey Victorian style with balconies and sometimes even stained glass. Their builders made use of the wood that flourished naturally in nearby forests rather than brick and mortar as would have been the case in Europe. Eventually, however, bricks were imported for the chimneys and many interiors were decorated at least in part in the British fashion with Chippendale furniture, fine linen draped over the tables and around the windows, and a large array of ornaments and figurines.[7]

In many cases an Old World flavour developed too in an almost instinctive bowing by those at the bottom of the social hierarchy to what they believed were the sophisticated ways of their superiors. On the North Fork Ranch, for instance, the cowboys who occasionally dined with the owners normally showed respect to the mistress of the house by slipping a dinner jacket over their flannel work shirts before entering the dining room.[8] Many of the ranchers, large and small, frequently enjoyed European social activities; in Millarville, the British immigrants were quick to institute a typical English turf association and readily upheld the convention that deemed the annual races "the social event of the year."[9] Ranching families in a number of communities met friends and neighbours at European-style balls, the most prestigious of which in many peoples' minds were those attended by the British or eastern "elite."[10] There were polo clubs from the earliest days[11] in places like Millarville, High River, and Calgary, and in the Medicine Hat area Major George Ross, who started ranching in 1886, enjoyed widespread acclaim as "one of the greatest polo-players in the world."[12]

Moreover, British conventions were clearly not restricted to the cultural life of the West. They were influential as well in moulding some of the practical day-to-day operations of the ranches. This was particularly the case on larger ones that not only had the connections but also the capital to import British and eastern expertise.

Occasionally such propensities produced interesting results. For example, many ranches employed packs of dogs and used the hunt to attempt to control the wild animals that preyed on newborn calves and colts.[13] H.M. Hatfield, who started ranching northwest of Pincher Creek and then moved south to the Waterton area, periodically recorded in his diary that his staghounds had cornered yet another coyote, or sometimes a wolf, which they would kill or hold at bay for someone to shoot.[14] His hounds were so well trained that he was able to take them on cattle round-ups.[15] The Cochrane ranch too kept and bred hounds and often brought together friends and neighbours to join in the hunt.[16] Because of the time and energy required to kill

Coyote hunt on 44 Ranch west of Nanton, Alberta, February 1906

a single predator, this practice was of relatively minor significance in the overall scheme of things, but it certainly contributed a distinctly British flavour to the Canadian West.

Eastern expertise in animal husbandry was of more practical importance, especially in the horse business. During the short periods when breeders were optimistic about the trade, they sought to provide quality mounts for British customers and some of them imported specialists to train the horses to the standard desired "at home." One of the first and best examples of these breeders was the Bow River Ranching Company.[17] In 1888 the *Calgary Herald* announced that "this year ... [the ranch] will export from thirty to forty head of horses to England. This will be the first shipment of the kind from the Northwest. The company employs Englishmen to break horses for use in Great Britain, thereby adding not a little to their value in the old country markets."[18] Another such ranch was the Quorn, ostensibly named after the Leicestershire village known for a famous hunt.[19] In 1888 the Quorn bred English Thoroughbreds with Irish hunters in hopes of attracting demand from the imperial army for remounts.[20]

It is necessary, however, to be careful not to overstate the impact of Old-World influences through the horse business – primarily because that business was itself relatively minor. Most ranchers ran horses, but few if any in numbers that could compare to their cattle herds. This was mainly because of the market. From the beginning horses were better suited to the ranching methods used in southern Alberta and Assiniboia than most other domestic animals because they can look after themselves under the most trying rangeland conditions. In winter they grow a thick coat of fur and can withstand very cold temperatures. Moreover, unlike cattle, they are adept at rummaging through deep snow to get at the grasses below. The stockmen grazed them year round, did very little or no hand feeding, and tended them largely from the saddle.[21] If the demand had been big enough to sustain a trade comparable to that in beef, huge herds of horses would undoubtedly have emerged on the open range.[22]

However, demand was not big enough.[23] In the early days, notes L.V. Kelly, "Alberta had horses to burn. Everything was favourable to production, but for the want of a profitable market the business languished."[24] Then demand improved somewhat, first as a result of the British need for mounts during the Boer War and then primarily from farmers in the West requiring beasts of burden to work their fields.[25] After briefly reaching a peak in the early twentieth century, however, the market went into a steep decline as wheat became the pillar of prairie farming and competition from steam and then gasoline grew.[26] Consequently, a sizeable horse industry was never sustained for any prolonged period and on most operations the herds remained comparatively small.[27]

Some ranchers also at times imported Old-World technicians for certain specialized aspects of the cattle business. For instance, when they eventually decided to move away from grazing alone and take up grain finishing, they hired qualified Britons to supervise their new, more complex feeding programs.[28] Obviously as well, anyone from the East and overseas who had an agricultural background applied it where he deemed appropriate to the new setting. Much of this he would have to adjust dramatically to fit the conditions of the frontier, but at least it gave a familiarity with basic breeds, their mating habits, their feed requirements, and so on. One of the most substantial ongoing Old-World influences on the cattle industry came not so much in the form of day-to-day practices as through trade in livestock. Firstly, numerous Canadian ranchers invested in British animals in an attempt to improve the quality of their herds. They had been forced to obtain most of their initial stock from the nearby American frontier where the necessary quantities could be found and driven in relatively easily. The main problem with the American cattle was the prevalence of Texas Longhorn characteristics. Many of

Horse round-up on H2 ranch on Little Bow River near Gleichen, Alberta (ca. 1905)

these cattle were tall and thin, did not fatten well, and, because of a light hide, were unsuited to the colder northern climate.[29] Breed selection in the American West had been virtually impossible to control because, on the open range, all sorts of bulls were afforded access to all manner of females. As a result, Longhorn qualities had adversely affected most cattle, including even those whose lineage stretched back to the heavier-set European types.[30]

The prominent Canadian ranchers understood this, and many worked methodically to upgrade their herds by importing breeding stock from overseas.[31] Thus, for instance, as early as 1881 "the Dominion Line steamship S.S. *Texas* ... arrived at Halifax with the largest consignment of cattle ever brought into Canada. Included in the shipment were sixty purebred polled Angus, Hereford and Shorthorn bulls, and two Clydesdale stallions – all destined for the Cochrane Ranch."[32] Along with purebred Hereford, Angus, and Shorthorn cattle, the Cochrane imported less well-known Sussex[33] and Galloway[34] breeds in the search for a hardy type suited to the harsh northwestern environment. The Cochrane's relative success in breeding was also related

Bar U cowboys on round-up, 31 May 1901

to the fact that its ranges at Waterton were isolated and away from most of the scrub bulls that roamed other areas. As the years passed, many ranchers attempted to rise to the Cochrane's standards. The Bar U brought in several shipments of Angus bulls from Chicago as well as Scotland. The Stewart Ranch near Pincher Creek imported directly from Scotland.[35] A.E. Cross spent a fortune acquiring the best British bloodlines for his ranch near Nanton,[36] and F.W. Godsol began upgrading his herd in the 1880s by bringing in pedigree bulls from Ontario.[37] He fenced off four hundred acres on his twenty thousand acre lease and managed to keep his best cows inaccessible to outside animals.[38]

It is evident that the larger operations took the lead in herd improvement, but there seems to have been a general inclination in the ranching community as a whole to work in that direction. In 1893 Commissioner Herchmer of the North-West Mounted Police felt that Canadian quality was so superior to that on the other side of the border that incoming Americans should be forced to sell their own cattle and buy here. "This would provide a good market for our people," he argued, and "would prevent the country being flooded with a lot of inbred cattle, which years of careful breeding would not improve sufficiently to equal our own stock."[39] The overall quality of the herds seems to have oscillated much more than Herchmer thought. However, the effort to upgrade is indisputable. It was also related directly to the British market, which Canadian ranchers were anxious to supply. "Most of the cattle are of the Shorthorn type," the *Macleod Gazette* noted, "good animals for the trade in every way. There are still a good many of the old kind, all legs and horns, but the ranchers are getting out of them as fast as they can, for no shipper will touch them."[40]

British demand for Canadian fat cattle also made a powerful impact on the ranching industry. The importance of that market was augmented by a British embargo on U.S. cattle that had been imposed in 1879 as a means to prevent the spread of disease.[41] It required American cattle to be killed at the port of entry. This gave the Canadian cattlemen an advantage in that they could move their cattle directly inland and have them fed on feedlots for however long it took to regain pounds lost in the long voyage from the prairies. A fear in Britain of pleuro-pneumonia resulted in a similar embargo on Canadian cattle but not until 1891.[42] The Americans purchased Canadian slaughter animals too, principally from ranchers like the Spencers who also operated in the United States and had useful contacts there.[43] However, a 27 1/2 per cent *ad valorem* duty[44] on purchases from Canada made it difficult for Americans to be competitive much of the time.[45] Just prior to the First World War, A.E. Cross informed a buyer from Chicago that for "many years past I have shipped all my export cattle to Liverpool and other English markets through Messrs. Gordon, Ironsides & Fares, and have never had any experience in shipping to your markets."[46]

British and eastern forces thus exerted a strong pull on Canada's ranching frontier, not only on political, legal, and cultural levels but also in the spheres of finance and commerce as well. Something that must kept in mind, however, is that from the 1880s a strong American influence also made its presence felt as both companies and individuals from the south pushed across the forty-ninth parallel looking for new sources of land and/or work.[47] Some of these individuals were cowboys who participated in the early drives and stayed on to help out on the big spreads.[48] Others were small ranchers who first appeared in the 1870s and early 1880s as cattle traders and then took up land and started ranching on their own. They included T. Lynch, A.M. McFarland, P. Weinard, J. Munsinger, J. Harris, D. Akers, D.J. Whitney, and A.M. Hatfield.[49]

In 1886 a relative "invasion" of Americans began as new leaseholders such as the Powder River Cattle Company,[50] the Pioneer Cattle Company,[51] the Circle Ranch and Cattle Company,[52] and a dozen or so others took up or expanded their holdings to the east and south of the original great ranches. They were situated primarily in the valleys of the Bow and Old Man Rivers, along the Milk River Ridge and to the east of Fort Macleod, in the Wood Mountain and Cypress Hills regions respectively near Maple Creek and Medicine Hat, and further east still in the southern regions of present-day Saskatchewan.[53] In 1886 the Americans drove some thirty thousand head of cattle across the border. However, the terrible winter that year devastated the new herds and may have significantly diminished the American invasion in future years.[54] But some stayed, and over the years that followed they were joined by thousands of their countrymen.[55] A few American ranches, including the Circle and the Spencers from Montana, the McIntyres from Utah, and the Matador from California, were able to buy up very large holdings and/or to procure major leases,[56] operating on a scale comparable to that of the Cochrane, Walrond, and Oxley. The vast majority, however, along with the new British, eastern, and European immigrants who came west at the same time, took up homesteads, many of them combined with smaller leases of from a few hundred to a few thousand acres.[57]

The census figures for Alberta illustrate that the American influx continued until the war. In 1890–91 there were 4,335 British-born people in the province and only 1,251 Americans.[58] Ten years later there were 7,120 British-born and 10,972 Americans.[59] In 1916 there were 86,699 Britons as compared to 91,674 Americans.[60] The Canadian-born were naturally by far the largest group throughout. However, the Americans made up at least a considerable minority of the population. It is also evident that ranching society in western Canada rapidly became aware of its own duality and the consequent struggle of cultures for predominance. In 1888 the following dialogue appeared in the *Calgary Herald*. It had been started by an American journalist named L.S. Merchant who visited Calgary and then, upon returning home, published his impressions in the *Cedar Rapids Daily Republican*.

Merchant claimed, "Here as elsewhere in the province the majority of the people are anxious for annexation to the United States. I should judge at least nine tenths of the votes in Alberta would favour it. The fourth of July is regularly celebrated, and two years ago an enthusiastic chap read the declaration of independence amid the cheers and laughter of the populace at such an act on the Queen's soil. Even the Alberta seat in the Dominion parliament is occupied by an American although desperate efforts were made to defeat him."[61]

Someone of British descent, whose argument nonetheless demonstrates a general recognition of a significant American influence,

Milk River, Alberta area, 1911

immediately denied these assertions. Merchant, the second writer countered, was "decidedly mistaken when he states that the majority of the people here are anxious for annexation to the United States. Native Americans who have come here because they can more profitably engage in business than across the line ... would like to see the United Provinces and the United States one country. This is only natural. It is also natural that an American stranger coming to Calgary or any other Canadian town should be taken in hand by Americans residing there ... It was a manifest mistake however for him to take the opinions of his resident American hosts as the sentiments of the whole population, the overwhelming majority of which is British and native born Canadian."[62]

Evidence also suggests that on the whole Americans found the adjustment to the Canadian ranching frontier less difficult than the British or Easterners did. As a result, in the struggle for predominance, they were more successful. This made their impression on day-to-day life, relatively speaking, greater than their numbers.

One of the best ways to ascertain who is coping well in a particular society is to focus on the beliefs and the values of ordinary people. Anyone who does this for the prairie West during the ranching era finds an almost universal admiration for American frontiersmanship.[63]

This was to a considerable degree reflected in its flip side, a concomitant general disdain for individuals from Britain who were unable to discard their former culture and embrace the ways of the West.

People felt that the frontier environment was virtually the antithesis of that in the Mother Country. Where the latter was developed and refined and catered to a polite and courteous people, the frontier was rough-hewn, rugged, physically demanding, and unsophisticated.[64] A selection process thus militated against the sort of Briton who was unable for whatever reason to thoroughly alter his ways. "Though the spirit of sheer adventure has sent many young men to Canada, and there made good and contented Canadians of them," many of these men are not "of the quality that wears well," warned a writer from London after a visit to Calgary. "Among the derelicts … in the west," he saw "young fellows whose sole equipment was manifestly their spirit of adventure. They hung about the towns looking picturesque and with yellow leggings and cowboy hats on, inept … and, waiting for some pleasant leisure for shooting prairie chicken or catching trout. Doubtless they are home by this time, with little good to say of Canada."[65] Some people on the frontier learned to look with deep suspicion on almost anyone from Britain. "After residing here and reading your newspapers for a few months past, it would seem to me many take a keen delight in fanning the flames of hatred towards the British nation," A.E. Cross wrote to an editor in 1895. It was, he felt, "a pity one has to carry back such an opinion to one's native land to mar the respect and friendship due so great a nation."[66] From time to time employers advertised job openings with the stipulation that "no English need apply."[67] In most cases, however, such prejudices were directed towards a particular kind of Englishman. He was the spoiled, well-heeled remittance man who had been sent to Canada by his family because he was an embarrassment at home. The West was supposed to encourage him to mend his childish and indolent ways. Stories about remittance men were commonly repeated in the newspapers and in the correspondence of people who became part of the ranching fraternity.

The following story appeared in the *Calgary Herald* of 12 April 1904.[68] It begins with words supposedly spoken by just the sort of person described above: "Why I just saw 'Calgary' marked on the map, and in a book that came to the house I read that there were cattle ranches in that vicinity, and so I decided that was the place I wanted. I had to coax and coax, but at last they let me go … and now I'm going to shoot blooming well bears and all the rest of it." The speaker was Harry Northrop, an English lad of delicate health. One of the party of newly arrived Britons with whom Northrop was travelling spoke to a newspaper reporter in Winnipeg and told the boy's story:

> We came to know the kid on the boat coming out. He got so blasted sick in his bunk, when things began to toss a bit, that we felt kind of sorry for him. He kept moaning all the time and calling out, "Oh, why did I leave my little village? I had a nice home there" – like the girl heroine in a melodrama. My word he did have mal-de-mer all right. From what he told us, he is a younger son. His parents are dead and he is under guardians. He was born and brought up in some little bit of a hamlet – I can't remember the name – in the interior of England, and this is the first time he has ever been away from it in his life. I guess he worked consent out of his guardians. He is chock full of ideas about red Indians and cowboys, and feathers and sunproof war paint, and fringed breeches and big hats. His ambition is to become a cowboy. He told us that he tried to get an outfit in England, but that he couldn't find one like those in the pictures. He's only about 18 years old, and I think personally he has consumption. The doctor at Halifax very nearly refused to let him pass, and I think it would have been the best thing for the little fellow. He evidently has lots of money, and he carried two big leather trunks full of kit. He has riding pants and leggings, and coats and hats galore. He also has an English saddle with a clothes line attached to it, for use when he commences on the ranch.
>
> I never saw anyone so green in my life. Since he struck our crowd he's been so well mannered and goodnatured we've let him stay, and we've had no end of fun. At Halifax he ran across a fellow wearing one of those Stetson hats. Harry got talking to him and the first thing I knew he wanted to give the fellow three quid ($15) for his "sombreerior," as he called it, because the fine gentleman told him that to become a cowboy he must wear one, along with a kerchief round his neck. Next day he came down with a great big bandana for a cravat, and he's worn it ever since. When we got on the train we struck another cowboy, bound for Medicine Hat, and he's been jollying Harry all the way out here. The kid believes implicitly every word he tells him, and he fairly worships him. He'd do anything that fellow asked.
>
> I don't know how he's going to make out in this country. He hasn't a friend out here and he has no relatives living. He's too delicate to work hard, and too green to know how anyway. When he gets to Calgary he'll have 20 pounds, and he thinks he'll just walk over to a blooming ranch and commence chasing cows till he's tired.
>
> Such chaps should be kept at home, that's what I think.

The latter sentiments were reiterated time and again by numerous people. They were convinced that too many young men who were relatively well-to-do, physically weak, and naive about the workings of the world had come out from the mother country. Many were not just awkward and out of place but predestined to fail in a land where only the strongest could compete. "The slow-moving brains of some, the lack of initiative, of originality, marked the general run of them as hopeless for Western life, where necessity is ever forcing and developing the inventive genius, the adaptability, and the power to make one thing do work for a dozen other articles," remarked L.V. Kelly in 1913.[69] The problem was not just biological but also cultural. Most of these young lads, fresh from an English public school education, were thoroughly programmed by traditional values and education and closely tied to Old-World preconceptions. "The British training of feeling," the misguided belief in "all things learned in England" precluded their ever doing anything worthwhile in this trying land.

Most observers maintained that the well-bred had difficulty in attempting to come to grips with the harsh realities of an undeveloped frontier. Some, however, thought that the main problem was lack of breeding. How "innately different we are from the people of the British Isles," wrote a Canadian woman in 1884 who had settled into the foothills with her husband on one of the 100,000-acre leases. She too stressed that many Old-World types were not "adaptable" and thus could not cope with the rigours of frontier life. Some of them, she argued, "have a very fair Education … good homes, more money than many of us … and still they are far beneath us in every way." She thought that the difference was that "our parents and grandparents *were* gentle men and women" rather than mere claimants to that stature, and "in spite of the hardships of Canadian Life … [they] preserved the true spirit of gentle breeding."[70]

That the idea many British people were unsuited to the frontier was more than mere prejudice is supported by the fact that the disparaging comments often came from British ranchers themselves. Monica Hopkins, who along with her husband had a 640-acre ranch near Millarville, was one of these. Her descriptions of her rather pathetic neighbours, the Bolts, paint a grim picture. "I never would have believed that anyone could live in such discomfort in such an appalling place if I hadn't seen it for myself," she told one of her fellow countrymen. The house built by Mr Bolts

> is of course built of logs, the ends of which have never been cut off and stick out at various angles at each corner. The roof has a dip in the middle and the stovepipe sticks out like a crooked handle. Instead of plaster or moss between the logs, odd bits of newspapers have been shoved in and when I got inside I noticed the daylight could be seen between most of the logs. The inside is

almost worse than the outside … Mr. Bolts is hopeless out here, so stupid and ignorant of anything connected with country life. In Manchester where he comes from he would probably be quite an ordinary young man, dressed in blue serge and a bowler hat and travelling by train or bus to an office.[71]

Story after story told of British failure on the frontier. D.H. Andrews, a Briton with years of experience on the American range and the manager of the Stair Ranch at Crane Lake, wrote of a man who "could not make a success of his business and sold out at a loss." He had allowed himself to become so broke that when he "took the opportunity to go home" to England he was forced to ride with the "cattle in order to save the expense of paying for railroad tickets and passage on a steamer."[72] In 1903 the *Calgary Herald* published an article on a well-known British experiment – the Barr Colony – proclaiming that its colonists are "Rich in Everything Except Knowledge of Their New Condition in Life." The author's main conclusion was that "Education leads to Disillusion."[73]

Such examples were so numerous that at least one school was started to provide young Britons with a realistic idea of what to expect and how to cope.[74] A.E. Cross was told in 1906 of a scheme to bring together "the members of the British public schools in Canada"[75] to help and advise them. He liked the idea. "We have a large proportion of public school men coming from the British Isles to this part of Canada," he told the people behind the scheme. "Many of them do not seem to get along very well owing to their lack of knowledge of what is required to make a success in the new country."[76] Amongst the Cross papers there is a sketch of a plan for a facility "to educate young Englishmen of from sixteen to eighteen years of age for a three year's course, and prepare them for ranching life."[77]

It should be said that not all Englishmen failed horribly in the West. L.G. Thomas's work in particular demonstrates that many British people settled on the frontier and actively pursued the profession of ranching for a considerable period of time.[78] Monica Hopkins and her husband were two of them. They became proficient at all aspects of ranching and stuck with it until they retired.[79] What does seem evident, however, is that for numerous people from more developed societies the adjustment to frontier life was anything but easy. There was a tendency for some to come out ill-prepared and with very unrealistic expectations about what was going to be required. A large percentage gave up rather quickly and went home.

Comparing attitudes towards the British on the frontier with those towards Americans provides an interesting contrast. Anyone who researches the correspondence of this era or reads the newspapers cannot help but be impressed by the high esteem Americans were held in because of their affinity for, and ability to deal with, conditions peculiar to the cattle industry. Few cases of American failure were cited by contemporaries while a disproportionate number of success stories centre on families like the McIntyres or men like George Lane, E.H. Maunsell, John Franklin, John Ware, George Emerson,[80] and D.H. Andrews[81] who were born or had spent a considerable portion of their lives south of the border. The reason would seem to be that the Americans, unlike their European contemporaries, discovered in the Canadian West a life to which they were more or less already accustomed. Many came directly from Montana and other ranching states and already had first-hand experience in the business, either as hired hands or as owners. They had a pretty good idea what they were up against on the frontier and felt comfortable dealing with its challenges. This gave them a distinct advantage, and it also ensured that they would play a disproportionately important role in establishing the ranching industry.

The first time many Canadian cattlemen received first-hand evidence of the superiority of American technique was when they took part in the great cattle drives. Cochrane, Stimson, and others acquired their initial herds in Montana, Idaho, and other northwestern states and had to use hired men for the enormous task of trailing the cattle to their new homes. Some of these men were Canadians or Britons but a significant number were cowboys who had worked on ranches south of the border.[82] There was the famous bronco-buster Frank Ricks,[83] George Lane, who was the one-time foreman and eventually the owner of the Bar U, and John Ware, who was contracted by the Bar U to drive cattle from Lost River, Idaho, to High River, Alberta, in the spring of 1883.[84]

The advantage of having the services of such men must have been evident from the moment they and their valuable cargoes began the long journey north. It is difficult to appreciate just how much training and specialized knowledge it requires to trail cattle on great treks over open wilderness unless you have tried it. Riders must not only be expert horsemen: they must also be thoroughly versed in the nature and temperament of range cattle. No untrained group of men could possibly have got such large herds to their destination. When cattle are subjected to new surroundings on the open range they become insecure and deeply suspicious of any sudden movements or noise. If surprised or if pushed too anxiously by drovers, they can quickly be transformed from tranquil, contented animals into irrational, panic-stricken creatures stampeding wildly across the land. During the early drives the Canadians witnessed the American handlers

Alberta cowboy, 1909

carefully coaxing, rather than forcing, the cattle across streams, up the sides of steep hills, and past creatures like timber wolves and coyotes (which the bovine mind finds extremely disconcerting).[85]

There were two points on the trail when the risk of a stampede was particularly high. The first was in the beginning when the cattle were fresh, full of energy, and unused to and relatively afraid of the riders.[86] The second was at night when they were "night herded" or held in one spot by a few riders while the other men slept. The night-time danger remained for the whole of the journey. Stampedes that occurred after dark were the most likely to cause tragedy. From dusk to dawn the herd was normally maintained in one specific area near the chuck wagons, which carried the cooks and the food, tack, and other provisions the riders required. Usually the cattle chewed their cuds and slept contentedly during this period. However, almost without exception on every drive, there would be nights when the cattle were much more difficult to handle. When it is dark, cattle are relatively easy to spook. On the trail this could happen because a coyote decided to howl close by, or a rifle was accidentally discharged, or a cowboy fell out of his saddle after inadvertently falling asleep. It could happen because of a sudden loud clap of thunder.

Such noises might awaken just a handful of animals. All at once they come alive and begin to mill around. In a few minutes their fear sweeps through the entire herd. At this point they seem to become agitated by the sound of their own movements and begin to run to and fro. It is now evident to the cowboys that disaster is close. In the dark the frightened animals bolt one way and then the other. With each charge the cowboys back off somewhat and then race their horses alongside the lead cattle, attempting to turn them in a circle and back to the original holding area. Sometimes the stampede is too big and the cattle break around the riders to disappear into the darkness, leaving them with only the sound of hoofs pounding the range in all directions. On other occasions the cowboys succeed and the cattle are returned to the holding area. However, once this level of excitement has been reached, it can be almost impossible to calm them and the slightest noise sets them off again.

By this time the cowboys who were sleeping have been awakened to help out. Even so, the odds are not on their side. Usually on the drives there was one cowboy for two hundred to three hundred animals. The charges recur once, and then again – sometimes five or six times during the same night. Each time the cowboys find themselves racing their horses in the dark in a desperate attempt to restrain the now wild beasts. One rider stays with animals heading in one direction, another with a group heading in another direction. With each charge the cattle are more excited and more difficult to turn back. Each time some break away and are lost. The cowboys find themselves running their horses further and further on rough terrain that they cannot see. Occasionally a horse hits a stump or a fallen tree or jagged knoll. The tired animal falls, the rider flies through the air and lands in a crumpled heap on the ground. If lucky, he is unharmed and is able to get up immediately, mount his horse, and return to the fight. If unlucky, he has a broken rib or arm or a fractured skull. Sometimes he lies unconscious in the dark and is trampled by stampeding cattle.

The aftermath of a stampede is a depressingly difficult and discouraging situation even if no one is hurt. First, the cattle will usually be scattered for miles. The riders have to wait a day or so for the animals to calm down before they can start the difficult task of rounding them up. But now the cattle are even more suspicious and more easily excited than they were at the beginning of the drive, and they have learned that they are capable of getting away from their human tormentors and are even more likely to bolt. This is not only difficult for the riders but costly for the owner. Pounds of beef are lost when the animals run, and in their excited condition after a stampede they tend

Last big round-up, Cochrane Lake, near Cochrane, Alberta, 1909

to eat little and thus do not regain the lost pounds very quickly. Andy Russell remembered his father telling him of a stampede "when 400 big, fat steers blew up in a thunderstorm and lit out for the horizon." The next morning the "herd was milling around the top of a low butte bawling dismally" with steam from their overheated bodies "towering over their backs." "'By God,'" the round-up foreman said when he saw them, "'I'd like to have all the money that's gone up in that steam.'"[87] On top of the lost beef is the cost of more man-hours to round up the herd, and therefore more wages.

Newcomers had to defer to American leadership and judgment on the trail, respecting not only methods of droving the cattle but also the question of how far and how fast to push them over the entire trek. The Cochrane outfit in particular learned this lesson at a high price.[88] Cochrane's first manager was Major James Walker who had attained his release from the North-West Mounted Police to take up ranching. Walker was a strong leader, and he was used to a strict military approach to handling men. However, he had limited knowledge of cattle or anything agricultural. His first mistake was when he purchased the original herd in Montana in 1881. He bought the cattle late in the season, which meant that he had to push the thirty cowboys he had hired for the drive to get the herd to the Cochrane range before winter set in.

Despite the protestations of his experienced riders, he insisted that once the cattle had got over their initial skittishness, they should be pushed along at fifteen to eighteen miles a day – far too fast.[89] The cattle were grouped so closely that they trampled most of the grass they might have eaten, lost weight, and became exhausted. A large number died. The youngest calves were among the first to fall.[90] Many of the older calves as well were impossible to keep with the herd. Cattle identify each other by smell; if they are grouped tightly together, they all take on the same smell and thus become relatively indistinguishable from each other. Cows and their calves can be standing close together and not know it. The mothers seem to have a little more common sense than the calves and will usually stay with the herd in hopes of sorting things out, but the calves will often break and run, heading back down the trail towards the place where they remember being with their mothers.[91] Their homing instinct is so strong that the only way to stop them is to pick them up and carry them. Wagons followed the Cochrane cattle for this purpose, but so many of the calves turned back that the wagons could not hold them all. The cowboys were forced to leave a good percentage on the trail to die. Rumour has it that they also traded them to settlers for provisions like butter or milk or tea or dealt them to whiskey traders they met along the way.[92] When the drive finally got to the ranch at the Big Hill west of Calgary, most of the cattle that had survived were weak and dehydrated. A fierce winter storm broke out almost immediately and the animals, unfamiliar with their new surroundings, did not know where to find shelter or feed. Estimates of the dead were in the thousands.[93]

In 1882 Walker bought another four thousand to five thousand head in Montana. In part because of indecision by his board of directors, his purchase was in the late summer, again forcing a long drive under the threat of the onslaught of early winter storms. He seems to have listened to his cowboys this time and moved the cattle more slowly, but in late September, just as the drive reached Fish Creek south of Calgary, a fierce blizzard struck. The American trail boss recommended that the cattle be left in a sheltered valley for a month or so to regain their strength before pushing on to the ranch and offered to leave cowboys to watch over them for that time. Walker, acting under his orders from Montreal, insisted that the journey to the Cochrane lease continue. "Your contract is to deliver them at the Big Hill," he told the trail boss. The latter, "declaring that he would surely deliver them, sent men ahead, picked up some scores of lusty native steers, and jammed them south through the snowdrifts, turning them back again at Fish Creek and throwing the weak, trail-worn herds into the path they had made. Driving fiercely, they forced the herds to the Big Hill." The trail boss then told Walker, "count 'em now, because half of them will be dead tomorrow."[94]

The warning proved accurate. At this time, Frank White replaced Walker, who had tendered his resignation earlier. White also had little or no experience on the range and was also inclined to follow orders from Montreal without question.[95] He found himself contending with a storm that continued unabated until 15 October. A thaw and then very cold temperatures that formed a crust of ice on the snow followed. This cut the weakened animals off completely from the grass, and those that had not died earlier began to succumb. The steers tried to shift southeastward toward better grazing but the cowboys, again following strict orders from White and thus the East to keep the animals on Cochrane land, drove them back. The result was devastation. Dead cattle began piling up in the coulees where they sought refuge from the winds. "By spring it was said a man could walk across some gullies, or even along their entire length without stepping off the carcasses." Cochrane lost at least three-quarters of the herd.[96] One of the cowboys believed that after trailing in eleven thousand to twelve thousand head in the two drives, "there remained … but a scant four thousand, counting natural increase."[97]

It was immediately following this last disaster that Senator Cochrane took a new lease in the Waterton area near the American border. Evidence from eyewitness reports indicates that the lessons of American frontiersmanship were more closely followed in day-to-day ranching practices. On the trek south the animals were moved slowly – some ten miles a day – and the cowboys worked in shifts to see that they were closely guarded at all times and allowed room and time to graze properly. Losses were kept to almost nothing.[98] The lesson that the earlier setbacks could have been avoided had the managers listened to the cowboys seems to have circulated throughout the ranching community. The first calamity in particular was well known and, combined with the fact that the Bar U fared so much better in its first great drive, must have done much to convince people in general of the importance of using methods that had been tried and tested on the southern frontiers.

After the drives were over, it soon became clear that American practices were far more appropriate than anything imported from the East or overseas for operating the new ranches from day to day. Americans were hired whenever they could be found and eventually formed a crucial segment of the labour force. Some of them migrated north looking for work or land or both. Many of them were the same cowboys who had conducted the drives. They "drifted in from across the border with the various herds" and were induced to stay by "the bigger wages paid in the new country."[99] One British rancher who came to the Canadian West in the 1880s after living for a considerable period of time in California, Arizona, Mexico, and Texas, estimated that by 1886 "and prior to that date some of the Ranch Managers were Americans, all the foremen, nearly all the cowboys, nearly all the cattle and horses, all the saddles, rifles, revolvers and cowboy outfit in general were American."[100] The impact of American frontiersmanship thus became pervasive.

Specific examples of British and eastern owners hiring Americans to manage their herds are numerous. The Walrond brought in James Patterson from Montana as a foreman.[101] The Allans and Fredrick Stimson contacted the Montana Cattle Association to acquire George Lane.[102] In 1903 Lane would form a syndicate and buy out the Bar U himself, expand dramatically, and become for some twenty-five years the biggest rancher on the prairies. In 1884 Frank White followed the example of his predecessor and resigned "control of the [Cochrane] ranch shortly after the spring and early summer had shown the disastrous results of following orders from the East."[103] Responsibility for the herds at Waterton was then given to Billie Cochrane who employed the experienced cowboy, James Dunlap, as his foreman.[104] At the Big Hill near Calgary, control was turned over to W.D. Kerfoot and a man named Ca Sous. The latter was described as "a splendid stock hand"[105] who had worked on both the United States and Mexican frontiers. E.C. Johnson who took "charge of ... Stimson's herd" at the Bar U for some years worked for D.H. Andrews "both in Wyoming & this country." He was a "first rate cowman, in fact ... about the best all round cowman" around.[106] Andrews himself had had many years of experience on the American ranching frontier before he came north to manage the Stair outfit for British owners. His letters to London often demonstrate how directly past experience influenced his approach to operating in Canada. Frank Strong, who came to Alberta from Montana in 1880, ran the I.G. Baker stock business while operating a horse ranch of his own.[107]

John Ware is one of many American cowboys who helped make up the most highly skilled segment of the day-to-day labour force.[108] Because he was black, Ware had always felt threatened by vigilante groups in the United States that commonly hanged men suspected of cattle rustling. He appears therefore to have been somewhat more comfortable with the less subjective justice administered in Canada by the Mounted Police.[109] However, his decision to stay on at the

Mildred, Robert, Nettie, and John Ware (ca. 1896)

Bar U was also undoubtedly because his expertise was in demand there, just as it had been in the south. One of the same ranch's most famous hands was the notorious outlaw Harry Longabaugh, better known as the Sundance Kid. He was employed to break horses in 1890 and was considered to be very good at the job.[110]

American practices were thus instrumental in transporting the ranching industry to the Canadian West and in helping it to take hold. Inevitably this ensured that the Canadian version of ranching would have much in common with that which had recently taken shape in Montana and other northwestern states. Well-known cultural geographer Terry Jordan identifies a region that he calls the "Anglo-Gentile Rockies" running from the Canadian border to Colorado. In this region a "mountain ranching culture" was dominated from the beginning by the "midwestern system" imported from Missouri and Iowa. After undergoing certain modifications to fit the highland environment, it was conveyed to the foothills of both central Montana and Alberta and then it expanded along the Milk River and into southern Assiniboia. Jordan believes that with respect to the manner in which frontier ranching was conducted, Montana and western prairie Canada can be treated as one region.[111] The evidence in this chapter, when viewed with that in the one that follows, strongly suggests that Jordan is correct.

3 Frontiersmanship

An examination of the day-to-day operation of the first ranches in some detail leads to the conclusion that in the technical sphere (as opposed to the financial and political spheres) the Canadian cattle business was not just profoundly influenced by the ranching industry south of the forty-ninth parallel – it was virtually dependent upon it. This investigation has two other benefits as well: it allows readers to improve their understanding of the major obstacles that all ranchers had to confront when they turned to the task of shaping new businesses in the wilderness, and it helps clarify the image of the cowboy in western Canadian popular culture.

The primary impetus for the introduction of American expertise to the Canadian West came from environmental selection. In previous decades techniques for running and nurturing livestock on the open range had been brought to the American Midwest and Montana from more southerly regions including California, Texas, New Mexico, and Mexico.[1] Because these techniques had already been adapted to the northern climate and ecology, they were appropriate for the challenge of developing the Canadian ranching industry from its inception.

The earliest cattlemen on both sides of the border found managing their spreads more daunting than those who followed them simply because they were the first. As time went on, the amount of open rangeland decreased, primarily because extensive networks of fences had been built to restrict the livestock to particular pastures. Many of these pastures were exceedingly large and remote, but at least they enabled the cattlemen to know approximately where their cattle were, and to keep them separate from neighbouring herds. This gave them important advantages, particularly with respect to the time spent checking the cattle, treating the sick and wounded, managing breeding, and collecting the marketable finished product.[2] The earliest ranchers started with an open range. They soon began enclosing their home bases and, as time went on, a significant proportion of their deeded land where they kept brood cows during calving season and the best of their breeding stock throughout the year.[3] But, even after several seasons, many allowed most of their stock to roam over unfenced acres in both summer and winter. Their working lives were thus dominated by the sheer magnitude of the rangeland with which they had to deal.

In this situation expertise provided by proficient cowboys was invaluable. Men accustomed to spending practically their entire working lives in the saddle were well suited to keeping watch on the herds. They were willing to camp out under the stars when necessary to prevent the livestock from straying too far, they understood the difference between range cattle and the more domesticated type, and they could use a rope and handle a branding iron when occasion demanded. They were also able to conduct the round-ups that had to be undertaken in order to gather the livestock.

The late spring round-up was the big event of the season, as by that time of year the bulk of the calves had been born and could be branded. The male calves could also be castrated. This made them less excitable and ensured that they would spend their time nursing, grazing, and putting on weight rather than fighting with each other and attempting to breed. One of the striking features of the spring round-up was the immense amount of preparation it required.[4] The job of organizing all major round-ups normally went to the local livestock association. This placed responsibility primarily in the hands of the prominent spreads in each area that tended to dominate the association and had the most at stake. All member ranchers were expected to take part in the round-ups. However, those with five hundred head or less were required to send one man only. That man's responsibility was simply to attend and look out for his own operation's animals.[5] This system was not entirely fair. Obviously the smaller operations had very little control over it. Moreover, many (perhaps most) of the settlers and squatters could not afford to join their local stock association and pay its fees, and thus they were not represented at all. As will be seen, they were in a position to lose unbranded cattle that were caught as the riders swept across the country.

As time for the spring round-up drew near, all the leading ranches had to turn their attentions to hiring on extra riders, refurbishing and provisioning their chuck wagons, mending harness and tack, and coordinating plans with neighbours. The most demanding task was preparing an adequate contingent of horses. Horses tend to wear out if used on the trail every day for extended periods. It was usual, therefore, for each outfit to take between five and ten mounts per cowboy to the big gatherings. For a ranch the size of the Cochrane or Bar U, which employed about a dozen workers, a total of one hundred or so animals had to be readied. Over the winter all the horses except the ones the ranch hands kept for personal use were

Roping horses in corral, Milk River area, 1912

allowed to roam the open range. The first problem was to find them and bring them to a central holding area. This was not easy. The horses were usually spread out in small bunches all over the wilderness, and the ranch hands had to go out repeatedly and drive them in a few at a time.

When the horses were penned up it was also necessary to reacquaint them with the finer points of the "cowpony." The bulk of these animals, like the cattle, had been imported from the American West. They were sturdy, stockier "cayuses," presumably of complex lineage that had originated in Texas. Most of them were "small, tough, and active as cats," and had become quite wild and unruly after months of freedom. In the days before the round-up, the men had to ride them one at a time. Usually an expert roper would go into the corral, single out a horse, and throw a lariat over its head. He would then quickly tie the horse to a snubbing post or else two or three of his fellow cowhands would rush in, grab the rope, and help hold the animal. Sometimes to quiet it long enough to be bridled, saddled, and mounted, the cowboys would blindfold it.[6] Or one of them might jump up on its head and bite it hard on one of its ears. For some unknown reason, probably connected to the nervous system, this causes a horse to stiffen up and stand still. Once mounted, some of

Breaking a horse at Forster Ranch, Cessford, Alberta, 1909

the horses remembered former training and responded the way they should to the rider and his instructions. Often, however, all hell broke loose. The animal would suddenly come out of its paralytic state, its head would go down between its front legs, its back would arch, and it would buck for all it was worth while the rider clung to the saddle. If unsuccessful, he soon found himself sitting or lying in an undignified heap on the ground. Usually, though, he rode the animal to a standstill. The seasoned broncobuster knew what he was doing. He used specialized techniques such as steadying his stirrups by "hobbling" or tying them to together under the horse's belly, and setting the reins so that when the horse moved, its head was forced up and to one side.[7] This prevented it from bucking quite so hard and from going into the rapid "zigzag" pattern that makes it almost impossible for the rider to stay on.[8] In the short time available all the horses could be ridden only once or twice, and many were sent out to herd cattle in a semi-retrained or "green broke" state. This meant they were prone to break into a buck at any time and riders could be thrown when they least expected it.

While the cowboys were working with the horses, the owners and managers who were to be involved in the round-up would get together and plan. Each ranch was expected to contribute its proper

Horses in rope corral near Circle Ranch, southern Alberta (ca. 1903)

share of cowboys, horses, and a chuck wagon with a cook, food, and bedding. The men would commit resources, pick the place where they were all initially to meet, and appoint one well-thought-of individual as round-up captain and another to act as his deputy.

The greatest general round-up in southern Alberta was held in the late spring of 1885. A hundred riders, fifteen chuck wagons, and five hundred horses participated. The captain was Jim Dunlap. His second-in-command was George Lane.[9] Some sixty thousand cattle were gathered over several weeks from across a huge span of territory. This turned out to be too ambitious, and thereafter the general round-up was abandoned in favour of smaller district ones. Each district sent representative cowboys, or "reps," to each of the other districts to watch for and claim cattle from their area. The larger ranches sometimes held their own individual round-ups, but the usual procedure was for several in each district to combine forces.[10]

Out on the range each day began early – sometimes at 3 a.m. – with a quick breakfast around the chuck wagon. Then the "wranglers" who looked after the horses, or the "saddle band," as it was called, herded their charges into a corral made by stretching ropes outward in a v from one of the wagons. The best ropers would go in amongst the horses to catch the animal required for that day by each cowboy. When everyone was saddled up and ready to go, the whole camp headed off in a previously agreed on direction. Wagons, horses, and riders moved along until usually before noon, when they reached the new campsite for that day. The wagons then set up again, and the cowboys split up into two groups to begin bringing in the cattle. The usual practice was to divide the area to be swept into a huge circle with a ten to fifteen mile radius. Each group swept one half of the circle. Some riders took the outside while others combed the inside. All of them made their way to the outer extremity of the ten or fifteen mile limit and then gathered every animal they found on the way back.

This normally took until late in the afternoon. When the men returned, all the cattle were placed in a large open area so that riders from each outfit could go into the herd one at a time and pull out the animals from their respective ranches. This was a tremendous test of the skill of both horse and cowboy. Only the best-trained horses, the ones that individual men rode regularly summer and winter, could be used. Horse and rider had to move slowly and cautiously so as not to cause undue disturbance in the herd. Edward Hough, who worked herds on the American range, describes the daunting process:

> Before [them] stretched a sea of interwoven horns, waving and whirling as the densely packed ranks of cattle closed in or swayed apart. It was no prospect for a weakling, but into it went the cowpuncher on his determined little horse, heeding not the plunging, crushing, and thrusting of the excited cattle. Down under the bulks of the herd, half hid in the whirl of dust, he would spy a little curly calf running, dodging, and twisting, always at the heels of its mother; and he would dart in after, following the two through the thick of surging and plunging beasts. The sharp-eyed pony would see almost as soon as his rider which cow was wanted and he needed small guidance from that time on. He would follow hard at her heels, edging her constantly toward the flank of the herd, at times nipping her hide as a reminder of his own superiority. In spite of herself the cow would gradually turn out toward the edge, and at last would be swept clear of the crush, the calf following close behind her.[11]

The hardest part came when the cow and calf were finally separated from the rest. The herd instinct takes over at that point, and the animals wheel and turn one way and then another as fast as they can in a desperate attempt to rejoin their comrades. Horse and rider need to have not only speed to stop them but also "cow sense" in order to anticipate their moves.

Once the cattle of the various ranches were separated from the main herd, they were grouped in separate areas so that ropers could ride amongst them to catch the calves individually for branding and castrating. Again, skill and training were required of both cowboy and mount. Only the best horses were used. The top ropers would catch the calves by the two back legs, tether them to the saddle horn, and drag them over to the branding fire, back feet first and on their sides. Less proficient ropers used the easier method of catching the calves by the head. Two or three other workers then had to grab the animals, wrestle them to the ground, and help pull them to the fire. The calves that were relatively big could put up fierce resistance, bucking and kicking with all their might. The work continued until all the calves were properly marked with a red-hot iron and the males were divested of their testicles, usually by a man working with a simple penknife.[12] The following depiction by Theodore Roosevelt provides a glimpse of ordered chaos that prevailed:

> If there are seventy or eighty calves … the scene is one of the greatest confusion. The ropers, spurring and checking the fierce little horses, drag the calves up so quickly that a dozen men can hardly hold them; the men with the irons, blackened with soot, run to and fro; the calf-wrestlers, grimy with blood, dust, and sweat, work like beavers; while with the voice of a stentor the tallyman shouts out the number and sex of each calf. The dust rises in clouds, and the shouts, cheers, curses, and laughter of the men unite with the lowing of the cows and the frantic bleating of the roped calves to make a perfect babel.[13]

When all the branding and castrating was finished, the calves and their mothers were turned out on the open range again, in the direction from which the round-up had come so as not to become mixed in with livestock as yet ungathered. Cows, calves, and yearlings that were identified by the "reps" as belonging to ranches in other districts were kept back as part of the "day herd." These were eventually taken back to their home ranges.

The day herd continued to grow as the round-up proceeded, and each morning men were assigned to look after it. This was not considered a desirable job. During the day, its worst aspect tended to be tedium. From early in the morning until late in the afternoon, riders basically just sat on their horses, watching the animals and making sure that they did not stray. While their colleagues were scouring the countryside, discovering lakes and streams and sights they had never seen before, the day herders often had trouble staying awake. In the mornings, when they drove the cattle to a new site, the monotony was broken somewhat, but even the moves were usually uneventful. The cattle had to be trailed slowly to avoid unnecessary weight loss and they tended to lull along, grazing lazily as they went. Sometimes the tranquility was broken when something frightened the herd and it threatened to bolt. Usually, however, it was not too difficult to calm the animals in the daylight hours and driving them was almost as unexciting as holding them. After dark the job of looking after the cattle became a lot more stressful. As during the drives, the cattle became much easier to spook and thus more likely to stampeded.

Serious accidents were far from rare on the round-ups as a whole, though the "luck of the draw" always played its hand.[14] One rancher in the foothills of Alberta, Fred Ings, remembered that "there was plenty of danger around a herd of cattle but no one seemed to get [badly] hurt. Horses fell with their riders underneath them – men were 'piled' by bucking broncos – but beyond a few days stiffness they were able to carry on."[15] On the other hand, one Montanan recalled that on virtually every major round-up at least one cowboy died.[16] Sometimes lives were lost when ponies stumbled at high speed and accidentally threw their riders.[17] One of the best known accidents of this type on the Canadian side of the border ended the life of John Ware, whose horse fell while he was gathering stock to treat for the mange.[18] Another highly regarded cowboy, Jim Christie, was thrown from his horse and killed in the Nose Hill area north of Calgary in 1893.[19] In the spring round-ups swollen rivers may have been the most consistent danger. Charles Ramond, who replaced Dunlap as foreman of the Cochrane Ranch, was drowned while trying to cross the Belly River near Lethbridge in early 1889.[20] Saul Blackburne, a rider for the Walrond, was pushing cattle across the Old Man River in 1894 when "his horse suddenly rolled over," and he was lost in the raging waters.[21]

After the spring round-up, the cowboys' time on the open range did not end. Through the summer their responsibilities centred primarily on a long succession of smaller round-ups. First they would sweep through the out-of-the-way areas looking for cattle that might have been missed earlier. Then they would go through all the pastures again to separate out the grass-fattened steers that were deemed ready for slaughter. These they drove to the railhead for shipment to eastern markets.

There was always a final round-up in the fall to gather all the cattle again, to brand and castrate late calves and pull out the last of the fat animals. Once enough corrals had been constructed, the calves were weaned and then kept close to the ranch headquarters where

Bucking bronco, Milk River area, 1912

they could be looked after until they were able to be on their own.[22] The breeding bulls were also then separated from the range cows, and the cows and yearlings turned out to winter pastures.

By the late 1890s yet another round-up became standard practice on the Canadian ranges for a period of several years. This one helped the ranchers protect their industry from one of its most threatening adversaries – chronic infestations of the disease known as the mange. The mange round-up was part of a complex system of treating the animals that had also been developed and perfected south of the forty-ninth parallel.

On the open range the mingling of the herds facilitated the spread of all sorts of livestock diseases. Well-known disorders such as black-leg,[23] pink eye,[24] tuberculosis,[25] lump jaw,[26] and foot and mouth disease greatly concerned all the cattlemen.[27] Standard vaccines were imported from the East to resist the first of these diseases, as were medicines for the second, but the only way to deal effectively with the latter three was to destroy the infected animals. Among the horses, glanders, a highly contagious illness that attacks the digestive system, periodically broke out in one place or another. In 1891, 1892, 1893, and 1905 it made its way through the grazing country, and a number of animals had to be put down to contain it.[28] Mange was the most destructive of all these diseases to both cattle and horses. It spread through the Canadian herds on a large scale in the late 1890s.[29] The disease is a parasite

Round-up crew, Porcupine Hills area, Alberta, 1886

that attacks the hides of the animals, causing them tremendous discomfort. It usually manifests itself by gigantic sores because the animals tend to scratch against trees, posts, buildings, or anything else that they come across until their hair drops out and their hides are torn. In the late nineteenth and early twentieth centuries the only satisfactory way to treat the mange was to conduct a special round-up in the affected area and dip every single animal in tanks filled with a solution of kerosene and/or sulphur mixed with lime and water.[30]

The infestation among the cattle that were brought in from the United States became so ubiquitous that in 1904 the government began erecting tanks along the international border so that all imported animals could be dipped before passing onto the Canadian ranges.[31] This did not have the desired effect, and soon the livestock associations began to develop a communal approach to erecting vats and dipping the cattle on the Canadian side. In 1899 Billie Cochrane assembled one of the vats himself on government land at Kipp,[32] advancing all the money except $300 that the government contributed.[33]

Something of the persistent nature of this disease is evinced in the following letter written by Cochrane to A.E. Cross in 1906: "I saw George Lane on Saturday last at Cayley … he told me to tell you that

Dipping cattle on the Circle Ranch, Alberta (ca. 1915)

your cattle on the Red Deer – were badly affected with mange – If you think it necessary to do any dipping – Geo Lane said he had a good dipping plant at Bassano – There is also a man in the country who has a spraying outfit & has two carloads of Beaumont Texas oil & charges 25 cents a head … Your cattle were clean last fall when we put them through the Mosquito Creek Vat – with the exception of a few old bulls which we boiled plenty. They must have become reinfected by mixing with cattle from High River which were driven to Red Deer … last winter."[34]

The mange was costly not only in terms of the construction of vats and tanks[35] but also the round-ups that had to be undertaken specifically for the purpose of treating the animals. Thc following description by "Dude" Lavington of a mange round-up in 1913 conveys the wear and tear on the cattle:

There were two epidemics of mange in the area entailing extra roundups. Of the first, I can only remember Dad riding away with two saddle horses, one with a light pack on, as on spring and fall roundups. But the second mange epidemic produced one of my most vivid memories. I was seven years old at the time.

Every hoof of stock on the range had to be rounded up and dipped. The dipping vat was about forty miles away at Sam Savage's ranch. Being summer time I was out of school and allowed to go on this roundup. A lot of the ranchers in the area pooled their stock and drove together. Dad had close to four hundred head then and Ralph, my cousin, had about one hundred and fifty. Roy Seeley and Ralph and Dad and I went with our drive. We were soon joined by seven or eight of our neighbours, and their stock, and quite a few more riders.

The nearer we got to the dipping vat the more cattle we came in contact with, till, toward the last, the whole countryside seemed to be a moving mass of cattle. Somehow we had to hold ours separate from other herds till it came our turn to go through the vat. We moved our cattle in closer as other herds ahead of us went through, and the last day or so we had our herd in a fenced holding pasture and didn't have to night herd.

The vat was on the shore of a lake. Sulphur and lime were mixed with water and boiled awhile. A steady stream of the stinking mixture was being pumped into the vat from one side, and lake water was being pumped in from the other side. There were great big holding corrals which funnelled into a chute, and this in turn funnelled into the vat which, I believe, was forty or fifty feet long.

The cattle dived off a platform and went right under for a few seconds, came up snorting and blowing, looking like drowned rats, and then swam to the far end and walked out. This steady stream of cattle went through day after day for weeks and months. I felt very sorry for the poor miserable looking devils. After they had gone through once, we had to hold them again till our turn came around to run them through again.

I vaguely remember our camp. It was hot and clear in the day time and around the corrals a fog of dust all day. We had no tent and just spread out blankets on the ground at night. I can remember getting mighty chilly before morning, so I reckon our bed roll was pretty skimpy. I even seem to remember having frost one morning.

After the last dipping we started for home and when the herd realized they were not just being held, they really started to line out. There was a lake well over a mile wide right across our general homeward direction. These cattle had been forced to drink horribly dirty, riled up water all the time they had been held. Now they got the smell of this fresh water and a stampede started straight for the lake.

That huge mass of moving, running cattle, with their horns flashing in the sun and their hooves rattling, was really something to thrill anyone. The leaders were pushed a mile or more out into the lake by the very momentum of the herd, and must have caused a small tidal wave on the far shores of the lake. Soon they were all swimming; a sea of swimming cattle, and there was no turning them back.[36]

This was obviously no easy process. All the cattle must have lost substantial amounts of weight. Presumably as well some got sick during the ordeal and even died. The cost of treatment was therefore enormous. However, the cost of not treating was even greater. Few cattle die from the mange alone, but usually what happens is that the infestation causes them so much stress that they do not eat or sleep properly. As a result they lose weight, their immune systems suffer, and they eventually catch a fatal dose of pneumonia or a digestive tract infection. When infected range animals lived long enough to make it into the winter they often were so emaciated that they soon succumbed to exposure.[37]

The ranchers were not very successful at fighting the mange until the early years of the twentieth century, in part because it was next to impossible to find and treat all the carriers at any one time. In 1899 Duncan McEachran told the *Macleod Gazette* that "had he known how extensive was the prevalence of mange among cattle in Alberta, the New Walrond Ranch Co would never have been formed."[38] In the end, however, the dipping procedure appears to have saved the Canadian industry. In 1904 J.G. Rutherford, who had replaced McEachran as veterinary director-general, travelled throughout the ranching country lecturing on the dangers of the disease and the importance of dipping. In that and the following year nearly 300,000 cattle were treated in the Macleod area, over 275,000 around Calgary and just under 200,000 around Medicine Hat. Near Cardston some fifty stations had been erected, and many ranchers were treating their horses too.[39] By this time the Americans also seem to have got some control of the disease and it was no longer being transported across the border quite as persistently. The disease was never stamped out in Canada but major outbreaks seem to have occurred only intermittently until after the beginning of World War I.[40]

The mange round-up was organized in essentially the same way as those for branding new calves or marketing fat cattle. Clearly round-ups were vital to open range management. They were also a very efficient means for the development of a plethora of minor techniques required to run cattle on the open range. Managers, foremen, and ranch hands of varying backgrounds were brought together from all over the southern districts of Alberta and Assiniboia for days and weeks at a time. They worked in coordinated teams to achieve a variety of objectives and learned to admire those among them who best displayed cowboy talents. This in turn induced them all to work on improving their technical skills. During the course of the round-up the cowboys invariably took time off to vie with one another in riding bucking broncos, cutting out cattle from a herd, and, most of all, roping. The riders normally carried lariats on the trail, and they liked to show off their ability to use them when opportunities arose. At mealtime or in the evening they would compete with each other in roping stumps, large rocks, wheels of the chuck wagons, or almost anything else that looked appropriate. When a coyote or wolf happened along, there was a good chance that two or three of the men would entertain their friends by chasing it on horseback to see who could catch it first.[41] Usually the episode would end with the unfortunate animal being "dragged and bounced across the prairies and hills until … [it] was dead."[42] On occasions the riders were known to rope and kill bigger game too, like antelope or deer or even grizzly bears.[43]

Roping was a necessary ranching tool not just for catching horses and branding calves but also as a means of giving animals individual attention. When a brand had to be examined closely, or a wound needed to be treated, or a calf had to be delivered, it was sometimes necessary to catch and throw a full-grown animal. Two ropers on horseback usually accomplished this. One would catch it by the head and the other by the back legs. They would then pull from opposite directions until the animal lost its balance.[44] Sometimes an animal had to be caught and thrown by a single cowboy. He would simply rope it, tether it to his saddle horn, and then walk up to it, grab it by the horns, and twist it to the ground. This took nerve, considerable strength, and the background to know that it was possible.[45] In the early days the men with such expertise were most probably Americans.

If Canadian cattlemen had ample opportunities in the round-up process to watch the skilled and knowledgeable at work, they also had some chances to see the unskilled and ignorant. The difference could not have escaped them. The following rather comical description of what happened when the uninitiated were relied upon makes this point. The storyteller is a young English lad who came to the Canadian West, like so many others, looking for adventure as much as a career. He took a job for a time on a ranch in the foothills of Alberta with other young men fresh from Great Britain.

> When … some people who are not quite so experienced start [breaking a horse], they do things differently. The boss says to one of the men: "George" (or whatever his name may be), "will you do the roping?" "Don't mind if I do," says he. He then gets his lariat and swaggers into the middle of the corral, carefully coiling the rope up in his hands, gives the noose a preliminary swing and says he is ready. The horses are driven round; he runs round too, swinging the noose violently round his head. It knocks against the

Cowboys roping for sport, Milk River area, 1912

Branding on the Walrond Ranch (ca. 1893)

snubbing post in the centre of the corral and curls round his neck, and throwing it that same time, nearly yanks his head off. Then he stamps round and blasphemes till his eyes stick three inches out of his head, and two of the mares faint and have to be carried out.

Then George has to be untangled and the business starts again. He swings his rope more carefully this time, throws, and hits the horse across the knees. Then he curses the lariat, says he would have got him that time only the noose did not open. Next shot he misses again …

At last, just as no one is expecting it, George does catch the bronco by the fore leg [rather than the neck]. The colt plunges round the corral; George flies round after him, hanging on to the end of the rope and yelling, "Come on you d_____ fools, and hang on; don't stand there like a lot of boiled owls" and everybody else, too much surprised to think of stopping still, tear round after him.

At last the bronco is thrown, and after he has been halter broken is saddled. Then comes the momentous question, who is to ride?

It then turns out that nearly everybody has something the matter with him. It is at times like this that one finds out what fearful and noxious diseases your friends, whom you had probably considered perfectly healthy, are suffering from. I myself say that I could not risk my life, as if some dozen other people were to die there would be no male left of my race or name. Everybody jeers at this, saying that if they were not suffering from these terrible maladies they would enjoy nothing more than a ride on that particular horse.

At last some benighted idiot volunteers to ride and climbs on. The bronco bucks backward, forward, sideways, and round in a circle, his back arched and his head sticking out between his hind legs, while the poor devil on his back clings to the horn of the saddle and looks as if he would give all he possessed and a darned sight more to be sitting peacefully on the prairie.[46]

From this description it is possible to see how much men like Frank Ricks or the Sundance Kid were admired. Such men introduced not only all the arts of the cowboy to the frontier but also the specialized tools of the trade. Among these were first and foremost the highly trained horses they rode regularly and used to cut out animals for branding, channelling into the day herd, or sending off to the slaughter market. They were also the horses that made roping possible. A cowboy is able to lasso cattle on the range only if his mount has the speed to catch up to them and the training to stay close as they race along, turning from side to side and jumping over all sorts of obstacles. The horse has to be accustomed to the sound of the rope whirling over its ears and, in the case where the cowboy is alone and giving attention to a single animal, it has to be trusted

Cowboy at cattle dip on Circle Ranch (ca. 1900–03)

to stand riderless, holding the animal while it is being attended to.[47] The cowboys' personal horses were chosen for their cow sense, even temperament, and businesslike attitude. Some of the best of them seem to have been crosses of Thoroughbreds or Irish hunters brought in from Europe and the cayuses that had resulted from the widespread mixing of breeds on the open range.[48]

Canadians could not acquire the experienced cowponies they needed except from the frontiersmen to the south. It was the same with all the tack and equipment for running cattle on the open range. Most of this equipment had originated in Mexico and then been altered to suit the ranching cultures of Texas, California, Colorado, and Montana. It included comfortable saddles, suitable for long journeys and designed to allow the tethering of wild livestock; boots and chaps to protect the ranchers' legs from the weather and the sting of willows and other small bushes; six-guns to scare off predators; and miscellaneous paraphernalia like spurs, slickers, and saddlebags.[49] It also included the traditional cowboy hats. In the northwestern states these had been adapted to the cooler climate by trimming the brim. The northern ranchers did not need as much shade as their counterparts further south, and the more compact models did not blow off as easily in the wind or at high speeds.[50] It is no accident that almost all the pictures the historian now finds of Canadian cattlemen at work on the trail, or later during round-ups, display riders outfitted with such items. This equipment came to the Canadian West because it was suited to the task of handling livestock on the open, unfenced, and relatively wild frontier.

When American personnel took positions of responsibility on the ranches, they naturally imported more than just skills and equipment – they had a tendency to influence virtually all practical aspects of ranch operation. An excellent example is found in a letter written by D.H. Andrews to the Stair Ranch owners in London, England, in 1891. At this stage Andrews was in the process of building the important initial skeletal network of fences which was used to divide off particular private pastures from the open range. He reported to the British owners that his work crew was using a system of construction consisting of

> posts set in the ground 33 feet apart with 4 barbed wires, the top wire 4 feet 6 in. from the ground and others 10 inches apart, with 5 stays or droppers placed 6 ft. 6 in. apart, with one end resting on the ground and stapled to the wire in an upright position. I have had experience of these fences for the last 13 years in Texas, New Mexico, Colorado and Wyoming and have seen thousands of miles of it. I consider it the best and cheapest fence that can be erected for holding horses and cattle and a far safer fence than the present legal fence in this country, which consists of posts placed nearer together, and a top rail, either wired or nailed on to them. My experience of fences with top rails is that the top rail is being continuously rubbed off which then leaves a gap in the fence covered by nothing but wire, with no droppers in which stock, in running, do not notice it and are very likely to get cut against it.[51]

The four-strand barbed wire fence and other facilities like corrals, chutes and squeezes constructed of logs from the trunks of indigenous trees had been tested and perfected elsewhere. They gained acceptance because they worked and because they could be constructed cheaply and efficiently in the western environment.[52]

American practices were transported north through a number of vehicles other than ranch personnel. From the 1890s many of the Americans who took up homesteads or leases or combinations of homesteads and small leases put their practical knowledge to work on their own spreads. Thus they were also able to act as role models for other less accomplished cowhands and ranchers.[53] Commerce played a part as well. Some Canadian cattlemen formed relationships with established ranchers in states like Montana and Idaho during business negotiations to purchase cattle and no doubt asked questions about how to run their own ranches and how to deal with a

RL Ranch about eight miles west of Nanton, Alberta (ca. 1899)

host of problems that would emerge. It seems logical to conclude that over the years these relationships, along with further cattle dealings, were developed and in some cases became a regular source of information.

The printed word was also important in the dissemination of knowledge about the American frontier. Editors of local newspapers in urban centres including Pincher Creek, Fort Macleod, and Calgary recognized that readers wanted to be up to date with all the latest methods of sustaining cattle on the open range, and they made a habit of reprinting articles from American periodicals.[54] Information about how their southern neighbours were dealing with problems such as the care and feeding of calves in the winter, the building of fences on the open range, and breed selection and improvement thus became available. Furthermore, once they began to form their own stock associations and attempt a communal approach to mutual rangeland problems like the mange, rustling, and government settlement policies, Canadian ranchers began to work closely with American associations to coordinate their efforts.[55]

The earliest Canadian organizations, including those at High River, Millarville, and Fort Macleod, all came into existence specifically to organize the round-ups, and they all appear to have been developed on the American model in important respects. For instance, fees were assessed for membership and voting privileges according to the number of livestock a rancher owned.[56] There was also close American cooperation in the formation of the groups. In 1886 the Central Stock Association in Fort Macleod advertised a meeting for the election of its first officers and announced that "Montana Delegates" would be present.[57]

The degree of cooperation between the associations on both sides of the border was enhanced by the fact that they had to confront similar frontier adversaries. Among the greatest obstacles encountered by the ranchers were human and animal predators. Both found it easy to gain undetected access to the herds because they grazed over such vast areas. To combat the human type of predator, Canadian stock associations commonly attempted to supplement the work force of the Mounties by hiring stock detectives to police the herds of their members.[58] They also sometimes sent representatives to Montana and other northern states to participate in round-ups where cattle that had wandered or been chased across the border were likely to be found.[59] In 1886 the Macleod Association sent a "communication to the Montana Stock Association asking them to use their influence with the Montana legislature to have a law passed to punish any one taking stock stolen in Alberta into Montana."[60]

Many of the functions of the local and of the South Western and the North-Western Stock Growers Associations were taken over by the Western Stock Growers Association in 1896.[61] That association quickly became the single most important advocate of the cattlemen, and it continued the fight against all the most threatening elements on the Canadian frontier. In 1897 it and the North-West Territories government together combated wolves by offering a bounty of "ten dollars per head for every female … killed."[62] Four years later, when the "North west government wolf bounty fund … [was] exhausted," the papers announced that the "bounties are now being paid entirely from the funds of the Western Stock Growers Association."[63]

The impact of American methods and personnel was so pervasive on the practical level that it naturally made a powerful cultural impression as well. Admiration of frontiersmen from the south gave rise to a sort of second-level social elite, based on the romantic image of the cowboy rather than property ownership. British and eastern ranchers may well have had their grand balls and their polo clubs, but on the streets of Calgary and Fort Macleod it was the frontier cowboy who caught the public imagination. It was his special status in most everyone's mind that shaped and directed popular culture. In 1886 a London journalist wrote:

> The management of these ranches is generally in the hands of Englishmen and Scotchmen with Ontario men, but the foremen, herders and cowboys are

Day herders, Milk River area, 1912

mostly from the States. In fact, this district, its towns, and manners and methods are very American, so that it seems much like a section of the western American frontier ... The lasso and lariat, the broad-rimmed cowboy hat, the leather breeches, and imposing cartridge belts one meets at the frontier towns on the Union and Pacific railways are reproduced in this district in the same reckless and extravagant fashion. The cowboy dialect rules supreme in the talk of the people, while the American national game of "draw poker"... [and] stud poker flourishes exuberantly at Fort Macleod and elsewhere ... The cowboy who can ride the fastest and "round-up" the largest herd is the popular hero in this part of Alberta.[64]

Respect for cowboys was so deeply ingrained that people were prepared to forgive (indeed to eulogize) almost any sort of behaviour by them.[65] "The story of the stockmen and ranches is one that presents most interesting characters and characteristics," a journalist wrote in 1912, "men of ability, of judgment, of superiority in many ways." They were "rough, uncultured, crude, but with a mentality that often placed them superior to the most highly polished, for ranching was a big business and it required big men to handle it most successfully." The same writer was prepared to perform mental gymnastics to support his basic thesis. Cowboys, he opined, "might consider it was legitimate to brand a maverick, to round up a stray calf and put the sign of ownership on it, but his word was usually

Southern Alberta, 1907

unquestioned and statements were pledges." These men were "honest, clean and straight in all their money dealings even though they might pick up a calf."[66]

The contradictions in this statement are striking. Despite the fact that the ranchers stole from each other the very commodity upon which the survival of their industry depended, they were the epitome of virtue, loyalty, and honesty. Many of the cattlemen were, indeed, involved in a considerable amount of rustling and other dubious activities. However, condemnation of such activities was far from universal. Often the person who did not glorify the cattlemen's behaviour simply refused to believe any charges of impropriety. "The practice of laying all sorts of crime at the feet of the cowboys is a very grave mistake," another writer insisted. "In a majority of crimes where some dastardly act has been committed the paper reporting it says it was 'a cowboy from the upper valley' did the deed, with no thought of mentioning the name or the outfit in which he works." This is a serious injustice because "every puncher in the section referred to is more or less injured." Besides, "in nine cases out of ten these 'cowboys' who wear the long hair and 'paint 'er red' in a low down style are not entitled to be known as cowboys." They are, as a rule, "tin horn gamblers or outcasts of the lowest type – left the states for stealing chickens or sheep." The real cowboy "is a gentleman always. He is not given to indulging in 'wild and wooley' antics. There is not a more faithful or larger hearted class of labouring men on earth."[67]

Because men with frontier training were advanced in a range of important activities, and because they seemed to flourish in the cattle industry, people became blind to reality and raised them to hero status. They lost sight of the fact that cowboys were in most respects just a cross-section of humanity – some good, some bad, some in-between. Presumably many non-Americans who defended and eulogized cowboys were themselves ranch hands or smaller owners who actually worked on the spreads and learned through trial and error to utilize their techniques. One, named Newbolt, embraced not only the skills but also what he considered some of the most salient habits of his fellow workers. Late in life he relished the memory that after he had spent a number of years on the Military Colonization Company Ranch he had learned not only to "ride and rope with any of them" but also to "hold my own in a poker game, and had acquired a liking for good whiskey."[68] Billie Hopkins, who ran his own spread, became competent in all aspects of ranching and with time he too showed signs of almost complete cultural assimilation. Thus, for example, much to his wife's chagrin, when he attended social functions he preferred to wear a Stetson hat, a "large silk coloured bandanna," and a "buckskin coat that he got from a Stoney Indian" rather than a formal suit, collar, and dress shirt that he had brought from England.[69]

The frontier and its open and boundless setting were instrumental in determining the flavour and character of this new civilization just as they were in selecting the means by which its most important staple industry should be operated. They were a great determiner that influenced the way people behaved, the way they viewed and judged each other, and the manner in which they gained a sense of self. In a society with more men than women, it should not be surprising that men made most of the judgments. It would seem appropriate to point out that women who came west were inclined to accept these judgments. A lady who settled on a ranch on the Milk River in the early 1900s later remembered with unmistakable nostalgia, "I would ride out alone" to the round-up, "spend all day and old Sammy [my horse] would bring me home as I would be completely lost on the wide open prairies":

> After awhile I think the men felt if I were to be hanging around all day I may as well be useful so they put me to work helping hold herd. Then one day Jim Turner [the foreman] said 'Cut out that steer and put him out of the other side of the herd.' Was I ever scared but I did not dare show it. Old Sammy was a perfect cut horse so into the herd of one thousand or more cattle I reined the old horse to the one that was to be taken out. Sammy did the work while I was riding for all I was worth. The herd hold boys were all watching to see how I made out which must have met with their approval and satisfaction because after that, they really put me to work whenever I went to the round-up.[70]

The same woman married a man named Emery LaGrandeur who was hired to break horses on the ranch and later became a rodeo star. What first drew her to him? "I never saw a better exhibition of riding by any rider at anytime."[71]

4
Nature's Fury

WARREN M. ELOFSON
WITH JOEL W. BULGER

This is the only life! I have any number of troubles – in fact too many to mention – but I forget them all in this joyous air, with the grand protecting mountains always standing round the western horizon. They seem the very spirit of the lovely old hymn "Abide with Me – O Thou that changest not," and they are the dearest most constant of friends …

It is the spirit of the West that charms one, and I cannot convey it to you, try as I may. It is a shy wild spirit and will not leave its native mountains and rolling prairies, and though I try to get it into my letters I fail, but I must warn you that if it once charms you it becomes an obsession, and one grows very lonely away from it. No Westerner who has felt its fascination ever is really content again in the conventional East.

Mary E. Inderwick, 1884[1]

The words penned by the wife of a large leaseholder in the foothills of Alberta in 1884 provide a glimpse of how effectively the environment worked on the human imagination on the frontier. After little more than a year in the West, Mary Inderwick believed she could sense its essence and its special qualities. She felt that the great open expanses and rugged terrain were making an enormous impact on her life, and she struggled to put it into words. In a few short years the ranch failed because of financial problems. And then, no doubt, some of her faith in the West was shaken. It must have felt as though her "grand protecting mountains" had abandoned her as she and her husband were forced to abandon them.

Although the environment did not in the end shelter the young woman in the way she seems to have expected, it did, as she recognized, deeply affect not only her life but that of virtually everyone in her society. An important message in the remainder of this study is that just as a combination of natural and frontier conditions helped to construct the ranching industry, they also forced it to change. In the process they sounded the death knell for the majority of the largest operations. However, they also encouraged adjustments by many others that would prove crucial to the survival of the agricultural industry in general in a considerable part of the prairie West.

This and the succeeding two chapters examine the most important forces that were involved in this process. They illustrate with some precision how those forces exerted their influence on the ranchers and how they compelled them to modify their practices.

To comprehend the power of the environment over the early cattle industry, it is necessary to keep in mind how limited the human resources were which the ranchers had to rely upon in order to confront it. This illustrates two basic realities. The first is that the challenges all the cattlemen faced were immense. The second is that the largest of the ranchers were, in important respects, less well equipped than the smaller ones to meet them. To make the latter point it is necessary to compare the manpower respectively available to the large and the small operations. The cattle barons had big dreams, but they were also businessmen and they intended to achieve their dreams with as little expense as possible. Among other things, that entailed keeping the labour force down to a bare minimum. Even in the summertime, when the cattle on the pastures required regular attention because of the need to brand and castrate newborn calves and market the fat steers, the cowboy-to-animal numbers were maintained in a ratio of one to somewhere between five hundred and one thousand. And the bigger the operation, the lower the ratio was likely to be. The leaseholders with ten thousand cattle normally hired no more than some ten or twelve stockmen.

The modern cattleman will attest that it is extremely difficult to manage livestock under those conditions. Moreover, the modern cattleman has advantages that his frontier predecessor lacked. The most obvious of these is proper networks of fences that give him the ability to regulate the movements of his animals and to restrict them at any given time to particular areas. Because he has had generations to string barbed wire around and across his pastures, today's rancher always knows where all his cattle are and he can go directly to them and attend to their needs whenever necessary. He can take feed to them when they are short, treat them relatively easily for wounds or diseases, and sort them into different groups depending on age, size, and gender. He can even match specific bulls with specific cows. The first ranchers, of course, enjoyed no such luxury.

The usual practice on the great ranches was for the cowboys to watch the cattle as much as possible from their horses and drive them back more or less to within the parameters of the lease when they inclined to wander too far. This seems to have been done with varying degrees of success but, for the sake of comparison, assume that it was achieved. Assume also that each cowboy was called upon to look after one thousand animals on his own which were spread out over, say, twenty thousand acres.[2] On horseback that would have been a formidable task. Just to walk his horse around his domain (approximately eight miles by four miles, or twenty-four miles in total distance) at four miles per hour would have taken him six hours and would have kept him at any one time five to eight miles away from parts of it. On a single patrol, he would never have been able to be sure that he had even seen all his cattle, spread out as they would have been over such a large area. He could not possibly protect them properly from predators, he could not be there to help many of the cows with calving problems, he could not get feed to anything like all of them on short notice, and he certainly was unable to exercise much control over breeding. The cattle he was responsible for simply wandered most of the time, oblivious to his protective eye.

The difficulty of this situation was heightened by the fact that while the range was still open the great ranches often did not succeed in keeping the cattle on their leases. When storms came up, the cattle would turn against the wind and then drift in the direction it was blowing. Even when the badly outnumbered cowboys happened to be in position to attempt to stop them, they found it almost impossible. The animals would move stubbornly on while the men did little more than drift with them. As the storm raged, small bunches would inevitably break away from the main lot, and many of the cattle would become dispersed, sometimes ending up a hundred miles or more from where they had started out. Obviously, when this happened, the ranch hand's thousand head became scattered across a lot more than twenty thousand acres. John Ware discovered this the hard way when he was working for the Bar U in 1883. During an early autumn snowstorm he attempted to keep a number of cattle together on the lease and found himself pushed along with them for four days and some fifty miles. He nearly froze to death and could well have died from starvation had he not been able to shoot a deer. Fred Stimson and other cowboys eventually tracked him and the herd down. By that time, however, the cattle had gone too far from the ranch site to be driven back, even with reinforcements, until better weather prevailed.[3]

At the other end of the spectrum from the large lessees were the ordinary ranchers who came out to the West as squatters and settlers in the 1870s and early '80s or were part of one of the two waves of homesteaders who started to settle respectively in the early 1890s and just after 1900. To the modern reader the lives of the small ranchers on the frontier do not appear easy. Most of them did not normally hire any help, in part because they could not afford it. In many cases therefore they worked their herds entirely on their own. In the beginning

Brown Ranch, Queenstown, Alberta (ca. 1900–03)

of course they too did so without the luxury of fundamental facilities; initially few of them had wives. They found their plots of land, quickly erected tiny log, board, or tar-paper shacks, often with dirt floors and earthen roofs, and they began grazing their herds while starting construction on their first corrals, chutes, outbuildings, and fences.

Still, life was not nearly as problematical for the small rancher with forty or fifty cattle to look after as for the hired hand on the great spread with one thousand or more.[4] The small rancher could get to know all his cattle well, and he could, by putting down his tools and riding out for short periods every day or so, keep them for the most part close to home. His livestock would also tend to drift at times but with determined action, he was able to offer serious resistance even during storms. When he did lose some cattle, he could go after them with a reasonable chance of finding them and bringing them back, even if this meant scouring the prairies for days.

The small rancher is exemplified by William Brown, a man who established himself in the Queenstown area on the south side of the Bow River in the mid-1890s. He had come out to the Canadian Pacific Colonization Company Ranch from England in 1890 and shortly afterwards had been appointed general manager. When the company went bankrupt in early 1891, Brown was given a small salary to manage the stock as it was being sold off.[5] In 1893 he attained a settlement with the company which apparently gave him some land of his own. However, it left him with very little money to buy cattle.[6] Therefore, he had to be careful with his resources, trying to build up his own herd while looking after stock for other ranchers. In August 1893 he was tending over a hundred head. A few of these were his own, and the rest belonged to W. Middleton, manager of the Canadian Coal and Agricultural Colonization Company Ranch at Namaka.[7]

By May 1894 Brown was operating from his own place, and he turned all the cattle out on the open range close by.[8] That month, in the course of negotiating his pay, he stressed the extra work the Middleton cattle entailed as they were not fenced in and required a great deal of herding. "They are scattered over the prairie ... [and] need someone constantly amongst them till they are all calved, our own cattle stay and don't go far so they need no hunting." Brown was earning his money. There tends to be about a 10 per cent natural loss of newborn calves in any herd due to calving problems.[9] This, he understood, can be improved if there is someone to assist the animals in difficulty and protect them from wolves drawn to the birthing site by the smell of blood.

One night an enormous rainstorm struck and "scattered all the cattle in every direction." This was a huge setback as it forced him to take to the wilds in what must have seemed at times an almost hopeless attempt to recapture them. A letter of 31 May evinces his frustrations. "Up to this date I have been fifteen days in the saddle," he told Middleton. "In that time I have only had five days help – I have been twice down the Little Bow near to Lethbridge, from which direction I brought in 29 head yesterday – I have ridden the country over east, north & west – I collect the cattle but no one in my absence looks after them, and now I have to start out today again to gather strays from the bunch."[10] The first night of the storm Brown had corralled over eighty: his own, Middleton's, and some belonging to a neighbour. The neighbour "would have none of his cattle corralled and came over early the next morning" and turned all of the animals loose. Brown found himself faced with the frustrating task of climbing back into the saddle and spending a number of days gathering them up once again.[11]

Eventually he got nearly all the stock back, but not without tremendous effort. In June he wrote a letter to a rancher down on the Little Bow range, describing how his cattle had drifted into that area. He said he had lost an unbranded heifer about nine months old that he had hand fed and generally nurtured from birth. "I have only a few cattle of my own," he told the rancher, "and would not like to lose this heifer, I would feel much obliged if you will kindly help me to recover her."[12] It would be nice to think that this Englishman, a newcomer in a hard country, eventually retrieved his animal. These letters bring the basic situation into focus at an individual level. Here was a small operator trying to establish himself. He had little outside help and he was pushed absolutely to the limit. The point is, however, that he was managing. He was familiar with all his animals and knew when any were missing and exactly which ones. Consequently he was ultimately able to keep the bulk of his stock together.

Considering how difficult this was for him with such a small herd, it is clear that the ranch hand on the big outfit was greatly overmatched. The cowboy, swamped with a thousand cattle spread out at the best of times over twenty thousand acres, could not possibly give them the attention that ordinary ranchers could give theirs. He was forced to leave all the cattle for the most part to themselves and then trust to providence that he would get as many of them as possible back on the round-ups. It was with respect to protecting his herds from some rather formidable frontier crises that the odds were stacked most emphatically against him. Among these crises, the most overwhelming, which have probably got the most press, were the very severe winters. They worked in conjunction with other natural forces to devastate the cattle herds on the open range year after year.

The worst of the winters saw temperatures that plummeted and stayed low for weeks or even months at a time and snow that fell to such a depth that it covered the tallest grasses in the high country, cutting the cattle off from feed. In such winters the death loss in the herds from the dual effects of hunger and cold could be enormous. Indeed, the fact that severe winters occurred with some regularity in the frontier period eventually proved pivotal. It did much to alter the manner in which the cattle business was conducted, and at length it was decisive in putting an end to open range ranching in general and large-scale open range ranching in particular.

Once they had encountered some difficult winters and witnessed the destruction they could cause, most of the small cattlemen who came West stopped leaving their cattle to their own devices year round. They put up reserves of wild hay for feed and made sure their cattle could have access to it whenever necessary. Because their animals were few, it was not too difficult to find suitable supplies. They simply cut the native grasses growing in low-lying areas near sloughs, lakes, and streams and in the flood plains of the valleys carved by the Bow, Old Man, and Saskatchewan rivers as they headed east from the foothills and the Rockies. The grass was cut and raked by horse-drawn machinery and then loaded onto wagons,

Ranch hand mowing grass, A7 Ranch, Nanton, Alberta (ca. 1910–12)

hauled and stacked by hand. This did not prevent significant losses from occurring in the case where an owner was not conscientious enough to keep close track of his animals and thus was unable to find them in storms and get them to feed. Usually, however, the majority of small operators were able to avert catastrophe. Some eventually began penning up their cattle in log corrals when the weather was bad so they could feed and look after them on a daily basis until it was safe to turn them out again.

A full-grown gestating cow requires approximately thirty pounds of dry hay a day when she can get nothing else. In some winters in southern Alberta and Saskatchewan it might be necessary to feed her for up to one hundred days. To be safe, therefore, the rancher required about a ton and a half of hay per head per winter. A small herd of fifty animals would need about seventy-five tons. In low-lying areas of even the driest regions it was not unreasonable to expect a ton of hay per acre. Therefore the man with fifty animals had to harvest some seventy-five acres each year to be fairly sure of being able to maintain his entire herd. The labour for this he could pretty much supply himself, at least after he had got through the first few years and finished building some basic facilities. This was natural hay and thus he did not have to cultivate fields or do any sowing to attain it. Cutting and stacking is labour-intensive and especially when temperatures are high, it is physically demanding. But since only some seventy-five acres were involved and particularly since other traditional field activities were unnecessary, it was within the bounds of what one hard-working man could accomplish in a summer season.

The large outfits were far less well prepared to cope with the worst winters. The task of putting up enough feed to get a thousand cattle through the entire cold season was impossible for one hired man. It would have required him to hay some 1,500 acres. With modern technology an individual might accomplish that now, but with early twentieth-century equipment, he could not even have come close. Many of the big ranchers soon realized they were going to need supplies of stored feed for the occasions when the snow was deep and the chinooks failed them.[13] They thus turned to haying, but the amount they put up was extremely limited in comparison to their livestock numbers. The Cochrane had four hundred acres of hay land as early as 1883.[14] It needed something like fourteen thousand acres to be sure of getting all its cattle through.[15] During the harsh spring of 1903 one observer noted that "it is feared that the losses of cattle among large ranchers who do not feed hay, will be considerable here. The length of the winter has made serious inroads in the hay of those who do feed, some are even now without it."[16] When looking back on the 1906–07 winter a woman who had been a cowhand on the Spencer Ranch remembered that "the loss was terrific." In those days, "the policy of ranching was to put up as much [roughage] … as they could. But with so many cattle they could not begin to feed all."[17]

The great ranchers were taking a big risk. After the long, hard winter of 1886–87 most of the bigger spreads adopted the strategy of keeping their older cows and younger calves in corrals and small pasture areas fenced in near what hay they had.[18] However, they continued the practice of turning out the bulk of their brood cows and heifers and all the steers that were as yet not ready for market. These were always threatened with starvation during long cold spells.

The big range herds suffered during the winter months from one other relative disadvantage. Even with the passing of considerable time, most of them could not be properly fenced in. Again the reason was the manpower deficiency. If the average settler by the mid-1890s had a 160 acre homestead and a three-hundred acre lease, he had, to be sure, a lot of work to do in order to enclose all his pastures. However, it was possible for him to accomplish this much more quickly than the hired hands on the great ranches could. By the survey system established in 1872 the 160 acre homesteads were set up as squares with sides half a mile long. Therefore, the average homesteader had to build two miles of barbed wire fences to surround his deeded land.

By working at it consistently when he was not haying or hunting down dispersed livestock, he could expect to do so in one or two years.[19] Then he could use the open range for summer pasture and keep all his cattle near home in the wintertime where he could feed and care for them when necessary. If he continued to work at it, moreover, he might within the space of five or six years enclose his lease land too. At that point he would have his entire herd fenced and protected from the open range year round.

Many of the smaller ranchers fenced off their pastures very quickly. Along both sides of the Belly River southwest of Macleod a number of them had apparently completely enclosed an entire twenty-five-mile stretch as early as 1885.[20] By 1901 settlers' fences were already beginning to make district round-ups difficult everywhere except south of Medicine Hat, here and there in the hills, and along the Red Deer River southeast of Calgary.[21] For the man with twenty thousand acres under his charge, similar progress was plainly unattainable. He would have needed to string about twenty-four miles of barbed wire just to enclose his section. At a rate of one to two miles a year this might well have taken him nearly a quarter of a century and he would have needed decades more to construct cross-fencing to reduce his pastures to a manageable size. In view of this, what the men on the great ranches did in the earliest days was concentrate their efforts on assembling the fences and corrals around the home site that were needed for the older cows and young calves. After that they worked away slowly at enclosing any deeded land that the owners bought up. However, they never finished the job and they neglected the leases almost completely.[22] Consequently, a large percentage of the cattle owned by the big ranches was liable at any one time to wander far and wide. Even in years when there happened to be some extra feed on hand or when some could be purchased from neighbours, it could be impossible to find or to reach many of these cattle in the blinding storms and deep snow.

A close look at some of the losses that occurred illustrates the seriousness of this situation. The winter of 1906–07 is legendary for its ferociousness. It has been given considerable play in L.V. Kelly's book, *Range Men,* and in articles and stories based in large part on the memories of some of the people who actually experienced it.[23] Less well known is the fact that prolonged cold spells and blizzards overwhelmed cattle on the range year after year. When reading about this, it is difficult not to wonder why it took some ranchers so long to recognize the risks they were taking. The devastation suffered by the Cochrane outfit between the fall of 1881 and spring of 1883 has already been noted. No business could possibly have afforded such reversals. Yet when viewed with the losses suffered by many of the major ranchers in other years, the Cochrane experience begins to seem almost ordinary.[24]

The winter that began in late 1886 was remembered by some cattlemen as the worst ever. After a succession of storms had raged for months the *Macleod Gazette* sent a reporter out across the country on the Canadian Pacific Railway to assess the situation. He wrote that around Maple Creek the snow

> was about two feet deep and very hard and cattle were getting a rough deal … everything points to a very heavy loss in that locality … Between Dunmore and Lethbridge the snow is from eighteen inches to two feet deep, and quite hard. Cattle down there cannot begin to get through to the grass. As far as … the eye could reach on all sides of the track, there was not a bare spot of ground. We saw about a dozen head of cattle altogether down there … They were skin poor and seemed scarcely able to drag one foot after another sinking as they did each step up to their bellies in snow. In one of the section houses there were three dead animals, and there were several lying close to the track. The train we were on stopped half a dozen times in a few miles for cattle on the track, but they trot along ahead of the engine, and the shrillest whistle will not make them get off into the deep snow at either side, and they cannot be headed off on foot. In this way several have been run over.[25]

What had happened was that the range herds had drifted out of the hills and onto the plains as the icy winds had blown out of the northwest. One of the ranches that suffered very badly was the Quorn. In the previous fall it had brought out several hundred "dogies" or "stockers" – yearlings or two-year olds, in this case from Manitoba – that the management intended to graze, fatten, and sell for slaughter in one or two seasons. These animals had been raised on small farms and had been hand fed during much of their previous lives. They were therefore not at all capable when it came to fending for themselves and began to starve very quickly. Many of them soon gave up and just lay down in the snow to die. One of the cowboys later testified that on several occasions he went out with John Ware who was employed by the Quorn that winter. "When we found any buried in the snow-drifts or lying, too weak to get up, we drew our six-shooters and killed them."[26]

In the spring the ranchers had to confront the depressing sight of the bodies of dead animals lying all over the prairie. The spectacle was made truly dreadful by the fact that before they died groups of cattle had crowded close together in a pitiful attempt to shelter themselves. As a result hundreds could be seen in heaps – little mountains of rotting flesh, seemingly here, there, and everywhere. Close investigation showed that the throats and stomachs of many of the cattle were lined with the hair which, in their hunger, they had sucked off each other's hides. Some also had their throats "punctured and torn by sharp splinters from dried and frozen branches and chunks of wood which they had swallowed in their anguish."[27]

Contemporaries were shocked. Kelly believed that "the average" loss was "about twenty-five per cent in the Calgary district, fifty to sixty per cent from High River to the Old Man's River, twenty to twenty-five per cent in the Pincher Creek country, and fifty per cent in Medicine Hat."[28] A.E. Cross himself in later years offered the opinion that "few of the ranchers lost less than 40 per cent, some losing 100, many losing 75 per cent."[29] The Quorn lost "nearly every hoof." Tom Lynch who had imported nearly three hundred stockers the previous summer, was left with eighty. The N Bar N outfit had just started operations in the Wood Mountain area the year before with six thousand cattle. Its cowboys pulled out of Canada in the spring trailing a scant two thousand.[30]

It was this particular episode that prompted many big cattlemen to change their ways as they began to comprehend that smaller men had avoided losses comparable to their own. Around Pincher Creek and in the Davisburg district south of Calgary, a number of the latter had put up sufficient supplies of hay and had fenced in their herds. They apparently "managed to come out in good order."[31] A few years later the North-West Mounted Police report for Macleod and Lethbridge areas indicated that all of the ranchers "no matter what class of stock is their specialty, now cut large quantities of hay, and nearly all have shelter of some description for weak stock. Some of the more advanced cow-men are now yarding up their calves in the fall and feeding all winter."[32]

This of course was only a partial solution for the biggest ranches. In March 1892 "the bitterest blizzard in twenty years, killed many cattle in every district."[33] On 24 April it began to rain in the evening and poured steadily through the night. The following afternoon the rain turned to snow, which continued to fall all through the next night and the following morning. A strong and bitterly cold north wind magnified the effects of plunging temperatures. Great numbers of cattle that had been thoroughly drenched and chilled by the rain were stressed to the breaking point. As the storm raged "the poor creatures could do nothing but drift before [it] … turning neither to the right hand nor to the left, and if any obstruction, such as a fence, barred their onward progress, they simply stood there till they died with the snow drifting over them."[34] Charles Craig had purchased thirty-five head of dairy cows and turned them loose on his pasture west of Macleod. They disappeared in the blizzard, "neither hide nor hoof remaining, the conjecture being that the entire herd was driven over a cut bank and perished." The Circle Ranch lost five hundred calves and thirty cows.[35] Later, when warm temperatures melted the snow near the ranch, the "water in the springs and small streams was very bad, owing to contamination from the putrefying beef."[36] As so often happens after a tough winter, the losses also vastly exceeded the immediate body count. Many of the surviving cows that suffered and were subjected to stress in the storms later aborted or produced stillborn offspring. This appears to have been by far the greatest financial blow to many of the ranchers.

Natural disaster sometimes seems to have a way of striking when the agricultural industry is least able to take it. This is precisely what happened in the early 1890s. The 1892–93 winter was even worse than the previous one. In the early weeks of 1893 at least eight thousand cattle succumbed in the foothills districts south of Calgary. And the losses were not confined to the foothills. In writing about their holdings in the Cypress Hills, D.H. Andrews told his British directors that this had been "the worst weather I ever experienced; the Tuesday morning … the thermometer went down to 64 below zero, the next day it was 56 below and a wind blowing there. For 12 days it averaged over 40 below, with snow storms every third day. Three bulls froze to death in the sheds one night and six calves were lost, at Crane Lake 5 bulls and 12 calves, we had to feed everything all they could eat during the storm, and had to feed inside … we shall have a big loss on range cattle."[38]

Andrews went on to estimate losses at the Stair Ranch holdings from Balgonie and Maple Creek in present-day Saskatchewan to Mosquito Creek in the foothills of southern Alberta. A few weeks later, he informed his owners that he might actually have underestimated the damage: "the loss in the Cypress Hills & Mosquito Creek [districts] … you will think a very heavy one. What the loss is in the Cypress Hills no one can tell, as we have not been able to ride to where the cattle have drifted since November and cannot tell what the loss is until the snow goes & we can get a wagon & outfit down there; I hope I have over estimated it, but am afraid it will be more than I have taken off. We have had a worse winter than has ever been known before in this country, it has been almost impossible to move about." This letter also provides evidence that small-scale husbandry was proving less risky than large-scale grazing. "Our loss at the farms," Andrews said (where the cattle were fenced in and close to plenty of hay), "has not been heavy except at Crane Lake where we had the weaned calves, and ran out of feed about the middle of February."[39]

In the later 1890s the problem of weak cows losing their calves again brought springtime losses that many ranchers previously had not figured on. The "very cold and stormy weather in November 1896, was expected to have disastrous results on stock in some sections of the country," the police commissioner recounted the following year. While "this fear was not directly realized, there was "a considerable decrease in the calf crop."[40] In 1898 similar circumstances prevailed. An officer at Macleod reported that "the calf brand is smaller than usual," and he explained that "a great number of deaths occurred among young stock in the early part of the year. From the depth of snow on the ground during March the cattle became emaciated, and were unable to withstand the cold." The second half of March was especially stormy, "trails were blocked, travel in many localities impossible, and horses as well as cattle showed the effect of the weather."[41]

When cows did not produce calves, it meant of course that all the expenses that had gone into buying, maintaining and pasturing them, and supplying them with breeding bulls, went to waste. Moreover, pastures would not be filled in the spring with newborn calves. It was when that happened that the risks derived from winter grazing shot up as the ranchers were more likely to import dogies from the East or, depending on the market, from the southern states and Mexico.[42]

In the early spring of 1902–03 it was principally both the dogies and the newborn calves that were diminished. Talk among the cattlemen themselves set the losses at about fifteen thousand, mainly in the foothills south and west of Calgary.[43] Near Maple Creek,

> severe weather [in February] compelled ranchers to begin feeding hay to their stock, and March was a severe month: the snow was heavily crusted in some parts, and cattle were reported to be getting low in condition. April opened with snow, followed by rain, and heavy frosts were experienced at the end of the month. A very severe storm set in on May 16, and lasted for nearly a week; a great deal of snow fell, particularly in the western part of the district, where it was very deep. There was considerable frost at night, and as a consequence of this storm, stockmen sustained considerable loss, chiefly amongst … young calves. A great many of the "doggies" [sic] … died from exposure, some in railway cars, some in the stock yards, and larger numbers on the prairie.[44]

The next spring another late storm near Crane Lake brought considerable destruction to yearlings imported from Mexico and Texas. In

Dead cattle on Bow River Horse Ranch after severe winter storm, 22 May 1903

an interview with a reporter for the *Macleod Gazette* Andrews gave a clear indication that many of his operation's cattle were still out in the elements away from human contact when the storm hit. "No attempt has been made to hunt up the stock as yet," he said, and therefore no adequate picture of the losses could be attained. He estimated, however, that the average everywhere on the southeastern cattle ranges would be between 10 and 20 per cent. "The storm was so heavy and continuous that in many cases even if the cattle did get shelter under a cut bank, they would starve for the snow was so heavy that they could not travel."[45] How close to the mark the 10 to 20 per cent was is unknown, but Andrews, as noted previously, could, in his concern for the financial well-being of his own ranch, incline to guess low rather than high.[46]

The winter of 1906–07 was the last straw for many of the cattlemen, and after it was over most of the great ranches and a good number of the smaller ones were liquidated.[47] The disaster actually began in the autumn of 1906 when fires resulting from an extremely dry late summer and almost unending hot winds from the west damaged much of the pasture across the entire country south of Calgary.[48] This situation was made worse because many ranchers happened at that time to be overstocking their ranges principally by importing dogies once again.[49] As a consequence the cattle generally had not been well fed over the summer and fall, and many were already suffering from improper nutrition before winter set in. This was compounded, moreover, because there happened that same year to be some severe outbreaks of the mange.[50]

Ironically, in late October and early November when it was too late to affect the amount of growth in the pastures, it began to rain. It continued to do so for two or so weeks and then on the night of November 15 the rain turned to snow and the temperature dropped to 15 degrees below zero Fahrenheit. Some three feet of snow fell in only a few hours. Then temperatures climbed above freezing for a short interval and when the blizzard began again and the thermometer dropped, there was a layer of hard crust under the fresh snow that made it even more difficult for the cattle to graze. That year the chinooks did not return. One blizzard followed another until late spring.

By the middle of December all the available hay that had been put up for the range cattle was either gone or covered by gigantic snow drifts.[51] The cattle began to die from starvation and cold. Soon many began to push south in a futile attempt to escape the northern winds and to find food. Some ranchers attempted to hold them back in vain. By the thousands the cattle were cut off by the fenced-in rail line of the Canadian Pacific Railway where they were found dead in the spring. Others pushed down the fences and staggered out onto the flat and treeless prairie. They ate everything in their path – supplies of hay in farmyards, small sapling trees sticking through the snow, the hair off the backs of one another. Near Fort Macleod, Charlie Brewster and his wife spent much of the winter fighting off starving cattle from the Red Deer River. "They almost walked over his buildings, and desperately tried to get at his small feed stack." The couple spent many hours in the bitter cold "urging the moaning animals past their home. No matter how much they loved animals, there was nothing they could do."[52]

Carcasses began to pile up all over the prairie against fences and in river valleys or low spots between hills where many had taken refuge before dying. For weeks starving cattle strayed hopelessly through urban centres including Fort Macleod and Maple Creek. In Medicine Hat, supplies of hay were brought in to help the cattle but still many died on the city streets or became so emaciated that they had to be shot. "At Fort Macleod, the town water carrier dragged a frozen carcass to the dump each time he returned from his deliveries."[53]

There are numerous eyewitness accounts of various traumatic events from this celebrated winter. One of the most eloquent, and most often quoted, is that supplied by L.V. Kelly respecting the town of Macleod.[54] The following description of conditions near the present-day border between Alberta and Saskatchewan helps to demonstrate that the arm of the tragedy stretched a long way beyond the foothills.

> Beginning in early fall … a raging blizzard that caught stockmen unawares, lasted into the next summer. At Sounding Lake the storm had broken on the 16th of November. Snow driven by high, fierce winds commenced to fall that day and fall steadily for three days. By that time it was three feet deep on the level and packed hard.
>
> The frightened cattle splintering into bunches began to drift before the storm. They kept on travelling until they were far from their home range …
>
> Riders who were to suffer the torture from the bitter cold that followed … took out after the wand[er]ers and tried to drive them back. All such efforts though valiant were unavailing. The creatures exhausted by hunger and exposure refused to move … Breaking through and cutting their legs on the crust or the hard-packed snow worked untold hardship on the horses, causing such lameness among them it was cruelty to force them to work any longer. So the struggle to save these drifters was given up.
>
> The hunger-maddened and shivering cattle-creatures at first bellowed frantically, drifting and milling in a frenzied search for food, for protection from the freezing gale, and finally some began to weaken and then to fail. The cries grew fainter and fainter and finally ceased. Soon they perished in twos and threes, in scores and at last, in hundreds. The cowboys, helpless and sick at heart, turned their tired, crippled ponies homeward and left the unhappy drifters to their fate.[55]

Bizarre stories about this winter abound. Ranchers noticed that even when they got hay to starving animals that were still on their feet, it was sometimes too late to save them. They just stood in one spot and stared with glazed eyes, too weak to devour the feed.[56] In the spring the owner of the Turkey Track Ranch in the Cypress Hills discovered that he had been "cleaned out." When the snow was finally gone he and his nephew "started out to look the situation over."[57] They must have known approximately what to expect. Still what they saw astonished them. "Three hundred carcasses in a ride of less than two miles, five hundred on the river flats, eighteen more in a log shack they intended occupying themselves that night." A person who had taken up residence at the Spencer Ranch that summer later remembered that "there were so many dead cattle from the hard winter, that I found them very useful in helping me find my way about the prairies." For instance, "at the fork of the road there was a dead Texas steer with huge horns and that was my sign to turn to the river bottom on the trail that led to the … camp" below.[58]

But what was it like over the entire winter for individual ranching operations? It is possible to piece together a fairly accurate and detailed picture from the Cross letters in the Glenbow Archives in Calgary. These demonstrate not only the severe damage that many ranchers incurred but, once again, that it was sustained mainly by those who were still relying on the open range. The letters also illustrate the extreme pressures that the weather placed on the shoulders of men who attempted to attend the livestock daily. Cross was keeping cattle in two different locations. The majority, on the A7 Ranch at Nanton, were under the foremanship of Archie McCallum. Another 630 were on unfenced land Cross had leased from the Canadian Pacific Railway at Bassano.[59] Charlie Douglass,[60] who also had a small ranch of his own on the Red Deer River, was handling them.[61]

At Nanton a close-management approach had been adopted from an early stage. By this time there were corrals and fences to control the livestock. McCallum wrote in February 1907, informing Cross that there was more snow at the ranch than he had ever seen. "We have lots of poor cows," he said, "but hope we won't lose many. Am feeding most of the herd now but if snow would get lighter I could turn quite a few of them out."[62] This indicates that he had a large holding pen for the animals. The fact he could gather them into the corral when the weather got bad and that he was prepared to turn them out when it improved indicates that he also had fenced some relatively small pastures where the cows could be observed and kept accessible throughout the winter. Cross had done enough fencing at his home ranch to keep all the cattle off the open range. He had also made provision for enough roughage to feed the entire herd through very long spells. Overall, losses at Nanton were small.

There is evidence that the A7 was far from alone in the amount of fencing it had accomplished by this time. In a 1908 letter Cross notified his foreman that he had bought three Hereford bulls and was having them shipped out to Nanton. "I shall telephone to Peter McIlroy to look after them so that the man coming from the ranch can find them in his stable, and I would advise his having them led out of Nanton and as far as the fenced road allowance about a half a mile or so, so that he can get a straight shoot to drive them in the lane, otherwise there will be trouble around town."[63] Thus fence construction was general enough in the countryside that there was a closed-in road allowance. All the man had to do once the bulls were out of town was stay behind them and keep them moving until they got to the ranch yard and the corrals.

At Bassano, by contrast, the land was still not fenced, and the country was open between the Red Deer and the Canadian Pacific Railway mainline running through Bassano about thirty to thirty-five miles to the south. Cross's management here was much less close and refined. Indeed, for much of the preceding summer the cattle appear to have run without any supervision at all.[64] Douglass had been preoccupied with haying, ploughing fireguards, and in other respects getting ready for winter on his own place.[65] Cross himself was totally out of contact with the herd. It was on 23 October that Billie Cochrane wrote the letter informing him that George Lane "told me to tell you that one of his men who is reliable, told him that your cattle on the Red Deer were badly affected with mange."[66] Cross was surprised to hear this news and immediately sent a letter off to Douglass asking him to check into it. At about the same time he was also apprised that one of his fat steers from the same area had strayed into a herd owned by a rancher named Scott near Gleichen.[67] It was unfortunate for Cross that the upcoming winter was to be one of the worst ever, but the fact that he allowed his animals to wander unprotected demonstrates that there was more than just bad luck involved.[68]

When the first winter storms began, the situation at Bassano was impossible. Douglass and Billy Maclean, who had been hired to help with all the extra work this winter created, spent much of their time in temperatures of 30 to 40 below zero Fahrenheit. They first fed up their meagre hay supplies and then they hauled hay, chopped oats, and greenfeed that had been purchased from neighbours. On a particular morning in November they were both nearly killed when a sudden storm caught them by surprise. Maclean went out alone to feed some cattle. About midway through the morning it started to snow, and the temperature which for a short time had been mild, suddenly fell dramatically. He was probably unprepared and poorly dressed and, ostensibly suffering from hypothermia, he left his horses and wagon at the stacks and set out across the prairie on foot. When he did not return at noon Douglass went after him. He soon came across Maclean, pulled him up on his horse, and started for home. The blizzard was now fierce, and Douglass found that he could not head directly into the wind. He made his way instead to the river and then under the protection of the steep banks was able to follow it to the house. They were two very lucky men. Within three hours one side of the house was completely drifted over. There was of course no way they could venture outside again until the storm began to subside.[69]

When the storm did let up a bit they realized that they were fighting an enormous battle.[70] From November things got progressively worse. "It was a daily occurrence to see dead animals being hauled out of the sheds where they had been trying to shelter."[71] On 20 January, Douglass wrote to Cross informing him of the situation on the Red Deer. He commented that the losses were bound to be heavy, as the cattle had drifted off their respective pastures into the

Feeding cattle on Wineglass Ranch north of Brocket, Alberta, 3 May 1907

river valley and were all mixed up. Those ranchers "that have hay can't get their cattle to it."[72] Douglass had been rounding up the Cross cattle to get as many as close to his ranch as possible. He had two teams busy hauling hay to about three hundred head at this time and he thought they had enough feed to last to the end of January.

A letter of 27 January illustrates that this bad situation quickly deteriorated. The cold weather and blowing snow continued, making it more and more difficult to haul feed. The cattle along the river were starving and eating brush. Douglass now had only about one hundred head of Cross's animals in the field and these were "all I can possibly manage so its no use looking for the poorest any more."[73] He reported on 16 March that they were skinning the hides off the dead animals that were not too mangy and selling them for six cents a pound. This he realized was not very profitable but he offered the commiserating observation that at least it helped defray the cost of some of the chop he was buying.[74]

Cross himself seems to have lived through this winter in great agony – unsure of his losses but terrified they were going to be severe indeed. His worst fears seem to have been realized. Early the summer of 1907 the CPR offered him free of charge a lease on land that he had paid good money for the year before. The railway company's agent explained that the railway was prepared to do this to help offset "the losses to cattle during the past winter … on land held under lease."[75] Cross declined, however. He was obviously discouraged. He thanked the company agent "for the kind consideration … for the welfare of the ranchmen who have been unfortunate enough to lose a large quantity of cattle" but said he had "made arrangements with Mr. George Lane to run my steers on his lease at Bassano."[76] Between the two of them, he and Lane now were running only enough cattle in the area to fill the one lease. "We got through about the hardest winter that there ever was in this country," Cross later told a business associate; "cattle at the present time are very cheap owing to the hard winter, and heavy losses."[77]

Contemporaries understood that the biggest ranches which were still dependent on the open range were the hardest hit everywhere. Early the next summer the commanding North-West Mounted Police officer at Macleod recollected, "Last winter was an exceptionally long and cold one. It was said to be the coldest in twenty years. Cattle in consequence suffered a great deal, and large losses had to be recorded, especially by the owners of large herds who could not feed and look after their stock in the way small owners could. These latter suffered very insignificant losses."[78]

It was estimated that the Calgary district lost 60 per cent of its stock; Lethbridge and Maple Creek 40 per cent and Pincher Creek 25 per cent.[79] "The Turkey Track Ranch, the Bloom Cattle Company, the Matador Land and Cattle Company, and the 76 Ranch all suffered equally."[80] Within a few years almost all were gone. The Bar U outfit lost at least nine thousand head.[81] Wilkinson & McCord lost three thousand and left the country. The Walrond lost five thousand head and sold out the following year.[82] The Two Bar Ranch near Gleichen apparently lost eleven thousand of thirteen thousand.[83] The Smith & Mussett outfit started the winter with 3,200 dogies and ended up with 250. The Glengary Ranch went from four thousand to 2,500. Bob Patterson lost a third of his 1,500. The High River Trading Company had pastured 1,200 cattle on the Red Deer the previous fall and had seventy-five left in the spring.[84] The weather of course had no respect for political boundaries, and much of the American northwest suffered a similar fate. In total, "some $11 million in stock perished."[85]

The information available with respect to all the most severe winters on the ranching frontier merely provides glimpses of the horror. There can be little question, however, that in the overall scheme of things, these winters were critical. Similar experiences today, when a death rate of 3 or 4 per cent after spring calving is considered the norm, would wipe out most producers. The winters that were harsh enough to really hurt a substantial number of the early ranchers were not infrequent. Those that have warranted our attention are 1881–02, 1882–03, 1886–07, 1891–92, 1892–93, 1896–97, 1897–98, 1902–03 and 1906–07. Nine winters out of twenty-six, or over a third of those that followed the opening of the era of the great ranches, brought great distress to what appears to have been a relatively large percentage of the cattlemen.

Cows and steers not only died in the winters but at times drifted so far that their owners never recovered them. Presumably in many instances they were taken into distant herds or were simply stolen by rustlers.[86] In November 1906 all the cattle in the vicinity of the community of Dorothy, some six thousand head, were being held for their second dipping for mange when the first storm hit. Despite the best efforts of the ranchers the cattle scattered towards the south in an attempt to evade the awful wind. Many perished when they were driven over cutbanks. Some were found two years later as far away as North Dakota.[87] Most, however, "were never seen again." The problem of drifting cattle on the open range could be costly to the ranchers in any winter that brought severe blizzards. In the late spring of 1890 D.H. Andrews wrote to Thomas Clary in Montana inquiring about cattle from his herds that had strayed across the border the previous winter. His riders had found thirty-five of them, but forty-three were still missing. Andrews wanted to know if Clary would gather and sell any of the strays he or his men found.[88] In September he wrote another letter to acknowledge the receipt of a cheque for $440 for the sale of seventeen steers. He offered thanks and help for Clary on the Canadian side of the border should he need it, and concluded by commenting, "if you should find any more of our steers if you could sell them with yours I would be very much obliged."[89]

Obviously the Stair was in the position that should the missing twenty-six head not show up, it would take a loss. In the area south of Crane Lake where the ranch's cattle normally grazed, a minimum of thirty acres was needed to maintain a steer for a year. The fact that these animals were sold ostensibly for slaughter suggests that they probably averaged around four years old. Thus they represented the profits off 780 acres over a five-year period[90] or a total of 780 5 or just under four thousand bovine acres. For a big ranch like the Stair, which was running several thousand head of cattle at the time, this could be absorbed. However, if it happened regularly it could also be one of the straws that helped to break the camel's back. The Stair Ranch was eventually liquidated in 1909 because of its depleted financial position.[91]

The immense impact of the harsh winters would have been bad enough for the industry had the cattle been able to get through the rest relatively unscathed. However, they were not. The truth is that life for the herds on the open range was anything but secure in the best of the cold seasons, simply because wandering cattle were not watched closely, nurtured, and protected the way they needed to be. Cowboys rode amongst the animals when the weather permitted and even cut out some of the sick or hurt ones and brought them to shelter where they could be looked after. However, they were not able to get to anything like all of the cattle with any regularity. It should be remembered that cowboy numbers were cut to the minimum after the final fall round-up was completed.[92] The following are entries in the daily journal of Billie Cochrane for the exceptionally mild winter of 1884–85.[93]

13 Jan found dead calf in bush.
17 Jan John Smith ... reported that a 3 year old bull had fallen into their well in milk house and broken his neck.
22 Jan another calf died. Bull dying on Kootenai.
26 Jan Dunlap found two bulls dead in Brown's stable and one in brush this side.
28 Jan a fine black bull calf [born] last night.
5 Feb crop eared wolf came up after dead calves.
6 Feb an outfit of Indians came up after the dead calves and have camped in the brush.
8 Feb saw cow near town with 3 calves [thus two of the mothers were missing and can be presumed dead].
10 Feb Lize found another dead cow today.
21 Feb Indians ... are skinning dead calves down by the river to take the meat.
28 Feb Dunlap found a polled grade heifer today dead, that had slipped her calf a week or two ago.
8 March Dunlap found a dead cow up by the Matt Dunn place.
26 March boys found a dead cow in the morning, and another shot by Indians on the Kootenai in the P.M. Baker found a spring calf killed by coyotes near Kootenai.
28 March Indians killing cattle, a cow dead calving at Stand Off.
31 March two more cattle have been found butchered by Indians.
3 April 2 year old heifer mired at Spring Coulee, roan cow dead up there too. Fell down bank into creek.
5 April cow mired near Smiths.
27 April shot the sick Hereford Bull.
9 May Lize reported a Bull dead on Kootenai supposed to be killed by Indians.[94]

Cochrane, who had thousands of cattle at this stage, was not reporting, nor did he know, all the deaths among them. He was just listing those he happened to find out about for a short period of about three months. Presumably there were heavy losses from sickness and a number of other things that went unnoticed.

The destructive power of winter was significantly enhanced on the cattle frontier by two other rather formidable natural phenomena. Of these the one that most directly contributed to winter losses was wolves. They preyed on cattle year round, but they were particularly likely to do so when snow covered the ground and wild game was scarce. The grey wolves grew to a great size and sometimes ran in packs. At such times they were known to kill full-grown cows.[95] The wolves plagued the young and relatively defenseless calves and colts. They would sneak up on a small animal away from the herd or on the periphery and pounce on and kill it before the frantic mother had a chance to intervene.[96]

The ranchers discussed methods for dealing with this problem almost routinely in their correspondence.[97] The beasts were also given a considerable amount of space in the frontier newspapers. "Timber wolves are more destructive every year, and numbers of young stock have been destroyed by them," the *Macleod Gazette* declared in 1892.[98] Some two years later the same paper reported that wolves have "created immense havoc amongst the cattle ranging in the country during the present winter."[99] It also announced that one huge beast that had killed "about $1000 worth of young stock" within a two-mile radius in the Porcupine Hills to the northwest of the town had been hunted down and shot.[100]

Cross told reporters that he commonly lost 10 per cent of his colts to the wolves.[101] In 1891 Commissioner Herchmer noted that they had done "considerable damage, particularly in the Porcupine Hills and in the vicinity of the foot-hills of the Rockies. In the Porcupine Hills Mr. Cross lost about twenty colts, as many as eighteen large timber wolves having been seen in one pack."[102] Individual ranchers tried several methods to eradicate the predators. They shot them with rifles,[103] hunted them down with hounds, and roped them from their horses.[104] Strychnine pellets placed in the carcasses of dead cattle found on the range seem to have been the most effective measure, as sometimes numerous wolves could be destroyed when they devoured a single carcass.[105]

In the 1890s the stock associations also enabled the ranchers to unite their resources to defend the herds through a bounty system. The bounties were paid for out of an annual levy on association members of twenty cents for each colt and ten cents for each calf born to their herds each year.[106] The bounties unquestionably enlisted a lot of people other than ranchers in the fight. The most active were Indians who took the opportunity to turn their hunting skills into cash. In August 1894 the bounty inspector in the Macleod area paid out on thirty-six wolves for the single month.[107] In a three-month period in early 1895 the Stoney Indian Band killed and collected on 120 animals. In the winter and spring of the same year the amazing number of 1,600 wolves were reported to have "bitten the dust" at the hands of both Natives and non-Natives in the territories as a whole.[108] The wolf problem has never of course been solved. Ranchers experience losses to them even today. However, their numbers have been depleted by the encroachment of civilization, and ranchers no longer see the carnage that their predecessors experienced.

The other major natural (or at least primarily natural) phenomenon that threatened the early ranchers in conjunction with harsh weather was prairie fires. It is well known that fires swooped down on and destroyed livestock from time to time during warm, dry summer months; they also substantially boosted winter death rates in two principal ways. Firstly, by obliterating pastures they badly reduced the food supply and the health of cattle, making them more susceptible to blizzards and cold spells. Secondly, in some years they wiped out hay crops that ranchers needed to save their herds when the snow covered the ground for prolonged periods.[109]

The destructive power of fire has also diminished with time, but it has not been eradicated. As recently as 1997 bush and grass fires between Pincher Creek and Granum destroyed some seventy thousand acres of pasture, numerous horses, 120 cattle, and close to a thousand kilometres of fencing. An untold number of cows also aborted in the area after the "stress of fleeing the deadly flames."[110] Forests and prairie grasses become highly volatile after they have been parched in the sun, turning ranch lands into tinderboxes ready to explode into flame at any spark. On the frontier they exploded more often than today, however, because there were more sources for such sparks. Then as now, they were started mainly by lightning, with vandalism and careless camping doing their share.[111] But they were also started by sparks from smokestacks of steam-driven trains[112] and by small landholders attempting to burn off the grass in specific areas to find buffalo bones to collect and market to fertilizer manufactures in the United States.[113]

Fires were not only more plentiful on the frontier than they are now, they were also capable of doing more damage. This was because of the speed with which they could spread across lands that were not dissected by gravel and asphalt roads or dotted with occasional cultivated fields. Along with pastures, livestock and hay, the fires often took ranchers' wood houses, barns, and other buildings.

Sometimes an outbreak singled out a few victims. In late 1885 a blaze near Stand Off burned the buildings and hay supplies of ranchers Pace and Murray as well as a police post nearby.[114] At other times a lot of ranchers were affected. In December 1884 Billie Cochrane reported to one of his foremen that "nearly the whole country between the Kootenai and Old Man's has been burned off, above Slide Out and Macleod which will make it pretty bad for us if the weather is too bad."[115] His chief concern was the loss of pasture. A few weeks later he reported to his father in Quebec that "the range over the Kootenai being burned off is a very great detriment to us as our cattle cannot go beyond Stand Off without crossing miles of burned ground or crossing on to the reserve."[116] This proved to be a very difficult year throughout the entire Waterton area.[117] Two disastrous fires occurred on a homestead owned by a man named Rathwell in January. Rathwell saw much of his pasture go up in smoke. However, the extent of his damage went well beyond that. In the first fire his stacks were destroyed, and, in the second, his barns were lost.[118] A number of his neighbours' properties appear to have been damaged as well.

In 1889 prairie fires depleted much of the grass around the Circle lease in an enormous area between the Old Man and the Little Bow Rivers. "This country is all burning up," the Circle manager, Howell Harris, said at one point: "if we don't get rain soon we will have to take the cattle away from here for the winter."[119] Successive years in the early 1890s brought further extensive damage. In 1891 it was the area north, south, and west of Calgary that was most severely affected. The main outbreak started on 5 October near a coal mine on the south fork of Sheep Creek. "It burned … about a township in extent, between the forks of Sheep Creek and up to the mountains, ruining a great extent of winter feed for stock, and destroying quite a large amount of timber and some hay." Other fires then did severe damage at Sheep Creek, the Stoney Reserve, Ghost River, High River, and along the Little Bow.[120] A vast area in the foothills west of Lethbridge was also damaged. Fire devoured parts of both the Oxley and the Circle ranges.

Some twelve months later, a "very severe" fire swept out of control for several days along the St Mary's River in what is now the Cardston district. The river valley was a great natural wind shelter in the otherwise flat countryside, and it offered a regular supply of drinking water for both humans and livestock. Therefore, a number of ranches were headquartered there. Along with their pastures some ranchers lost buildings, others supplies of hay and/or straw, and some lost both. That fall, the Macleod, Lethbridge, and Halifax Lakes areas were all hit.[121] A Mountie at Macleod recounted that "the whole country has been literally burnt up."[122] The outbreaks, he said, were "numerous and destructive,"[123] and they wiped out the "greater portion of the hay" in the entire Macleod district.[124]

Serious though mostly localized damage occurred in one place or another over the next few years.[125] Then just after the turn of the century large-scale destruction returned. In October 1901 an area on both sides of the American border became at one point a vast sheet of flame covering hundreds of miles. In that same month a fire attacked the prairie between the railway and the South Saskatchewan River west of Medicine Hat, while another one destroyed the winter range in the Plume Creek area. But the worst fire erupted near Gleichen when a man named Dan McNelly carelessly threw away a match after lighting his pipe. The flames swept south and west, covering some fifty square miles of grazing land all the way to the mouth of the Bow River. L.V. Kelly estimated that by the time it was over, the Bar U had lost $15,000 in property and stock, Pat Burns $3,000, T.C. Langford $5,000, and George Ross $2,000.[126] Hundreds of "horses, cattle and wild animals … perished outright or were so badly marred that they were killed or dragged themselves off to some secret spot to die lingeringly. Whole bands of horses and cattle were burned to death in the bottoms along the Little Bow, the majority of them having their eyes burned out, or else their hoofs and legs burned off, many being still alive when the range riders found them after the fire and mercifully shot them down in scores."[127]

One of the ranchers watched in 1901 as a blaze approached his area south of Claresholm from some forty miles away. It was moving with the speed of a "freight train." In the beginning, he said, "we could see nothing but the dense clouds of smoke." However, when suddenly "the rolling bellows of smoke and flame broke over the top of Black Spring Ridge … it was a terrifying sight … Nobody dared to get into the path of that raging inferno. All the animals in its path perished: cattle, horses, antelope, coyotes and jack-rabbits."[128]

Both fire and wolves should also be seen as factors in the decline of the big ranches. The smaller herds were not immune to either, but close to their owners' protective eyes, they were not as vulnerable as those that wandered great distances on the open range. The man who had a small herd was able to defend it with a rifle from predators and move it out of the path of flames. This was particularly so after he had surrounded his cattle with barbed wire and thus knew exactly where they were at any one time. In the case of fire, moreover, it stands to reason that any pastures he had fenced off were likely to be in places where the bush was relatively sparse and the open ground with ample grazing, large. Therefore, even when he was unable to get to his herd on time, his losses were likely to be comparatively light. A grass fire can spread rapidly and harm livestock, but it is nothing like the type that builds up in forests with thick underbrush. That type often produces an inferno with flames shooting forty and fifty feet in the air and a great deal of heat. Few animals caught in it survive. The ordinary rancher was also in a position to protect his entire winter feed supply by ploughing fireguards around his relatively small hay lands and stacks.[129]

As with so many other things, it is impossible to estimate in precise terms the exact number of cattle the ranching industry lost to all the most damaging forces of nature. Unfortunately the extensive collections of account books that would be necessary to make such a calculation are not available. Few of the ranchers' books have survived, and those that have tend to be disappointing.[130] Some outfits like the Walrond went years without taking even a rudimentary count of their livestock, and the Stair Ranch, the A7, and many others allowed cattle to fend for themselves for months on end. When animals disappeared, the owners in many cases could offer only a hypothetical explanation. Therefore the historian is left with general impressions of the magnitude of the destruction. Based on such evidence, however, it would not seem unrealistic to suggest that the impact of weather, wild predators, and prairie fires, frequently working in combination with each other, was substantial enough to make the frontier cattle business, at least at the top, an extremely difficult and potentially unrewarding proposition.

Devastation from natural causes also at times went beyond what can be described in the purely economic sense. It has to be calculated in more abstract and much more personal terms of human suffering. Fires that destroyed their homes or woodlands sometimes burned people too. "Several deaths and many injuries were reported by the Mounted Police."[131] There are also recorded cases of ranchers being attacked by wolves.[132] It was the winter weather, though, that caused by far the most human suffering. Almost every year brought stories of cowboys freezing limbs or dying in the cold. Perhaps the best known cattleman who paid the ultimate price was James Dunlap, foreman-manager of the Cochrane ranch. On 23 October 1887, Dunlap, "one of the best cowmen in the country," badly froze his feet while riding across the Cochrane range between Macleod and Waterton.[133] He was taken to the hospital at Macleod for treatment and was expected to survive. However, after both his legs were amputated, he just seemed to give up and within a few days he was gone.[134]

In November 1891 a man who had a large herd in the Cypress Hills lost two sons who were attempting to bring the cattle in out a ferocious storm.[135] In the winter of 1906–07 Nat Scofield, a cowboy from the Mexico Ranch, failed to return from an outing. Three weeks later his horse wandered riderless into a neighbour's home place. The next spring Scofield was found on the range with his head resting on his saddle. He had undoubtedly suffered hypothermia, lost his ability to think straight, and decided to lie down in the midst of the storm and get some sleep.[136] Lee Brainard had just begun ranching in the Hand Hills area in the autumn of 1906. He set his seventeen-year-old son and a crew of cowboys to work constructing corrals and a shack for themselves, but they did not have the facilities to hold their large herd. The cattle tended to drift, and the Brainards and their men had to ride out every day to drive them back to their lease. One evening when they were attempting this, a severe storm hit with a deep fall of snow, a strong wind, and virtually no visibility. They soon found themselves stranded and lost. In stumbling around, the hired hands happened across a homesteader's shack. It was not until they were inside that they discovered that the boss and his son were not with them. Incredibly, they went back out. They found the elder Brainard caught on a barbed wire fence and near death. The lifeless body of his son was lying nearby.[137]

Such tragedies help to demonstrate that in many ways the Canadian frontier was a rough and dangerous place. A privileged few including the Cochranes were insulated from the wilds by grand Victorian houses and Old-World elegance, but the men who were part of the labour force regularly faced the elements and sometimes paid for it with their lives. The North-West Mounted Police, as will be seen, faced disadvantages of scale in terms of the man-to-area ratio similar to that of the cowboys on the big ranches. They sometimes also suffered heavily. On a bitterly cold day in March 1891, Constable Herron was making his rounds in the countryside around Lethbridge, and in the glare of the afternoon sun experienced snow blindness. Unfortunately, he somehow got separated from his horse and was left "wandering aimlessly over the wide prairies, sightless, frozen by the cold winds, staggering along until about a mile from the Brown Ranch … he finally gave up in exhaustion and despair … With his remaining strength [he] placed his revolver to his head and killed himself."[138] Winter weather was a constant threat to any men who, like the cattle, were required to spend a significant part of their time on the immense, open, and sparsely populated range.

5 Two-Legged Predators

Another substantial adversary with which the early ranchers struggled was criminal activity. Investigation illustrates that the big ranchers were again affected by it more severely than were the small ranches. There are two principal explanations for this. One is that under frontier conditions the big operations with their wandering and relatively unsupervised herds were inordinately vulnerable to crime, just as they were to the destructive forces of nature. The other is that the frontier environment itself both facilitated criminal behaviour and made effective law enforcement exceedingly difficult. In the process of illustrating these statements it is necessary to argue directly against one of our most cherished myths about Canadian western society and the North-West Mounted Police.

Over and over again students of Canadian history have been told the legend of the Mounties who brought law and order to the frontier.[1] In the early 1870s government leaders in Ottawa supposedly recognized that Ontario farm families would soon expand into the prairies. To guarantee a peaceful transfer of land from the Indians to the white settlers, and to avoid the range wars and other violent and chaotic conditions south of the border, a hand-picked group of young men was sent out in 1873. They built forts, began regular patrols, and made sure that private property was secure. When settlement ensued, they also saw that "police posts and patrols ... were constantly increased to keep pace." By 1889 "a vast surveillance network thoroughly covered the south-west." Five divisions served the cattlemen: D and H headquartered at Macleod, K at Lethbridge, A at Maple Creek, and E at Calgary.[2] These were said to exert such a pervasive influence that potential conflicts were diffused, western towns became centres of tranquility, and rustlers, along with the whiskey traders, were either arrested or chased back to the United States.

At times the Mounties themselves helped to develop the image of the peaceable Canadian West, in part to rationalize their own worth to their superiors and to the public back East. The contrast between the Canadian and American frontiers usually figured prominently in

Sir John Lister Kaye with rifle and cartridge belts at his Namaka Ranch, Namaka, Alberta (ca. 1884)

their efforts. In 1894 one of the commanding officers wrote in his annual report:

> The prospect for settlers in the North-west Territories of Canada would, without the protection of the mounted police, be far from pleasant. In the American press we constantly read of "railway trains being stopped and robbed," "stage coaches being held up," etc. Take for instance the depredations committed by the "Cook gang," and compare that with the total absence of such crime in Canada. Yet there are persons who go so far as to advocate that the entire force be disbanded. With the North-west Mounted Police in the country a settler may go away from home on a trip of fifty or sixty miles and leave his wife and family in perfect safety and security, but one can imagine what his anguish of mind would be if he was obliged to leave home, knowing that his wife would have to depend upon her own efforts alone to protect herself from Indians, tramps or outlaws who might feel disposed to raid the ranch …

> The policy of establishing the means of obtaining law and order, before settlement, has been most beneficial to the country at large, and makes "vigilant[e] committees," "white caps" and "lynching gangs" impossible. By such committees gross injustices have, and always will be perpetrated, and many innocent persons shot and hanged.[3]

There is considerable evidence in the reports themselves that society on the Canadian side was not quite so secure.[4] Indeed the officer who wrote the above words had in the same breath to admit that he was witnessing some deterioration. "I regret to say," he owned rather sheepishly, "that there has been a slight increase in crime during the past season. From the annexed classification you will notice the total of the magisterial cases is 241, against 190" during the previous reporting year.[5] The numbers were for the district of Macleod alone and did not, of course, include crimes that had not been brought to trial. The increase of approximately 27 per cent was not slight.

It is not difficult to imagine how historians anxious to tell readers what it was that made Canadians unique and – equally important – different from the Americans picked up the "tame West" image, embraced, and reiterated it. Over time a modest dimming of this image has transpired as some scholars have provided specific examples of criminal activity on the cattle frontier. Stanley Hanson has uncovered extensive rustling in the Wood Mountain area, although he insists that ultimately the enforcement techniques of the Mounties along with the law-abiding character of the pioneers won out.[6] Thomas Thorner has shown that in southern Alberta crime increased throughout the period 1878 to 1905[7] and that around Calgary property crimes, liquor offences, prostitution, and gambling flourished in the final decades of the nineteenth century, while incidents of "extreme violence against persons were few."[8] More recently Louis Knafla has drawn our attention to the Holt-Dubois gang which was involved in rustling and intimidation over an immense area stretching from their spread at Stettler all the way to Montana.[9] And Hugh A. Dempsey has provided numerous descriptions of thieves and outlaws in his exciting monograph, *The Golden Age of the Canadian Cowboy*. He concludes that while lawlessness and violence were not as prevalent as they were south of the border, the Canadian West itself was not "entirely docile."[10]

Still, the myth of the orderly society has for the most part remained intact. Along with journalists and museum moderators, the latest (and otherwise very informative) study of the North-West Mounted Police perpetuates it.[11] The major shortcoming in the image is its tendency to underrate the frontier setting in moulding ranching society. This setting placed the Mounties in no better position with respect to imposing law than were the cowboys on the great ranches when it came to controlling and protecting the cattle herds. The Mounties' strength, based on numbers of men stationed within the five divisions, fluctuated as follows: in 1873 it was three hundred; in 1885, one thousand, because of the Riel Rebellion; in 1895, 750; 1898, 500; and 1901, 450.[12] These men were stationed in small groups in detachments located some forty miles apart. At the turn of the century, in "organized" areas of the North-West Territories, this was equivalent, according to the estimates of the police themselves, to about one officer for every five hundred square miles and for every 350 people.[13]

Moreover, roads were non-existent or very poor, and travel was by horse and unsupported by two-way radios or even a satisfactory telephone system. No one working under these conditions could do a proper job of keeping crime under control. David Breen has pointed out that extensive networks of regular patrols were instigated to prevent rustling. However, there is reason to have serious doubts about how effective they could possibly have been. For one officer just to ride around five hundred square miles (approximately 120 miles) on horseback at five miles per hour would take twenty-four hours or three days working eight hours per day. After such a patrol the officer might have acquainted himself somewhat with the periphery of his area, but not at all with the interior which would stretch the equivalent of ten miles across and fifty miles in length.

Furthermore, the frontier had very limited facilities for servicing the basic needs of the population. Consequently the Mounties had to shoulder an inordinately heavy load not only to ensure their own and their mounts' survival but also to provide for the well-being of the civilian population. The North-West Mounted Police were sent west with a double mandate. They were supposed to keep law and order while acting as agents of the federal government in the process of nation building. This required them to settle the Indians on the reserves, protect the civilian population from "natural disaster and human disruption," and provide state services normally offered by specialized agencies in more mature societies.[14] To comprehend the degree to which this complicated life for them, it is appropriate to turn to the mileage log that was kept for Fort Walsh in 1881. It shows that out of a total of 14,978 miles travelled by the detachment staff, 1,283 miles or 8.6 per cent were for what was termed "Indian issues," and 12,865 miles or 85.9 per cent were for the physical survival of the post. A mere 830 miles or 5.5 per cent were for what the police themselves termed law enforcement.[15] Construction, laying in their own food supply, firewood cutting and hauling, care and feeding of the horses, medical services to the men and the community, and governmental duties such as collecting weather data and conveying mail occupied the majority of their time.[16]

The police also had to devote a considerable portion of their energies to dealing with emergencies such as putting out prairie fires and helping people caught in floods or blizzards. This could be extremely time-consuming. In 1891 the commanding officer at Lethbridge sent out a party of men to defend the ranches from fire on the ranges west of town. He hoped they would be able to help out briefly and then return quickly to their duties in law enforcement. He found out the hard way that in such a big country the task at hand could be a lot greater than it appeared. He "sent a party of men under Corporal Edwards to the headquarters of the [Circle] ranch at the little Bow, distance about 20 miles." There the men were informed that "the nearest point of the fire" was still "about 12 miles off." They pushed on further but by the time they got to it they had travelled "nearer 25 miles." In the end the intervention used up nearly two full days of the men's time.[17]

Moreover, because the frontier was a new and unfamiliar land, the Mounties sometimes found themselves dealing with circumstances that must have taken them completely by surprise. This included periodic inadequacy of the water supply. "The police … are melting snow for their own use, and also for their horses," it was reported in the *Macleod Gazette* in the spring of 1883: "the little water that is still in the creek is so bad that it is unfit for use."[18] More frequently the police had long hours of duty protecting Canadian ranges from inundation by hungry American herds that were constantly pushing their way across the border.[19] "The ranchers of Wood Mountain and Willow Bunch complain of the herds of cattle from Montana that have crossed the border, and are a constant source of trouble to those who have to put up food for their own stock," a newspaper editor acknowledged in 1896. "The Mounted Police have had a pretty hard season, and in order to relieve them, several cowboys have been appointed to assist in driving the cattle back."[20]

In comparison to their modern counterparts the frontier police thus worked under a formidable disadvantage not just in terms of manpower but also because for most of their time they were precluded from even turning their attention to crime prevention.[21] This seems to have been an important reason for low morale in the force. Young men, many of them educated and from "good families," no doubt came out to the West with a certain amount of idealism about what they were expecting to accomplish.[22] When they got to their destination, high ideals and romantic notions were dashed by crude living conditions, isolation, in particular from family, a dearth of female companionship, and the frustration of being unable to concentrate on the job of keeping law and order. One manifestation of low morale was a prodigious desertion rate. Between 1881 and 1907 this fluctuated between 1 and 8 per cent, and it was not uncommon for thirty to eighty men to desert their posts in a given year.[23] Successive annual police reports for all the divisions are rife with instances of men leaving without permission or taking the opportunity of a journey away from their posts to disappear.

News of such incidents was often reported in the newspapers and much public opinion was expressed about it.[24] Interestingly, there seems to have been a general recognition that one problem might well be the fact that police work had so little to do with law enforcement. "May not the desertions from the police posts be traced to the same cause," it was argued, "as a general rule young fellows enlist through a strong inclination for military life, and become thoroughly disgusted and desperate when required to do all manner of dirty work."[25] It may be that some of the seemingly numerous police suicides in the Canadian West were related to the same factors.[26]

Along with the relative weaknesses of the police, the attitude of much of the citizenry worked against efficient law enforcement. It is not feasible to attempt to compare levels of respect for the law on the Canadian cattle frontier with that south of the border or even in the East. As one respected legal historian recently declared, this is partly because "quantification of crime in early western Canada is impossible."[27] The main reason is that the available data is insufficient. There are the files of the justices of the peace in the provincial archives and the reports of the Supreme Courts respectively in the attorney-general's office in Alberta and at the archives in Saskatchewan. These, however, are very large collections that will require years of scholarly work before they can be used to illuminate frontier crime in western Canada as a whole. Moreover, the records show only cases that were tried. As will be seen, the police themselves often lamented that much of the criminal activity went undetected and unsolved specifically because of the obstacles they themselves had to face in administering to the needs of society in the vast and undeveloped frontier setting.

However, it does not seem critically important to make comparisons. What Canadian scholars really need to do is look closely at circumstances on their own side of the border in an effort to determine if previous assertions of an orderly culture can be supported.

Cowboys beside log house, Cochrane Ranch, ca. 1892

Our problem is simply to decide whether epithets used in the past such as "law-abiding" or "tame" say something germane about, or in any sense specific to, the Canadian West. Do the members of this society deserve to be singled out for their refusal to stray from the path of justice, integrity, and civility? There is a great deal of evidence to suggest that they should not. Indeed, under a variety of circumstances many people north of the forty-ninth parallel seem to have had a strong, maybe even a pervasive, tendency to evade the law, disregard the North-West Mounted Police, and live a raucous and reckless existence.

One of the qualities that underlines a relatively low concern on the ranching frontier about "civilized" standards was a general propensity to carry and use guns, particularly six-shooters. It is possibly true that Canadians were less likely to resort to firearms in disputes than Americans. The Mounties expended considerable effort to control guns, and they attempted to prevent people from openly using them or threatening to use them against each other.[28] Thus, as one cattleman who moved north in the late 1870s or early '80s put it, "the American cowboys, coming to work on Alberta cattle ranches, shed their six-shooters at the boundary as trees shed their leaves in the fall, and were glad to do so."[29] However, anyone doing even the most rudimentary research finds it difficult to avoid the conclusion that gunplay was anything but uncommon here.

If cowboys did take off their six-shooters when they crossed the border there is also every indication that they were not at all reluctant to put them back on again when the situation demanded. One of the men who initially came north on the great cattle drives of the early 1880s, George Lane, often carried a six-shooter.[30] Lane had spent a considerable portion of his life ranching in Montana, and no doubt picked up the habit there. One of his fellow countrymen, Jim Patterson, who became foreman respectively of the Walrond and Oxley ranches, was renowned for his prowess with the gun.[31] The well-known bronco buster, Frank Ricks, a cousin of the celebrated outlaw Jesse James, apparently was almost never seen without a sidearm.[32] The six-gun culture was passed on to non-Americans as well. Billie Cochrane, who became manager of the ranch at Waterton, had a revolver that he thought important enough to replace when it was stolen at a hotel in Macleod in 1885.[33] A lot of less well-known cattlemen also kept guns near them if not always dangling from their hips. The ranch hands usually did not wear their side arms when working the herds because they were heavy and an impediment to roping, branding, and otherwise handling the cattle.[34] However, many of these men were willing and able to strap them on at a moment's notice. One distraught young Englishman on a cattle drive for the Military Colonization Company who found his fellow herders using his bowler hat for target practice observed this in 1894.[35] In the late 1880s a cowboy from the Cresswell Ranch looking for stray horses in the Wood Mountain area came across two Canadian ranchers, and as he approached them found himself suddenly looking "into the bad end of a rifle and six-gun." The two had heard about Montana outlaws holding up some of the "boys from the Seventy-six" outfit, and they weren't taking any chances.[36]

A Mountie stationed in the Wood Mountain area between 1884 and 1888 summed up the situation in a few words when he surmised that cowboys "are invariably armed, owing to the exigencies of a nomad life in a wild country."[37] By any standards, furthermore, there was considerable gunfighting and it, rather than traditional legal authority, was frequently the means of dispute resolution. The following incidents involving guns are a small representative sample of those found in newspapers and annual reports of the North-West Mounted Police.

Sometimes such incidents entailed only the threat of violence by men who had consumed too much alcohol. In 1885 a cowboy with a revolver was found menacing citizens at a tavern in Fort Macleod.

Armed ranch hands at Lucas, Eastman and Waller Ranch, Porcupine Hills, 1886

Mounties were notified and compelled him to give up the gun. He was thrown in the North-West Mounted Police guardroom for the night and fined $25 for disturbing the peace.[38] At other times serious repercussions of gunplay were not so successfully avoided. In March 1904 a cowboy in Calgary got into a dispute with some local men and when the police intervened, turned his gun toward them. The Mounties had no alternative but to shoot him.[39] In 1886 several men held up the Calgary-Edmonton coach at gunpoint[40] and got away with $400. A short while later "the cowardly murder" of a young man named Clinker Scott occurred, apparently in relation to this crime. He was shot through the window of his shack west of Calgary while he was making bread. "Dead men," it was noted "tell no tales."[41]

There were gunfights too of the type shown time and again in American movies. In July 1885 at Medicine Hat Ben Hale, "a well known cowboy," shot a man named Bob Casey three times. The two had been drinking heavily and got arguing about something as insignificant as whose horse was the faster.[42] In early 1891 a cattle thief named Edward "Tex" Fletcher shot and killed a man named Peter

An evening's relaxation near Walsh, Alberta (ca. 1902–05)

Dacotah in a rancher's home near Battleford after a night of revelry and illegal whiskey. Fletcher later received a twenty-year prison sentence for murder.[43] In November 1895 John Lamar, foreman of the Walrond ranch, and Gilbert McKay, a former ranch employee, got into a heated dispute over a personal matter. Some days later McKay rode out to the Walrond and challenged Lamar to a gunfight. Lamar had his revolver on at the time, but in the hope that the other man would go away, he retreated into the house and remained there for some time. When he came out, however, McKay was still waiting for him, and immediately drew his gun. Lamar was a faster draw and got off the first shot, wounding McKay in the arm. He then fired two more shots in an effort, as he himself explained, "to disable his opponent." Unfortunately McKay "changed his position in the saddle," and "one shot took effect in his chest and the other in the abdomen."[44] Miraculously, he seems to have survived after a stint in a North-West Mounted Police hospital. On 12 June 1896 two long-standing enemies named Godin and Ducharme met on the Bow Marsh Bridge in Calgary. One grabbed the pistol from the other's holster and shot him in the abdomen. The aggressor then attempted to flee but as he turned, the wounded man, having wrenched his gun back again, shot him in the back. Both men died of their wounds.[45]

A few years later a ranchers' feud in the Pot Hole district brought a similarly tragic end. Two men named Lee Purcel and Dave Akers disagreed over the question of the ownership of some cattle. Purcel took the dispute to heart and decided to seek revenge. One day he got his rifle and waited for his old friend to approach the cattle in a corral. He then put a bullet through Akers's head. Purcel was later arrested and tried for the crime. He was eventually convicted of manslaughter and given a paltry three years in the penitentiary by a generous judge.[46] This episode was recorded in the newspapers and, in 1916 Captain Deane related it in his *Mounted Life in Canada* along with the equally emotive Tucker Peach, Benson, and Watson murders.[47]

It is usual to think of Canada as the law-abiding kingdom to the north of the forty-ninth parallel that resisted the violence and chaos so integral a part of American society. On numerous occasions, so the story goes, the Macleod district was infested with horse and cattle thieves from the south. Furthermore, the Mounties often took the liberty of escorting men with bad reputations back to the boundary line and telling them to stay at home or else prison would result.[48] These assertions are not in dispute. It should be recognized, however, that this worked both ways. On frequent occasions Canadian disorder, like stolen Canadian livestock, spilled over into American society and had to be solved by peace officers there. In 1895 a Constable

Heading to town, de Winton, Alberta area, early 1900s

Richardson followed stray horses across the border to Middle Butte, Montana. While there he was shot in a fight with a man named Long whose acquaintance he had first made on the north side of the line. Long then quarrelled with American authorities and was killed in a gunfight.[49] On a number of occasions riders toting six-shooters successfully held up the Canadian Pacific Railway train. In at least one of those cases Mounties formed a posse and attempted to track the thieves down, but they made their way across the border and were never found.[50]

On the frontier men were drawn to the gun in part because of a culture that was anything but tame. At night their instincts drew them to urban centres large and small where they sought booze and various forms of entertainment. Inevitably this got some of them into fist-fights and shoot-outs. In 1912 L.V. Kelly illuminated this fact with some elegant prose when extolling the virtues of Canadian ranch hands. Cowboys, he eulogized,

> might go on hilarious "busts" when in town, they might "shoot-up" a barroom and smash every light in the place, they might ride into stores on the backs of frantic horses, but they were good men, the kind who worked for their employers. If a flooded river must be crossed to save some of the cattle carrying the brand of the outfit they worked for, they plunged in and braved the torrents with their driftwood and their deadly "drag". If a fifty-mile ride was necessary in order to save a horse they took it. If an all-night vigil beside

a herd of freezing stock was necessary to save those animals the vigil was cheerfully undertaken. Many and many a night the cowboys sat on their horses, bundled to the ears, while the bitter winds of ten and twenty below zero swept across the prairies; and there are known instances where cowboys whose feet and legs were frozen remained by the herd and pulled it through until relief came. The employer's stock was their own; a theft was a personal loss ... They were "good," men – rough, ready and true.[51]

Kelly, a contemporary of the men he was describing, was merely expressing values that prevailed among them as they helped forge the ranching frontier.

An episode that occurred in Macleod in 1891 suggests that bar-room gunfighting was entwined in the popular culture of the cowboy. Previously two men named Murray and Leeper had met on the banks of the Kootenay River. They got arguing and pulled their guns. Leeper beat Murray to the draw, "thrust the muzzle of his six-shooter" into the latter's ribs, and then humiliated him by forcing him to take a swim in the river.

Some days later the two happened to be drinking in separate saloons in Macleod. The town was "full of round-up cowboys who were certainly not worrying a bit about the serious side of life." The ranch hands knew about the enmity between the two men and decided to have some fun with it. One crowd of them formed around Murray and the other around Leeper. Billy Stewart did everything he could think of to spark a conflict. He spent time separately with both, telling each the dreadful things the other had said about him. As the liquor flowed, "white-hot rage soon took possession of the two, and they talked darkly of dire happenings if only the other could be met with, Stewart and the two parties of cowboys sympathizing with each wronged individual and telling just how to kill most painfully and disgracefully." The cowboys also got both men's fire-arms out of their holsters, secretly removed the bullets, and replaced the guns. Then they brought the men face to face with each other in the Queen's Hotel. In an instant "the big guns leaped like magic to the ready hands." The men "stepped into the clear, and advanced slowly, the 'clickety-click' of the futile hammers on their weapons indicating just how earnest they were." When they realized that their guns were empty the men both tried to "bend the steel frames against each other's head." At that point "the hilarious spectators intervened and patched up a truce that remained unbroken, if strained."[52]

Stories are often told of American cowboys coming north and causing trouble in Canadian bars. Lots of them are true. Among numerous others, the occasion when the Sundance Kid pulled his gun to settle

Charlie Millar at the Pekisko Ranch, foothills of southern Alberta, 1892

a dispute with his partner in a tavern in Calgary bears this out.[53] However, Canadian cowboys also went south and returned the favour. One night Tom Lynch, Bob Newbolt, and a group of British, Canadian, and American riders on a cattle drive went drinking in a bar on the Montana side of the border. After they "had several drinks they proceeded to shoot up the saloon."[54] Admittedly the tendency towards this kind of behaviour was tempered somewhat in Canada by the police who were known to confiscate six-guns from men they did not like or trust.[55] Even so, it clearly cannot be argued that shoot-ups in general were rare. "Blazing away with a pistol, whenever a man gets drunk, whether it be in the hands of a policeman or a citizen is getting monotonous"[56] a reporter complained in 1886.

In 1885 the editor of the *Macleod Gazette* wrote that "shooting seems well on the highway to becoming a common past-time,"[57] and in the 1930s an elderly pioneer who had witnessed the ranching frontier firsthand remembered that "most cowboys had only one aim, that was to buy as much ammunition as they could, become as 'quick on the draw' as possible, and become deadly accurate shots."[58] The gun culture even had a tendency to spread to young men who were far removed from ranching – sometimes with disastrous results. After work one night in Medicine Hat two young clerks aged fifteen and sixteen strapped on six-shooters and went down to the train yards to practice the draw. They got clowning around and staged a mock gun battle. A gun accidentally discharged and one of the boys was killed.[59]

Thomas Thorner, who has undergone some of the arduous task of searching through the Justice of the Peace files for southern Alberta, estimates that between 1878 and 1905, 10 to 20 per cent of all crimes were "crimes against the person," and they increased throughout. In the periods 1878–98, and 1900–05 respectively, approximately nine cases and twenty-seven cases of murder, manslaughter, or wounding were brought before the courts on average each year. In most of these cases a gun was used; there were also a number of stabbings.[60] Thorner points out, moreover, that the "dark figure" of unsolved crime is not reflected in the files. It may well have been large. In one of the years in which there were at least eight murders, only two were recorded in the files. Frank W. Anderson presents a number of individual episodes of gun violence in his brief book *Sheriffs and Outlaws of Western Canada*.[61] Anderson's style is journalistic and he does not document his sources; because of this, scholars have largely ignored him. However, his descriptions of gun-toting cowboys and shootouts are vivid and detailed and can be verified in the frontier newspapers, court records, and police reports.[62]

If this comes closer to a Hollywood depiction of the Canadian West than might be expected, so does the cowboy-versus-Indian violence that erupted from time to time both before and after the celebrated Riel Rebellion of 1885. There were four Indian tribes located adjacent to, or in the heart of, ranching areas where the range remained open for many years: the Bloods bordered the Milk River Ridge and the foothills southwest of Lethbridge; the Peigans were in the Porcupine Hills northwest of Fort Macleod; the Stonies inhabited the foothills west of Calgary; and the Blackfoot were situated along the Bow River near Gleichen. Knowing that the tribes had ready access to their herds, the ranchers often blamed them for stealing and killing cattle.[63] The Indians were undoubtedly wrongly accused at times,[64] but particularly when the winters were long and the buffalo scarce, they did seem to have been willing to take livestock to survive.[65] It was relatively easy for them to avoid detection when taking cattle that wandered conveniently into or near their communities and they were seldom caught and brought before the Justices of the Peace. However, incidents involving Native rustlers appear quite regularly in the press, and in many of them "exchange of shots" between the thieves and the cattlemen is said to have "produced casualties."[66]

In August 1887 a rancher near High River caught two Blackfoot Indians slaughtering his cattle. A gunfight ensued in which the rancher shot one of the Indians dead on the scene and "fatally wounded the other."[67] The fact that there was little shock or dismay expressed in the media about the deaths suggests that there was a general and widespread value system that inclined cattlemen to use the gun to protect their stock from Natives whenever necessary.[68] In late October 1903 James L. Taylor, who ran a spread just north of the international border, sent his youngest son, George, out to find some steers that had strayed from his home range. The boy found them on the other side of the boundary, rounded them up, and headed them for home. Before he got back across the line, a "half-breed" attempted to take the cattle, firing several shots at him. "The bullets whizzed in dangerous proximity, and one of the deadly missiles punctured the crown of his head gear." The boy refused to give up. He "determined to return with the cattle or leave his bones for the prowling coyote." That night he saw the cattle safely back to their Canadian pasture.

A few evenings later the boy was out on the range again and caught the same man trying to make off with the same steers from the Canadian side. The fellow opened fire on him and the boy returned home. Early the next morning he armed himself with a revolver and headed back to the range. He found the man driving the steers just across the line. Both riders opened fire. The man appears to have been the better marksman, and he managed to wound Taylor: "One of the shots went through his coat that was being flapped by the breeze," and another hit him in the foot. The would-be rustler fled the scene heading south at a gallop. The Taylor boy returned home, "the wound in his foot being very painful."[69] The wound and the near misses attest that both men were perfectly willing to see the other die.

While Canada saw no large-scale Indian/white massacres on the ranching frontier of the type once glorified by American film, there was a great deal of bitterness and racial animosity that often manifested itself in violence and death.[70] In 1887/88 Kootenai Indians embittered by the loss of land in the foothills and white settlers upset over the murder of two miners near Cranbrook narrowly averted armed conflict.[71] On 10 February 1897 Charcoal, a member of the Blood tribe, was hanged for shooting Sergeant A.B. Wilde of the North-West Mounted Police. Charcoal had previously murdered a fellow tribesman and shot and severely wounded a white farm agent.[72] In the same year Sergeant Colebrooke of the Mounties was shot by a Cree Indian named Almighty Voice.[73] Over the next two years a total of four more policemen were eventually killed by the same man.[74] Almighty Voice was hanged after an extensive and much publicized manhunt. Some years later the newspapers reported a gruesome discovery on the Blood Reserve: a prospector's dead body was found with the legs severed and clothing burned.[75]

In white society strong feelings against the Native community were unquestionably as prevalent in Canada as to the south.[76] In 1884 the wife of one of the large leaseholders tried to sound enlightened when referring to Indians in a letter to her friend in Ontario. However, she could not conceal her own pronounced prejudices: "I think if the Indians could have been isolated in the mountains and left with their own laws and ways of living, and never been allowed to eat of the fruit of the tree of knowledge as revealed by the white men who came to live among them," she wrote, "they could teach civilization a great deal, but our inconsistencies are too subtle for their minds and when they try to follow, they are lost and, under existing conditions, the sooner they become extinct the better for themselves and the country."[77]

In many of the cases where white/Native violence occurred, the consumption of whiskey undoubtedly played a part just as it did in white/white violence. To those investigating the propensity towards lawlessness in the Canadian West, one of the interesting things about the fact that so much of it was associated with the consumption of spirits is that until 1892 the liquor trade itself was illegal. It is testimony to a common willingness to break the law that the trade infected frontier society at all levels, traversed all ethnic lines, and fostered extensive commercial activity both across Canada and across the United States border.

In the early 1870s the federal government determined to quash the sale of liquor to the Indians. The North-West Territories Act of 1875 prohibited intoxicating liquor in the territories except by permits issued to individuals by the lieutenant governor. These permits were meant for the importation of a small quantity on a yearly basis for personal use only. The permits were apparently intended for the wealthy and influential and were granted in the beginning to a select few.[78] However, as a result of a thriving smuggling trade, the ranching frontier was anything but dry. The first smugglers were Americans who concentrated on specific locations such as Fort Whoop-Up and had supplied the Indians before there was a considerable white population. In time much larger numbers of Canadians replaced the American smugglers. Most of the liquor seems to have come from Montana, but a considerable amount was also transported from Ontario via the Canadian Pacific Railway after 1883.[79] The Canadians were not racially biased in their commercial dealings and supplied anyone who could afford it.

In 1884 the trade was greatly facilitated when the government, in recognition of the fact that settlement was increasing rapidly, started issuing the permits to practically anyone who applied. Then the system was open to a great deal of abuse. First, many people took out the permits, imported the whiskey and, since the permits were never collected and cancelled, kept them to justify the illegal liquor they would in future buy from smugglers. Before long, public carriers began to bring whiskey in from Fort Benton. The carriers were careful to use permits to cover every bottle they transported. They also managed to acquire them from all sorts of people who did not intend to use them. The permits were made out to "the bearer" rather than named individuals and the police had no way of telling who the original holders were. This enabled the carriers and other middlemen to acquire a sizeable amount of surplus liquor to put on the open market.

Abuse of the system was also crucial to a burgeoning illicit saloon business in every ranching community from Fort Macleod to Calgary, Lethbridge, and Maple Creek. An entrepreneur would acquire numerous permits, purchase a liquor inventory, and then sell across the counter to anyone who could afford it, claiming that he was supplying licensed liquor to permit holders only. One of the highest-ranking North-West Mounted Police officers in the territories reported with obvious frustration in 1888:

> Some of the newspapers are continually agitating on the liquor question, and not without great cause. Under the present system there are undoubtedly the gravest reasons for complaint. In the towns there is a great deal of liquor, and consequently more or less drunkeness among a certain class of people, generally a class who will drink anywhere… A saloon keeper of any experience keeps about enough liquor on his premises to fill his permits and whenever "pulled" by the Police he produces his permits, or those of his friends, and keeps his reserve stock of contraband liquor in hay stacks and manure heaps, [and] closets.[80]

The strength of the whiskey trade was to some degree a product of the weakness on the frontier of law enforcement agencies and the numerical predominance of single young males who were inclined to seek the pleasures of alcohol as a staple in their rather limited entertainment regimen.[81] If in the following depiction the writer is guilty of some embellishment he cannot be charged with representing the ranching frontier in anything but its true colours:

> Whiskey rolled into the land in every conceivable way. It came branded as red ink, it came in bales of hay, in loads of oats, even in kerosene cans, boots, boxes and kegs. A shipment of Bibles arrived at one town, and the settlers

purchased them so avidly and hastened away so rapidly to commune with themselves and the book's contents that the Mounted Police smelled a rat, the study of the Bible not being a pronounced habit of the majority of Westerners in those days. Upon purchasing one of these coveted volumes the Police smelled more than a rat, for the 'Bible' was a little metal cask, formed like a book, branded like a book and entitled 'Holy Bible' in gilt letters, but filled with whiskey![82]

Arrests were difficult to make because the permits were preserved religiously by a very thirsty society. Even when there were arrests, convictions were often virtually impossible to achieve because of collusion by all the men who supported the trade, either because it supported them or because it brought them one of their principal items of entertainment, or both.[83] "Conviction after conviction was quashed" by the inability to get reliable witnesses or by understanding male judges.[84] Many of the single male police officers themselves participated in the trade, and consumption within the ranks became a real problem.[85] Colonel James F. Macleod concluded that "for every successful (whiskey) patrol there were many unsuccessful ones."[86] In 1884 one of the few married ladies in the Pincher Creek area described her experiences on a social occasion in Fort Macleod. It is possible to visualize not only how endemic the illicit whiskey trade was but how closely bound to the seamier side of life on the frontier. She remembered that when she and her husband first arrived at the town they went to a ball at the police barracks. They "knew very few people as none of the men we knew had come in, and only a … woman for whom I do not care; but … a young Canadian … and his … wife were greatly in evidence, and he had been bracing himself by some of the very bad whiskey which prohibition produced in dark corners about the town … he came up to me and asked me to dance. I said I was engaged but … [my husband] did not appear, and he was growing cross and I desperate, when a broad shouldered officer turned round and said to me 'Ah! This is our dance …!' I felt that he should have had the Victoria Cross."

Later, the same lady returned to the home of local townspeople with whom she was being billeted for the night. She "found my hostess in tears. It seems she was engaged to a Protestant against her brother's wishes and, through the uplifting influence of some smuggled whiskey," he had "decided to send her home." He had "confirmed this decision by selling the house and everything in it to some man he knew."[87]

In 1892 the Licensing Act provided for the sale of liquor in licensed premises. Respectable citizens including A.E. Cross then got into the brewing business,[88] and drinking became even more general than before.[89] Selling liquor to the Native population was still illegal. As might have been expected, that trade grew enormously with the coming of cheaper and even more abundant supplies.[90] Convictions for the offence of selling to the Indians increased steadily, except for a brief decline in 1895–96, peaking in 1903 when ninety-three such cases were heard.[91] Contemporary accounts acknowledge that this crime grew with the settlement of the regions. Primary responsibility for the increase, the police believed, were "low class whites" who felt that the high profits made the risk of being caught worth taking.[92]

Another illegal activity that was largely uncontrolled on the ranching frontier and which went more or less naturally with the illicit whiskey trade in a society numerically dominated by single males was prostitution. As James Gray has pointed out, this was carried on regularly in the urban centres and the farming communities and there is no reason to argue that the ranchers and cowboys did not partake.[93] A host of young women with a great variety of names and sobriquets operated in the cattle towns. In Calgary there were Rose Ann Fulham, Jennie Ringold, and Nellie Webb.[94] Frank W. Anderson describes some others in the city in the early 1890s:

> Among the sixty odd prostitutes who made their headquarters in Calgary ... the two most famous were Carrie Hough and Lizzie House, both of whom employed several girls and both of whom operated lavish establishments on the banks of the Bow River. The furnishings were said to rival those of famous houses in the East. But, of all the girls police ... kept the closest watch on May Buchanan.
>
> In January and February of 1891, several charges of keeping a disorderly house and of selling liquor illegally had been brought against May Buchanan and as a result of the steady pressure, she had vacated her house on the Edmonton Trail. Taking her girls – Trixie Livingstone, Tillie Willis and Violet Decarmin – she had moved down the line to Canmore, but within three months she was back at the old stand. This time she had added Nellie McPherson, a Nettie McDowell and a Lily Reeves to her trio of doxies.

Buchanan, like so many of these women, got into deep trouble with the law for serious crimes and quit the trade of a madame to become a prostitute on her own, operating from a restaurateur's premises at Sheep Creek to the south of the city. Again like so many others in the trade, she came to a violent end, axed to death by a client in 1893.[95]

Prostitution, like the whiskey trade, was prosecuted irregularly by male police officers and judges, who felt there was a need for it at this stage of western prairie development.[96] Neither the Mounties nor

Houses of ill-repute, Nose Hill area, Calgary, 1911

the urban police forces consistently did much about it in the early years before family life became more widely established. The annual reports of the commanding officers stationed at Calgary, Fort Macleod, Lethbridge, and Medicine Hat show that prostitution laws would go largely unenforced for years and then suddenly, presumably when some of the townspeople raised objections, there would be something of a crackdown.

In the Calgary area in 1891 "keepers of disorderly houses, inmates and frequenters," were indicted forty-one times, by far the highest number for any crimes except liquor offences during that year.[97] In the same city four years later, indictments for the crime were half that number.[98] Then for some years little action was taken. From 1905 to 1909, when Calgary's population grew from a few thousand to around 15,000,[99] the police "arrested on the average three keepers, twenty inmates and ten frequenters of houses of ill fame each year. Only one prostitute (streetwalker) and two procurers were arrested in an entire five year period ... for the entire E division, which extended from Calgary north to Red Deer and east to Tilley."[100] When irate citizens demanded in 1906 that Police Chief Thomas English shut down the brothels, he told them that "there is less gambling and less prostitution in Calgary, than in any other city of its size in the U.S. or Canada. There may be houses of prostitution in Calgary, but I don't know of them." Two days later, the *Morning Albertan* observed that there were at least nine such establishments within the city whose locations were known to everyone "except the chief of police" and that further construction was currently underway.[101]

Prostitution flourished in all the towns. In Macleod it went unmentioned in the annual reports of the Mounted Police and then suddenly for a short period it was front and centre. In 1897, when the population of the town was still under eight hundred,[102] thirteen keepers and inmates of houses of ill-fame were tried. The other major prosecutions also suggest a raucous frontier town. There were twenty-one trials for assault, thirty-four for being drunk in public, thirteen for theft and larceny, and ten for gambling. In 1898 the largest number of criminal cases tried was assault, fourteen, causing a disturbance by being drunk, 111, desertion of employment, fifty-three, creating a disturbance (other than drunk), fourteen, Indian Act offences, twenty-two, keepers and inmates of houses of ill-fame, twenty-seven, non-payment of wages, twenty, theft and larceny, fifteen.[103]

In 1906 the police instigated a campaign against prostitution in Maple Creek after years of indifference. Though the town had only 687 people, no less than thirty-eight cases against keepers, frequenters and inmates of houses of ill-fame were brought to trial.[104] These were second only to drunk and disorderly at fifty-five. Between 1906 and the war, police policy in that town then continued as elsewhere to oscillate between strict enforcement of the law and almost total relaxation.

The files of the Justices of the Peace provide an opportunity to generalize about prostitution in the southern prairies as a whole, and they confirm the same pattern of enforcement and relaxation that is discernable in individual urban centres. The crime was prosecuted infrequently in the 1870s and early 1880s. Then in 1884, nineteen cases were recorded. In the years that followed, while inconsistency in bringing cases to trial is evident, the upward trend predominated, culminating in 1904 with 137 cases.[105] Considering the reluctance of police officers to take effective action against prostitution, this would seem to point to a flourishing and probably greatly expanding commerce throughout the entire southern territories.

Neither gunfighting, nor the whiskey trade, nor prostitution did much direct damage to the cattle business. Indeed, with respect to the latter two, the opposite could be argued – that they were necessary to the establishment of a frontier industry that required a large male work force. The same cannot be said of other crimes. Among these, livestock rustling was the most destructive. It became a major detriment to ranching and, like winter weather, wolves, and fire, has to be seen as a significant factor in the decline of the open range approach.

Because so many cattle and horses roamed free and therefore were neither properly guarded nor fenced in, thieves had little difficulty stealing them and moving them swiftly over long distances. Extensive evidence of rustling is plentiful. L.V. Kelly refers to it frequently,[106] the *Macleod Gazette* and the *Calgary Herald* often gave it a public forum, and the ranchers themselves mention the crime repeatedly in correspondence now preserved in the Glenbow Archives.[107] Moreover, the annual police reports present it as a more or less insoluble frontier manifestation.[108]

There was in fact so much rustling going on that it can be categorized into several clearly recognizable types. Much of it was done on a quick-grab basis where a few men got together, made off with a herd, and then disposed of it as fast as possible as far away as possible. This system was particularly well suited to horse theft because of the mobility of the stolen object. The prolific prairie historian Grant McEwan tells the story of a hundred head of horses "whisked from the nearby range" along the Highwood River in 1885. The animals belonged to Duncan Cameron, John Sullivan, and Fred Ings. Most of them had been turned out just a year or so earlier. "There were no clues except that a big band of unidentified horses was known to have been driven across the … [river] and herded northward."[109] The thieves were never caught. Captain R. Burton Deane describes another case from the late 1880s and early 1890s. A particularly brash young cowboy in the Lethbridge area regularly encouraged five hundred to six hundred horses to graze near his home. On a moment's notice he and presumably some helpers would gather a number of the horses and drive them to a distant market. It took many years for the police to get enough evidence to lay charges against the ringleader.[110]

Often rustlers nabbed livestock in the northern states and ran them into Canada. The most famous of the American rustlers was probably the Dutch Henry gang. At one stage in cahoots with the celebrated Sundance Kid, its members transported American horses into southern Assiniboia – there to be sold to homesteaders needing them to start up their new farms.[111] Just after 1900 Henry and his cohorts joined forces with the Nelson-Jones gang[112] and set up headquarters in the Wood Mountain area south of Swift Current. This region was ideal for rangeland criminals, "heavily wooded terrain, with hills and minor mountains whose canyons and gulches offered ample concealment" for "horse thieves, cattle rustlers and wanted outlaws." The rustlers instigated a reign of terror to prevent local ranchers from helping the police against them. Apparently, at times there were so many criminals in the area that it was "difficult to tell the 'good guys' from the 'bad guys.'"[113]

While the Dutch Henry and Nelson-Jones gangs were in Canada they were regularly pursued by the North-West Mounted Police.

Ultimately, however, only a few were ever arrested by the Mounties. In 1904 Edward Shufelt was tried and "brought to justice in Canada," another gang member escaped after being arrested and was never recaptured, and two others were apprehended and turned over to authorities in Montana. The rest scattered to various places in the United States where two of them were murdered, two were arrested and imprisoned, and two were shot by law enforcement officers.[114]

If trafficking in stolen goods often traversed the international border from south to north, there were also lots of cases of it going the other way. In 1885, for instance, two southern Albertans – one a North-West Mounted Police constable – were arrested in Montana with stolen Canadian horses. They quickly learned that Americans were opposed to such tactics – in the process of being taken to Fort Benton for trial they were intercepted by a party of cowboys and after "very few preliminaries," were "taken to the nearest tree" and directed to "the hempline route to the great hereafter."[115] In 1902 Sheriff C. Wallace Taylor of Choteau, Montana, arrested James Fisher, wanted for helping to steal thirty-one dogies from ranchers near his hometown of Okotoks, Alberta. Fisher waived extradition and came voluntarily to Alberta for trial. He was found guilty and sentenced to five years in jail.[116]

Other forms of rustling were subtler than the snatch-and-run method. Ironically, some of the most highly respected Canadian ranchers themselves habitually practised one of them. The big operators adopted the convention of stealing cattle from the small operators by branding and taking possession of every unmarked animal they found on the range at round-up time. This practice started with the very first great ranch to make an appearance on the Canadian range.

In the spring of 1882 Major Walker of the Cochrane outfit set out with his cowboys to gather all the stock that had not been killed by the previous winter storms. The cattle had been branded only superficially before the trek from Montana, and the main objective was to do the job properly. In gathering the cattle the cowboys were assisted by settlers in the district who seem to have been a bit awed by the big ranch and therefore got some satisfaction from helping out.[117] Some of the settlers also had unbranded cattle scattered on the range and wanted to retrieve them. They soon realized that in fact the Cochrane had no intention of helping them. Walker had orders from the East to put the Cochrane brand on every unmarked animal he found, and he intended to follow those orders to the letter. One rancher owned a cow and calf that he had "made pets of" and kept around his home place.[118] He saw them being swept into the corrals and roped for branding. With strong support from one of the foremen, the rancher objected. Walker refused to be moved.

This lost him the sympathy and support of the settlers who immediately stopped helping and began heading home. On the way a good percentage of them gathered every animal they came across. "Many a secret coulee, many a distant ravine and sidehill, still held Cochrane cattle, and these settlers knew the country much better than the Cochrane men did." The settlers "kept on gleaning, until a very respectable number of the big company's animals were diverted to individual ranches, without the exchange of a dollar."[119]

Other large operators seem to have used the Cochrane precedent as justification for rounding up cattle that did not belong to them for the entire duration of the ranching frontier. Fifteen years after the first Cochrane round-up Sergeant A.F.M. Brooke at Calgary observed that "it is the general custom of the large ranchers and ranch associations at the spring and fall round ups to either brand or sell all stray and unbranded cattle, including calves which are known as 'Mavericks' for their own benefit." Brooke believed that at any one time many of the larger ranchers thus had cattle "in their possession that legally they do not have the right to." A significant portion of these cattle, he estimated, "belong to some of the smaller ranchers who are not members of any association and do not have nor attend the roundups, and have no representatives." These people he believed were the ones who "become heavy losers." He said that "numerous cases of cattle being lost have come to my notice, and although extreme efforts have been made to find them, only a small percentage were ever recovered."[120]

In an open range system where all the herds were mixed together and there were so many newborn and therefore unbranded calves, it was much easier for the cowboys to brand all the animals they found rather than attempt to sort out which animals did not belong to them. Therefore they commonly took any unbranded animals, or "mavericks" – newborn or otherwise. It was next to impossible for the police to decide which livestock was the property of which ranchers. The large ranchers knew that at least some of the cattle they were gathering were not their own as they would often slaughter mavericks for the chuck wagon or brand them to be sold later. In the latter case the revenue usually went to the association to be used to cover round-up expenses.[121]

The practice of branding mavericks was dealt a severe blow by the courts in 1903 when a German settler laid charges against the captain of the Plum Creek round-up for taking a steer.[122] The presiding judge ruled in his favour and ordered that the steer and a heifer belonging to another settler be returned. The case received a good deal of coverage in the press and after this the taking of mavericks at the round-ups seems to have waned.[123]

Up to that time, the fact that many of these animals had been used "for the general good of the association" appears to have cleared the consciences of many big ranchers.[124] They could at least feel secure in the belief that they were working for the good of their kind. Evidence also suggests, however, that some of them needed no such rationalization. They were prepared to steal from any operation, large or small. Moreover, it was not just unbranded cattle they took. In 1892, D.H. Andrews of the Stair Ranch wrote to the Glengary Ranch Company with some rather serious charges. These seem to implicate at least one very important middleman in the frontier cattle business. "We have found one of our three year old steers," he said, "branded 76 & plain earmark … vented with your brand[125] & also with Mr. [Pat] Burn's brand on it. I hear you have delivered a number of cattle to Mr. Burns during the spring months & that most of them were killed before the spring round up [and] also that three other firms have found their cattle branded as our steer has been."[126] Whether or not this matter was ever brought to the attention of the authorities is unknown.

While it appears that the taking of mavericks by the big ranchers decreased after 1903, there are also indications that it did not end. In 1909 John F. Dubois, "a stockman of long and varied experience in all the range country on this continent," was tried on several charges of stealing cattle from the Hatley Ranch Company. C.J. Sifton, the presiding judge at one of the trials, summarized the evidence:

> No honest stockman will brand a 3-year old steer, without careful examination, unless he has lately purchased it from a known and reputable person, and even then it would be much wiser if he did exercise care and see that so-called accidents do not occur. According to the evidence, it would appear that alleged respectable ranchers and stockbuyers do sell, do ship, do kill and do brand cattle which do not belong to them, and, when they are found out, pay for them, which raises a strong presumption that there may be numerous cases which not being found out, soon enough result in financial benefit to the so-called respectable people, and undoubtedly place them in the position of being cattle thieves under sec. 989 of the Criminal Code. And I am unable to see that the evidence given places Dubois in any better position.[127]

Dubois was acquitted on several of the charges but found guilty on at least one and sentenced to nine months imprisonment and hard labour.[128] It seems unlikely that many of the large operators robbed each other very often. It would have made little sense to most of them to risk the wrath of their peers, particularly considering the fact that both individually and through the livestock associations, they were engaged in a common fight to defend their herds from rustling. This was no easy fight. After the incident with the Cochrane in 1882, many of the ordinary ranchers assumed the right to pick away at the big herds year after year, mainly by taking the newborn calves before they had been branded. From there the conflict escalated. The great ranches took every unbranded animal they could find at every round-up, and the smaller men actively claimed any calves they could get their hands on whenever they came across them. In some areas mavericks came to be "considered the property of the first man to run his brand on their virgin hides."[129]

Many of the ordinary ranchers seem to have got their start this way. They came out to the ranching frontier with little or no capital and no cattle and got into the business principally "by stealing the beginnings of a herd of their own from among the strays from the great herds on the open range."[130] In 1893 the *Macleod Gazette* noted the "extraordinary manner in which some men's herds" tend to "increase out of all proportion to their original size." It was about time, the paper declared, that ways be found to "stop the depredations of certain unscrupulous white men who never legally owned a head of stock in their lives but who are waxing fat on what they can steal from their neighbours."[131]

Some quite sophisticated schemes were developed to take calves. In one area in the foothills three young men on two small ranches became adept at it indeed. On one ranch they had "a log cabin, a stable, a corral with a spring in it, and a closed in shed." A coulee ran "a couple of miles" from the corral to a creek bottom. The men would head out with their six-guns strapped on. When they found a herd in the valley they would chase the calves up the coulee using the noise of their guns to scare off the mothers. The calves were quickly herded into the corral and then deposited safely into the shed out of sight of any passers-by. In a few days, when the calves were properly weaned and there was no fear that they would recognize their mothers, or vice versa, they were branded and turned out to pasture once again.[132]

The chief way of stealing calves, however, was to pick them up one at a time and subject them to the so-called "running" or "round" iron. A rustler would travel the range with a branding iron short enough that he could slip it into his bootleg when he needed to conceal it. The iron had a round edge on one end that the rustler could use to fashion any brand he desired.[133] In 1906 the police officer in charge at Lethbridge told his superiors that he was not sure whether or not rustling had increased in the past year, but that he was

> inclined to think it has, judging by the rapid increase of some of the herds in this district, and from the numerous reports received; this is not the same class of work as is done by the horse thieves, who take chances and drive their ill-gotten gains north for sale. The cattle rustler rides the ranges with a running iron strapped to his saddle generally in stormy weather and picks up calves which have arrived at the age to be easily weaned from their mothers. It is only a work of a few minutes for these experts to rope the calf and drive it to some place where it is held till it would not be claimed by the mother, or recognized by the owner.[134]

As time went on, virtually any unmarked cattle – not just those from the great herds but from all the ranches, large and small – became fair game. The Mountie quoted above added that "fortunately" for the running iron rustlers, "a number [of ranchers] have settled in the district with small bunches of unbranded cattle."[135] These cattle, he was insinuating, were being pilfered.

This measure was not just used on mavericks. The rancher who had previously branded his cattle was not safe from the running iron as it was useful for changing brands. Sometimes the rustler would simply obliterate the original mark on an animal by burning over it and then would replace it with his own brand. Or he might alter or "vent" the existing mark. The letter E could, for instance, be turned into a B by closing up the open side; or a D could be made into a B by adding a dividing line in the middle; Vs became Ws, Cs became Es, Ps became Bs and so on. In the 1870s and '80s the police acted as recorders and distributors of brands, but many were not recorded.[136] Therefore, one caught in possession of cattle with a particular brand could claim that he had used it strictly for the purpose of telling his own animals from neighbouring herds.

Another form of rustling on the open range required organizing networks of thieves over large areas. The participants were, for the most part, squatters, homesteaders, ranch hands, and/or professional rustlers. A group would go into a certain area, pick up a small herd of either horses or cattle, drive them out as quickly as possible, and then trade them to thieves in new localities for commodities such as cash, grain, or more livestock. When the livestock were traded, both the travelling and the local thieves needed to move on again to negotiate further trades with men in other places. "At present we have under arrest, committed for trial, one Brewster, who is accused of stealing over 30 head of cattle near Red Deer," Commissioner Herchmer reported in 1896. "This Brewster was found at Green Lake after a long search, some 800 miles from the scene of his alleged theft, in possession of a large band of horses, which we held for some time."[137] These horses may have been well out of their original territory, as the police could find no ranchers willing to claim them.

The advantage of this type of arrangement for both the travelling and the resident thieves was that they found themselves in possession of livestock that they had not stolen. The local man had animals that could not be traced or identified easily, and the travelling thief, if caught, could argue that he had bought his herd. The latter gained a second advantage: he normally came out on the better side of the deal. The local thief was working his own area and was likely to want to get rid of his merchandise as quickly as possible for fear of having to face his neighbours. Therefore he was not in a very good bargaining position. It was the "custom," Herchmer noted, for horse owners "to send out parties in charge of bands of horses through the northern and eastern settlements, in order to trade them off for any merchantable commodity." Two young entrepreneurs named Parslow and Dalgliesh who were residents of Calgary got into this trade when they went to Prince Albert on one of these expeditions. "Some time after their departure" from Prince Albert a "considerable number" of cattle were missing. "As it transpired that they had taken out three car-loads of good cattle in return for two of very indifferent horses," the matter was brought to the attention of Staff-Sergeant Brooke. Ultimately "three-fourths of the missing cattle were found west of Calgary, and 650 miles from where they were stolen, some having been already sold." When tried for theft Parslow was acquitted but Dalgliesh, "a cow-boy," was found guilty and sentenced to time in jail.[138]

Large ranchers from the northern states conducted another form of livestock theft that required considerable planning. The best known of these ranchers were the Spencer brothers, respected cattlemen from Montana. In 1901 they leased land on the Milk River Ridge on the Canadian side of the border in order to gain access to the open range there.[139] Then they developed and perfected two fraudulent methods of exploiting the opportunities it offered. First they would bring far greater numbers north than their lease of land could support. They would legally ship a few hundred head of cattle across the line at the beginning of the grazing season, declare them at the border, and pay the duty. Then they would smuggle in hundreds more with the same brand on them. They would turn all the cattle loose and allow them to disperse into small groups spread out across the open range. Any of them that were sighted by the Mounties could, of course, be claimed to be part of the original legal herd.

To make this even more profitable, when the Spencers rounded up their animals to take them back to Montana in the fall, they had a tendency to incorporate any Canadian mavericks found grazing with them (or, one presumes, that the Spencers could encourage to graze with them). The Mounties figured this out fairly quickly by doing some rather simple mathematical calculations. Under the open range system, Captain Deane estimated, "the ordinary … expectation in the matter of calf crop," was "one calf to three cows or thereabouts." Therefore, John Spencer's "claim, that every one of their cows had a calf, was a sheer absurdity."[140] To confirm this the police visited one of the herds that was in the process of being shipped home and they found "a goodly number of dry cows" that clearly had either lost their calves or had failed to give birth.

The Spencers were far from the only American outfits conducting business in this way.[141] Numerous ranchers grazed cattle close to the border and leased land on the Canadian side. One of the best known of these was the Circle Ranch on the confluence of the Belly and Little Bow rivers.[142] Other American ranchers simply drove their cattle north allowing them to drift over the border as if by accident.[143] Thus they too accessed the plentiful and inexpensive crown lands and ostensibly picked up stray cattle when it came time to take their herds home.[144]

The picture that emerges with respect to the problem of rustling in general is not one of law-abiding ranchers and cowboys working hand in glove with the Mounties to ensure that property on the frontier was safe. Indeed, it is just the opposite. Both published and manuscript reports indicate that the herds were anything but secure.[145] The police insisted on numerous occasions that a great deal of livestock crime was being conducted that they were unable even to detect. They also pointed to the frontier environment as the principal reason. Captain Deane believed he should spell this out in some detail to his readers when publishing his recollections after over thirty years in southern Alberta. "It is necessary to explain," he wrote, "how it was possible for peripatetic cattle to be gathered and stolen in such a large way." The main explanation he offered was the ranchers' practice of leaving livestock to "run at large on the public domain." Deane had a good basic understanding of ranching and it is no accident that in speaking of losses in the herds he also chose to mention the most substantial forces of nature. When unsupervised cattle happened to escape the thieves, he mused, they were often subject to the "depredations of timber wolves" or they were liable to be "overtaken by a severe winter."[146]

Other Mounties expressed genuine frustrations at their inefficacy in the battle against livestock theft. "This is an enormous territory to watch," Commissioner Herchmer complained in 1896 while lamenting the amount of rustling going on.[147] One year later he noted: "we have endeavoured ... to patrol the country as usual, and while we have been successful in arresting many cattle thieves and other delinquents, advantage has been taken [of our small numbers]."[148] By 1903 the commanding officer for Calgary sounded disillusioned in the extreme. "The convictions for cattle and horse-stealing are ... one more than last year," he wrote. "I can only repeat [that this kind of crime is] the most prevalent and ... the most difficult to detect. The way the cattle and horse business is carried on in a stock country such as this, lends itself to this class of crime. So many have been tempted, that it is very hard to get reliable information."[149]

Surely police opinion is compelling evidence. If the men in charge of enforcing the law felt that rustling was rampant, would it not be rather perverse of posterity to assume the opposite? A huge span of territory, relatively few policemen, and the sheer number of those who were regularly "tempted" were obviously crucial in the officers' eyes. These same factors made convictions extremely difficult to achieve when rustling was uncovered. The police simply could not give individual instances the kind of attention they required. "At present, no matter how carefully our cases are worked up, some technicality almost invariably causes the release of the prisoners," Herchmer told his superiors. "Every day the immunity from punishment, so clearly shewn, is encouraging rogues to increase their cattle stealing business, and under present conditions, no matter how many are arrested, we cannot stop this nefarious practice."[150] The next year there were "88 cases of horse-stealing entered" and "several bands of horses" were "brought in from the United States," which the Mounties "had every reason to believe, were stolen." However, "the brands were so well 'worked' that the owners could not be discovered, and, therefore, nothing could be done."[151]

Adding to the problem, many ranchers refused to help the police. Frequent complaints from the force noted that "the majority of stockmen, especially those doing a small business, will not try to help themselves, and give ... [us] little or no assistance ... although they frequently complain of the failure of the police to trace ... criminals."[152] Numerous ranchers seem to have followed the ancient biblical adage "let him who has not sinned cast the first stone." A clampdown on range crime was threatening because it would have implicated too many people. For those who were not involved in crime, a major obstacle to helping the police was the possibility of retaliation.

"I am bound to say, that more could be done by us if some ranchers were not so reticent in giving information, through fear of reprisals," the commanding officer at Maple Creek estimated in 1903.[153] It seems likely that the honest person, recognizing that great numbers of his neighbours were implicated, believed that he stood alone and was therefore particularly vulnerable to depredations and even to vengeance should he help the authorities. In the Wood Mountain area, the members of the Dutch Henry and the Nelson-Jones gangs seem to have taken turns terrorizing the smaller ranchers, and at times were able to force them into actually aiding and sheltering them. Those gangs are known to have "punished" informants.[154] In his recent article on violence on the western frontier L.A. Knafla has suggested that intimidation was one of the most persuasive tools used by the Holt-Dubois gang to prevent their neighbours from helping the authorities.[155]

Another major obstacle to efficient law enforcement was the scarcity of facilities for processing and punishing criminals. When men charged with crime were arrested, there was often nowhere except the guardroom at one of the North-West Mounted Police barracks in which to lock them up.[156] The usual policy of the magistrates therefore was to allow the prisoner to be freed on bail. When that happened, the accused normally did not stick around for the trial. Instead, he would terminate his local operations and simply slip away into the wilderness. There appears to have been some honour amongst thieves. If his neighbours or friends had given securities to back the bail bond, the accused would often sell whatever property he had and pay them back before hitting the trail. "A reputed cattle thief" would get bail, "say himself in $1000 and two sureties in $500 each." If he was guilty and "sure to be convicted," he was likely "at once to get rid of his own loose property and 'skip,'" or if his sureties were "too sharp for him," he had the chance "of squaring them, so that they suffer no loss."[157]

Convictions that might have had wide implications were sometimes lost as a result.[158] The point is made by the case of a man named McArthur accused of stealing a number of cattle from High River and Pine Creek, "and whose trial the police expected would involve several men who have been suspected of stealing cattle for years." After spending some considerable time in the guardroom at Calgary, McArthur had to be released on bail. He took the opportunity "to arrange his affairs and disappear."[159] That, of course, was the last the police saw of him.

Other problems of law enforcement resulted from the fact that conditions on the frontier were novel and that legal conventions had to be established to deal with them. One was the means of identifying cattle and their owners. From the beginning many of the ranchers used the age-old system of branding. In the 1880s they began recording their brands with their stock association, and the police acted as hide inspectors when cattle were being sold or shipped to market. However, a lot of the cattlemen – in particular those who were not members of associations and could not register brands – did not properly mark their animals.[160] The police insisted that in an open range where livestock was dispersed and where massive numbers mingled, branding should be both supported by law and made universal. "The man who owns a large number of cattle which roam at large over the prairie, is in all probability unable to identify one per cent of his property, except by means of the brand which he has placed upon them before turning them loose."[161]

It was not until the North-West Council hide ordinance of 1898 that all brands could be properly registered. The ordinance also made it clear that a man could be held criminally accountable for altering a brand or for venting it before sale.[162] A recorder of brands was appointed in Macleod[163] and a law was passed requiring that all cattle be inspected before being sold.[164]

To ensure uniformity and to prevent duplication, the territorial Department of Agriculture took over the issuing of brands.[165] In the following year the North-West Council ordered that all stock must be inspected before it was shipped or driven out of the country.[166] These laws seem to have had some effect,[167] but they did not immediately bring a flood of convictions for theft as the criminal code was not amended to establish that a brand on an animal was prima facie evidence of ownership.[168] Captain Deane, when Superintendent at Lethbridge, called attention to "the fact that for want of such provision cattle stealing is now increasing in extent and in audacity year by year." The current law, he said, "provides punishment for obliterating, altering or defacing the recorded brand of any other person [and] also for venting a brand in case of sale, the vent being then prima facie evidence of the sale or transfer." However, he pointed out that "these minutiae are of little importance when the brand itself is not recognized by the courts as prima facie evidence, and when a man can steal an animal branded with another person's well known registered brand, and cannot be called upon to account for his possession thereof."[169]

In 1900 a new ordinance made up the deficit. The remaining major flaw was the lack of an official publication that could be circulated widely to assist the police in identifying brands.[170] The first brand book appeared as early as 1888 and new ones were issued from time to time.[171] However, there apparently were few copies and they were poorly updated and distributed. That changed as a result of pressure from the Western Stock Growers Association.[172] By 1907 the provinces of Alberta and Saskatchewan were publishing their own brand books.[173]

Other factors undoubtedly helped to make the cattle frontier relatively conducive to rangeland crime in the early days. The impossibility of holding regular court sessions in outlying areas and reliance on poorly trained courtroom personnel, for instance, must have hindered due process at least somewhat. Legal historians will no doubt conduct more thorough investigation of the frontier legal system and crime in general in the future.[174] It should be said that the purpose here is not to suggest that everyone was a criminal or that the police worked entirely alone on the open range. While many cattlemen were involved in theft, others tried to help bring a semblance of security to their industry. Under everyday circumstances cowboys patrolled the herds in an effort to discourage rustlers, and when district roundups were organized, representatives or "reps" from ranches in neighbouring districts were invited to participate in order to pick up properly branded animals and return them to their original pastures.[175] There are instances, moreover, of ranchers taking it upon themselves to reimburse the owners of strays found grazing with their herds.[176] However, both published and manuscript reports indicate that from a legal point of view the frontier was anything but tame.[177] Theft mushroomed at times out of control as both ranchers and police grappled with the immensity of the country at a stage when proper jails and other facilities were lacking.

It is no easier to estimate how much rustling cost the ranchers than it is to grasp the extent of damage from winter storms, wolves, and fire since the livestock men who continued to use the open range system did not keep meticulous records and often did not know themselves which particular adversary was responsible for what losses. It is clear, however, that overall destruction from these four sources was very great indeed. Captain Deane's belief that it took three cows to produce a single calf seems to have been justified. Kelly observed that in the earlier period "it was found that a goodly number of cows" were needed to bring a single calf through one season[178] and Edward Brado states that it was "possible to assume an annual increase of a herd of range cattle at twenty-five to thirty-five percent."[179] Today, some of the cattlemen who have run herds on large ranges support that contention.[180]

It also seems reasonable to deduce that rustling by itself must sometimes have been destructive enough to bring the individual rancher to the edge of bankruptcy. The following recollections of a cowboy working in the British Columbia interior in the 1930s when it was still a frontier illuminate this. They also highlight the fact that large-scale theft is a predictable occurrence in a situation where cattle are turned loose to graze huge, open pastures for extended periods.

> We found on arrival that things were quite a little upset over at Butch's. When he made his summer roundup to brand, he found nearly a hundred head of cows and calves missing. Somebody had gone to rustling with more than just a long rope and a running iron. They must have known Butch's schedule fairly well and run this bunch off the range soon after the cattle were turned out, when there was no one in that whole county for a couple of months. Lots of rain had washed tracks out completely and, since it was done in the height of the growing season, the places they had held the stock didn't show much sign. Butch took two Indians – Johnny Sam, the best trapper and tracker in the country, and Lexie, who knew the whole country. They travelled for about three months trying to locate the bunch. They found two or three holding places, enough to establish the direction the cattle were being taken, but then the rustlers crossed through range that had lots of stock on it. Tracking from there on was useless.
>
> A lot of the cows came back home fairly early in the fall, but some not till after Christmas. However, the cows were all dry. Their unbranded calves had been weaned off them and mixed into someone else's herd. We tried back-tracking the cows that came in after there was snow, but they had invariably stopped at meadows any places there was feed enough to hold them awhile. The closer they got to home, the longer they were apt to stay, and tracks back from there were unreadable. Also, they came in from different directions as though they had been held and probably turned loose in small bunches from different localities at differing times, so there wouldn't be any well-defined trail of a herd to follow.
>
> Whoever did the rustling planned well and never slipped up on even the smallest detail and must have had a lot of cow-savvy. Poor old Butch was out two-thirds of his calf crop and several cows, also his time and wages for two men for three months, and all to no avail.[181]

Ranching in the British Columbia interior at that time was carried on under much the same conditions as in southern Alberta and Assiniboia some three decades earlier. The following year the owner, Butch, sold what remained of his cattle and terminated operations.[182]

6
The Evolution of Technique

The downplaying by Canadian historians of the importance of both the frontier and the natural environments in shaping ranching history may be one reason why very little investigation of day-to-day practices has been undertaken. These pages have argued that the American cowboy made a major impact on popular culture on the frontier because he, better than anyone else, had the skills, equipment, and knowledge to work the herds in an open range situation. The main contention in this chapter is that while adjusting to frontier and environmental conditions, cattlemen had to change their agricultural practices from the form of ranching that many of them expected to maintain to something that could more appropriately be called mixed farming.

The movement towards farming and away from ranching started almost from the beginning, and it continued right through until the First World War. In the process the ranchers had to alter their methods and in many cases, it would seem, not without some regrets. When they first arrived on the Canadian range many cowboys were determined to keep up the distinction between ranching and farming. This was important to their self-image as well as to their public image. They believed the line separating ranching from farming was the type of work one did, and they had a clear picture about that. A rancher was someone who worked with "his horse and lasso and branding iron" and stayed away from chickens, hogs, and milk cows and from such devices as rakes or pitch forks or "ploughs and binders and threshing machines."[1] In part because of the high esteem he was accustomed to enjoying on both sides of the border, the cowboy resisted any pressure to get out of the saddle for extended periods during the working day. The ranch hands "all say they have not time," it was observed in 1888; they "will not work on foot," and they have not as yet shown a willingness to "cut hay … [or to] garden and attend domestic animals."[2]

Within a few years all this changed as ranchers found themselves slowly but surely forced to embrace a number of farming practices in order to meet major environmental challenges. The changes appeared first as a product of the movement away from year-round grazing. Initially, the ranchers allowed their herds to roam in winter as in summer because they were relatively ignorant about their new environment. They made the mistake of assuming that the chinooks would appear faithfully every winter and that, along with other favourable environmental conditions, this would enable the herds to survive on the open range.[3]

This soon put the ranchers in a perilous position. Some sensed how dangerous it was from an early date. In 1884 the wife of one large leaseholder wrote the following depiction of a primary tension on the range to a relative back home in Ontario. In her words the general sense of helplessness in bad weather is unmistakable:

> There are times when a snow storm has come and spread a cruel depth of snow over the long grass and the cowboys ride late and early driving starving cattle to the nearest hay stack or at any rate driving them from the thickets near a stream where they go for shelter but remain to die ... This ... throws a shadow over our days for as long as it lasts – 10 days – even two weeks sometimes but not often – and every ear is listening for the happy sound of the first murmurings of a Chinook. One night we were sitting just as I have told you and suddenly some one said "the Chinook!!" We were all outside in a second, and there was the low roar in the mountains and in twenty minutes the wind had reached the house. We went in and made coffee and were a much more joyful party than an hour before.[4]

Plainly the fear of massive starvation among the herds and the need to supplement winter pastures with some reserves of hay were already factors at this woman's ranch. A year or so later the *Macleod Gazette* evinced the same sentiments when it advised the ranchers that "every cowman in the country should put up enough hay on his range to feed weak stock through any bad storm"[5]; if cattlemen would do this, they would "sleep better during the cold and stormy nights of winter." However, it was the winter of 1886–87 that convinced many of the serious ranchers that they needed to have large roughage supplies on hand every year.[6] Thereafter they learned to judge the ranching potential of any particular location by the tall natural grasses that could be cut and stacked.[7]

The recognized need for winter feed was a main factor in eventually pushing ranching out of the lower plains regions almost totally. This left it where the leaseholders had started, in the higher and more humid elevations of the foothills, the Milk River Ridge, and the Cypress Hills. The arid climate and lighter soils on the plains make it impossible to produce substantial hay crops without irrigation.[8]

Haying on Walrond Ranch (ca. 1893)

When there were few settlers and lots of land, it was feasible to find enough natural roughage for the small herds in low-lying areas. However, as more and more settlers poured in, beginning in the 1890s, these were too few and far between to sustain what would have been a lot more livestock. In the new century some ranching continued on the plains, primarily in the valleys of the major rivers, but elsewhere the cattlemen were replaced by an army of wheat farmers attempting to eke out an existence on holdings of 160 acres.[9]

In the high country, the fact that roughage could be put up in abundance improved the chances of a successful cattle industry but it also initiated the end of the era of the cowboy who worked only from the saddle. Harvesting hay was labour intensive. It required mowing and raking the grasses with horse-drawn implements and then many hours of work in the hot sun with pitchforks and wagons to stack and store the forage for the winter. The men who were employed on the ranches and rode the herds thus found themselves also spending a considerable portion of their time working in the fields. As time went on it was realized that the wild grasses could be improved upon by planting fields of mixed domestic varieties including brome grass, timothy, clover, and alfalfa.[10] That obliged the ranchers to break up and cultivate the virgin soils and then to work them again every four or five years to replant.

Increasingly, ranchers turned as well to the yearly planting, stooking, and stacking of greenfeed made from the stalks of oats or oats

Cutting oats, Buffalo Head Ranch, Longview, Alberta, 1908

and barley mixed.[11] This involved annual field cultivation and more plant husbandry. The small ranchers made the transition to hay and then greenfeed with relative ease. Within a few years many were able to put aside enough roughage to get all their cattle through prolonged winters. The big ranches did so with much less success. However, most of them did learn to put up some roughage and got to the point where they were able to protect their newborn calves and older cows. The North Fork ranch was gathering hay annually as early as 1884, and the Cochrane, A.E. Cross, and the Stair Ranches were growing crops of both hay and greenfeed in the late 1880s and/or early 1890s.[12] The Walrond was putting up enough roughage to winter all its calves and bulls by the late 1890s,[13] and American versions of the great ranches including both the McIntyres and the Spencers moved into the production of feed soon after they set up business.[14] This forced the cowboys to work on foot in the wintertime as well, when it came time to haul the feed and to distribute it to the livestock.[15]

To protect the cattle properly the ranchers also built fences on their holdings so they could prevent livestock from wandering too far from stored feed. All the cattlemen appear to have done some fencing, but again it was the smaller operator who did so with the more success. By about 1900 those who had not yet sufficiently divided up their lands were buying up wire – some by the "car load" – and in a few short years much of the deeded land, and a good percentage of the leased, was enclosed and cross fenced.[16] "Things in the foothills are looking well this year," it was reported in 1904, "although fences are going up in all directions."[17] Several months later in the Pincher Creek district the following words, written about fighting the mange, indicated both that the range in that area was now closed and that it was the small man who had completed the job:

> In a range country it is possible for ranchers to take prompt and effectual methods for prevention and cure [of the mange]. Where the range is not intersected with fences it is easy to handle large herds of cattle, run them through dips, and hold them until every head in that particular district has been dipped. But in [the foothills near Pincher Creek] … the building of public dips … would be almost useless. For one thing there … [is] not a large enough vacant space of land, unappropriated, which could be used for herding any large bunch of cattle; and for another thing, the cattle … [are] now held by so many people in small bunches, that it would be almost impossible to see to the treatment of all infected animals.[18]

The foothills districts seem to have been the first to see the completion of the closing of the open range. In other areas it proceeded more slowly. On the Bow and Red Deer rivers east of Calgary, for instance, little fencing had been done by the winter of 1906–07 and the community of Dorothy was still practising a communal approach to dipping cattle.[19] However, in most locations where the beef industry was to continue to predominate on a permanent basis, the open range disappeared in the decade or so before 1914. This brought new efficiencies in a number of areas. It is as important to the cattleman to keep undesirable elements out of his herds as it is to keep the herds themselves together. Fences allowed him to wage a better battle against the mange and other diseases because they gave him the ability to prevent infected animals from bringing it in from the outside.[20] Moreover, it allowed for drastically improved breeding patterns and breed selection.

This had been an enormous problem from the beginning. Initially, the quality of the Canadian herds was considerably less than perfect. Most cattle originated south of the border where indiscriminate mating on the open range had allowed characteristics of the least desirable animals to spread widely. Contrary to scholarly opinion, this seems adversely to have affected even the very large outfits.[21] In the beginning, one cowpuncher remembered, "the Bar U in common with other ranching enterprises … was compelled to purchase as its foundation stock, cattle of a low and inferior type." It took many years "to weed-out" the inferior animals and replace them with "a better type."[22] In the earliest period the Canadian range was as open, unfenced, and uncontrolled as the American and, despite commendable efforts by some ranchers to import pure and quality mixed-breeds from the East and overseas, the move to general improvement was slow.[23] Some progress appears to have come, however, when a few of the great ranchers fenced small portions of their huge pastures and were able to keep their best breeding stock separated from the run of the mill.

When smaller ranchers began to arrive in large numbers in the 1890s they too brought in most of their initial cattle from the American West, and this seems to have been a setback for overall quality. "It is a great pity that so much inferior stock has been brought in from the United States during the past season by settlers taking their residence here," the Department of the Interior recounted in 1895.[24] Because the smaller men also started grazing without fences, and some of the least efficient continued to do so for a number of years, this situation did not soon change. As late as 1898 the Mounties were reporting that "the class of cattle in the country is not generally as good as formerly. The steers offered show less breeding and are smaller … Many of the small ranches have too few bulls, and rely on the enterprise of their neighbours to provide new blood, and there are still many wretched looking bulls on the ranges; and indeed some of the young bulls imported are not likely to improve matters."[25]

Nonetheless, many of the smaller operators who did not accompany the great ranches out of business were quick to begin upgrading their herds.[26] They built fences around all their pastures as soon as they could, kept undesirable bulls out of their herds almost entirely, and controlled which of their own bulls were mixing with which cows. As a result of this, and the fact that they both bought up better bulls and culled their cows, they gradually replaced the motley range varieties with heavier-set, more uniform, pure and cross breeds of the Angus, Hereford, and Shorthorn variety. "There is no doubt," the above report continued, that the best steers come from areas where "the ranches are small, and stockmen feed hay all winter, and can attend to the breeding of their cows."[27]

Complete networks of fences gave the smaller cattleman the ability not only to prevent outside bulls from getting to his cows but also to regulate breeding by his own bulls more precisely. He was able first to mix his cows and bulls thoroughly in smaller enclosed areas so that whenever any female cycled into heat, there was a male nearby to ensure that procreation could proceed on schedule.[28] The ordinary rancher could also move bulls in and out of his cowherds with more precision so that they would produce calves at the right time of year. Most of the ranchers wanted to induce March to early April calving and thus put bulls with the cows in early July and removed them about six weeks later.[29] This prevented fall and winter births that were highly risky because of the potential for inclement weather.[30] It also avoided summer births that produced offspring that were too young at the end of the grazing season to be weaned and convert easily to, and grow well on, dry feed.[31]

The man with low numbers and small, well-fenced grazing lands could also see to the proper sorting of his cattle. He could keep some pastures for his older steers, some for his yearlings, and some for his cows. This prevented confusion and enabled him to do a better job of marketing and to keep better track of which cows were producing small offspring or none at all. The latter capability put him in a position to cull his brood stock more scrupulously. He could also weed out poor-quality heifers by spaying them and ensuring that they did not become pregnant and reproduce. Spaying is somewhat more complicated than castrating and is normally not done until the young females are about a year old and, therefore, are bigger and more difficult to handle than the baby bull calves. The heifers had to be thrown to the ground and held there for some time while a veterinarian or well-tutored cattleman cut through their flanks with a scalpel to remove the ovaries. The big ranches like the Walrond[32] did some spaying of poorer quality heifers and female dogies that were brought in for grass fattening. But it was next to impossible for them to be thorough with the heifers from their own cows, considering that there were so many dispersed so widely. The man who had only a handful of cattle confined by fences, on the other hand, could sort out any young female stock he did not like the looks of and see to the job reasonably quickly.[33] The neutered heifers were normally fattened like the steers and sold on the slaughter market.

The smaller rancher thus could maintain a younger, healthier, and higher-quality herd than his bigger counterpart and, therefore, he was almost certainly more productive in almost every sense.[34] When E.H. Maunsell bought the Cochrane cattle in 1905, L.V. Kelly could see that the industry had already demonstrated a distinct propensity away from the great herds mixing endlessly on the open range and towards small units. He was cheered, he said, to note in the face of the "wide decline of the grand old ranch industry which was fast giving place to mixed-farming and small ranchers, that all of the old timers had not given up hope."[35] Proper and precise care and management of livestock, which included feeding, fencing, and herd control, were crucial to the trend that was underway. These procedures

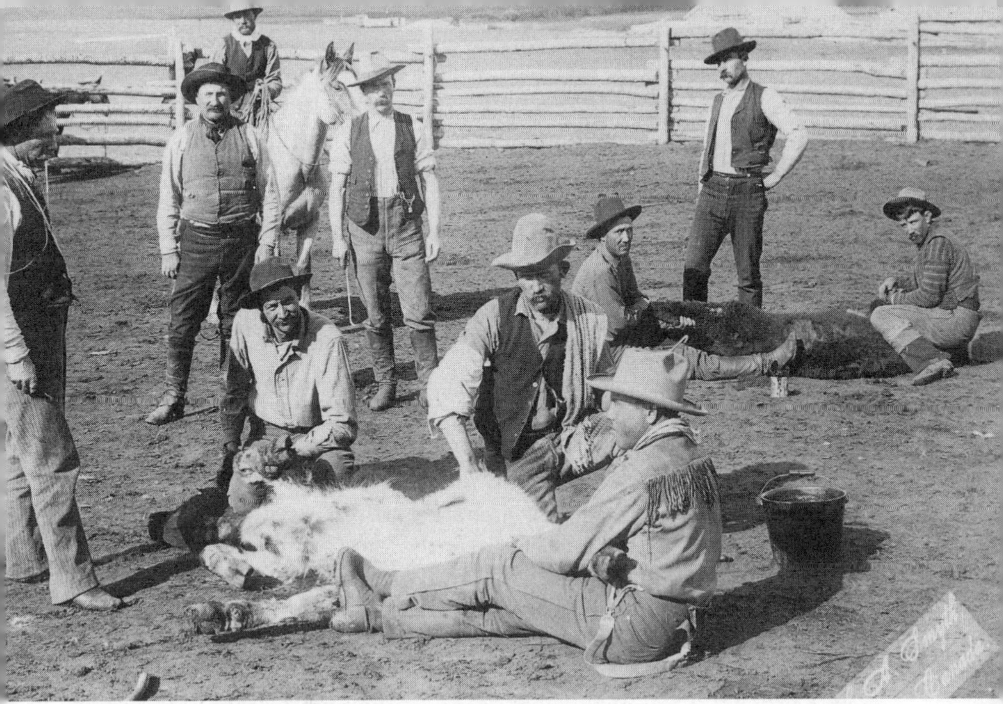

Spaying heifers on the Walrond Ranch, 1894

enabled the smaller ranchers to achieve modern calf crop returns of 80 or 90 per cent as well as better quality stock. As a result they became economic while the great ranches floundered. The latter must have improved somewhat on the one-in-three ratio as they too did some fencing and winter feeding. However, they continued to lose a lot more calves than they should have and to experience heavy losses among both yearlings and mature cows in the wintertime.

As early as 1884 some Canadian ranchers began to explore methods that were to push the beef industry significantly closer to its modern form. Experimenting with coarse grains as well as roughage, they found that the calves they were corralling over the winter prospered when given one or two pounds of ground oats or barley or frozen wheat kernels on a daily basis with their hay and greenfeed.[36] To attain reliable supplies of grain, they broke up new arable fields and began producing oats, barley, and feed wheat every year.[37] In time increasing numbers of ranchers began to do the same, and thus became farmers proper. Far from simply working livestock from the saddle, they were now toiling in their fields, sowing crops, putting up hay and greenfeed, harvesting, storing, and hauling both hay and grain, and working a good deal on foot caring for animals both within their barnyards and outside.[38]

Between about 1900 and the First World War, harsh winter weather, combined with geographical isolation from European markets, stimulated ranchers to refine their techniques a step further. Since they were keeping many of their cattle in corrals and on feed during the winter, it occurred to some that advantages could be achieved by providing very large daily doses of processed grain to the fat cattle in the weeks before they were shipped overseas. In so doing they ventured into what their modern counterparts would call the grain-finishing business. To grasp why livestock producers began to utilize this process in the pre-war years it is necessary to understand the obstacles to efficient marketing that still confronted them.

Each summer and fall, when the fat steers were gathered, the task of getting them to market was anything but easy, and it exacted a tremendous cost in terms of amount and quality of the beef. Cattle that had been loose on pastures over the summer months had become unused to close human contact and thus the round-up and initial confinement in corrals was stressful. When within days the animals had to begin the trek to distant markets, they were positively traumatized. The sound of whips whizzing through the air and screams of handlers when they were being loaded onto trains frightened them, and crowded conditions on very noisy railway cars did nothing to ease their anxiety. The Canadian Pacific Railway stopped the trains at regular intervals to give the stock rest as well as feed and water.[39] However, that entailed more handling, whips, and screams and probably relieved the pain only minimally.

Transshipment into huge ocean vessels and then once again to trains in Britain added to the ordeal. It is not surprising that shrinkage on the carcasses could be very great indeed. One expert writing in 1909 put it as follows: "Cattle wild, excitable and soft off grass, are driven to the railway, held sometimes for days on poor pasture waiting for cars, and finally, after more or less unavoidably rough handling, are forced on board … Is it matter for wonder that after a journey of five thousand miles, made under such conditions our grass-fed range steers arrive in British lairages gaunt and shrunken, looking more like stockers than beeves, that our Scottish friends think we have no feed, or that I should declare a business so conducted as sinfully wasteful?"[40]

Slowly, the cattlemen began to realize that since they already had built corrals as well as feeding troughs and other facilities for their calves, it was not that difficult to hold their "fats" for sixty days or so before shipping and to put them on a heavy grain ration. In this way, the cattle could be subjected more gently to regular human contact and, at the same time could be given a final coat of "hard" fat, which would not melt away so quickly en route. In adopting this system, the Canadians seem to have followed the lead of the American producers. Observed one government official,

Our friends in the United States long ago realized the folly of shipping to Europe, alive, steers direct from the range. Their range cattle are brought to the Middle West, dehorned, if this has not been earlier done, fed for at least sixty days on a ration comprising a liberal allowance of grain, then sent to market, generally in Chicago, and carefully inspected and culled. Those deemed fit for export are then taken to the seaboard by fast trains and in cars specially fitted for feeding and watering enroute ... As a result of these superior methods, United States cattle even when originally from the Western ranges, arrive in Britain in much better condition than Canadian cattle and, of course, command correspondingly higher prices.[41]

Canadian cattlemen began to realize as well that by extending the period of intensive grain feeding they were able to market their stock considerably sooner than was possible on grass and roughage alone.[42] The earlier practice had been to ship steers to market when their body weight reached between 1,400 and 1,800 pounds. On grain, however, carcasses could be properly finished when the steers were three years old or younger and weighed around 1,250 pounds alive. This significantly shortened the commitment to each generation of calves and cut down on expenses.[43] It also produced more tender and better-marbled beef, which could be expected to command higher prices.[44]

The cattlemen started the fattening process by feeding one or two pounds of ground grain per animal per day and then gradually increasing the amount to six or eight times that much.[45] Interest in grain finishing became widespread enough that in 1914 the government farm at Claresholm experimented to develop the best possible combinations of feed and conditions to sustain it. Their published findings demonstrate the close and careful barnyard management required. The experimenters used mostly "range steers two years old past, with a few threes and fours. Cattle were fed loose and in the open on the lee side of buildings and with eight foot high board fence shelter ... The feeds included hay, green-feed and straw for fodder, and oats, frozen wheat and barley for grain. The racks were kept filled with long feed, consisting of hay and green sheaves, chop[ped oats and/or barley] were fed on table tops twice a day. Salt and [warm drinking] water were always available ... Feeding began on November 1st and the cattle were sold about May 1st."[46]

By this point a degree of specialization in beef production seems also to have been achieved which saw some cattlemen concentrate their efforts either on the cow/calf operation or on pasturing and feeding the weaned calves. Those who preferred not to get into intensive feeding procedures made the decision to concentrate their efforts on keeping, improving, and developing their herds. They tried to produce the best possible calves every spring. These they would normally sell in the fall rather than wintering them, pasturing them the next year, and then feeding them through to slaughter. In many cases men who wanted to get out of the breeding end of the business purchased the calves. Eventually these men sold their cows, bought calves in the fall, wintered them on hay, put them out to pasture as yearlings, and then, often depending on perceived market conditions, either sold them to grain finishers or fed them to slaughter themselves the second winter. As this suggests, some cattlemen also specialized just in the finishing trade. They stayed away from both cows and calves and bought the larger yearlings. These they put on heavy grain rations and then sold them on the slaughter market after only a few months.

It is difficult to give precise dates for all the stages that ranching as a whole underwent in the southern prairie livestock regions prior to World War I. However, it would probably be safe to state that the so-called great ranches made the transition from pure ranching in the very earliest frontier period to what might be described as a combination of ranching and mixed farming by the late 1880s and early 1890s. Most of them never ended the practice of open range grazing before liquidating in the early years of the new century. Many of the modest ranchers did end the practice, and before 1914 they had enclosed their pastures and gone into roughage, grain, and finished beef production and were undertaking closely managed selective breeding programs. This does not mean that all the skills of the cowboy became redundant on their spreads. Summer pasturing continued to be important on a majority of the operations in the high country. Therefore, while the district round-ups on the open range disappeared, it remained necessary for each individual outfit to have expert riders who knew how to gather livestock on horseback.

Clearly, however, a cowboy could no longer be just a cowboy. After the turn of the century the minority of ordinary ranchers who were not prepared to embrace mixed-farming techniques sold out, like the cattle barons, and moved on. "Now is the time to buy, and there are numerous good ranches, or farms, we should say, on the market," a newspaper editor wrote in 1905. "Many of these farms have been listed simply because the owners, old time cattlemen, could not get down to farming, preferring to sell out and go to a country where the range is still unbounded and the pasture free."[47] People like Monica and Bill Hopkins near Millarville[48] and Claude Gardiner in the Porcupine Hills northwest of Macleod replaced those who did terminate operations.[49] They took up residence based on the 160-acre homestead and then acquired further holdings to grow their crops and pasture their small herds.[50]

Once they had developed all the agricultural conventions discussed above, many settlers also pushed on into forms of production that were not associated directly with the beef trade. This, to be sure, continued to be their primary or staple industry. However, the smaller operators needed to utilize any farming activity that would provide cash to pay the bills between seasonal cattle marketing.[51] As they responded to this need they embraced more or less the entire range of agricultural forms usually associated with mixed farming. One of these was dairying.[52] "Many who came to the West had little money but they had good health, ambition and strength," recounted a man who witnessed his own family's expansion into that as well as other sub-industries. In the 1890s these settlers "built up herds of cattle and acquired a homestead. As long as there was open range they depended largely on cattle." They had a "small herd of cows, dual purpose shorthorns," and some chickens. They made butter and collected eggs to "pay for groceries, the taxes and other incidentals of living." When the "Creamery became established, the cream cheque supplied the living."[53]

The operations that took up dairying must have been within a few miles of towns such as Claresholm, High River, and Maple Creek, since milk is a highly perishable commodity and had to be delivered without delay by horse and wagon over relatively poor country roads or trails. By 1908 there were private creameries in a number of towns and enough suppliers for them to advertise regular daily pickup routes. After one had been in production less than a single year, the local paper announced that "last season 14,797 lbs. of butter was made and $2871.83 in cash distributed among the patrons, after deducting all charges. It is, we consider, a very satisfactory showing considering that last year was the first season and the factory in operation only a few months. This year with a full season and the whole district organized the output ought to be tripled. [This paper] … believes in mixed-farming and hopes to see the creamery heartily supported by the farmers of this district."[54]

By this time the cream separator was available,[55] enabling stockmen to keep their skim milk for their own consumption and as a feed for pigs.[56] Most ranchers acquired their dairy stock by selecting from their herds Shorthorn crosses which produced milk, although not as efficiently as Holsteins or Guernseys, and also beef, but without the high carcass yields obtainable from Hereford or Angus varieties. The importation of the better-known purebred dairy types began prior to the war.[57] In 1913 the Department of Agriculture reported what it considered fundamental steps forward. From that report it is also clear that much remained to be done. "During the year there has been a phenomenal demand for milch cows," it stated, "and in the neighborhood of 10,000 were brought into the province. Many of them were fairly good cows, but there were also a proportion of genuine culls amongst them. All were sold at high prices – prices, which were only justified by the high returns obtainable in the cities for milk and cream."[58] At this time, few had separate dairy barns to keep and feed their cows indoors during the winter. Therefore, they did not milk year round.[59] During the summer, however, they pastured the animals in or near the farmyard and brought them into the regular stock barn every day to be fed and milked.

Many ranchers also eventually produced hogs. When they had first settled they had been restrained from getting into the business because of the physical characteristics of the species.[60] Hogs lack a heavy coat of fur to protect them from the elements and therefore were particularly vulnerable before the settlers were able to build shelters for them.[61] Once regular stock barns were constructed, however, hogs could be brought inside when the weather was bad.[62] The inclination of foothills cattlemen to commence pork production when they were able to offer some protection from the elements is reflected in a newspaper advertisement in the *Pincher Creek Echo* in the spring of 1904. It announced that "on the request of numerous farmers and ranchers," a local firm had decided "to assist in the formation of a joint stock Pork Packing and Cold Storage Company, having among its objects the acquisition, enlargement and carrying on of the business."[63]

The Department of Agriculture, Canadian Pacific Railway,[64] and a Territorial Swine Breeders' Association[65] sponsored importation from the East and Great Britain of purebreds including Berkshires, Tamsworths, and Yorkshires. What really brought movement into this industry, however, was the sudden growth in the export market just prior to the war when the United States duty on Canadian pork was removed and access was granted to Chicago and Seattle.[66] At that point ranchers and farmers alike set about the task of upgrading their breeds and their facilities with a new sense of urgency. By the Great War they had probably arrived at about the same stage of development as the dairymen. They had shed some of the crude frontier standards of the past but would need to continue to work in that direction.

Settlers also took up poultry. As with dairying and hogs, they turned to chickens in particular in order to supplement their incomes.[67] They were able to purchase first-rate stock once the provincial breeding station appeared at Edmonton in 1908 and to construct adequate shelter as one hundred or more chickens can be comfortably housed in very small coops.[68] Prior to 1914 numerous so-called ranchers kept chickens, protected them from predators, fed them indoors during the season of severe weather, and marketed the eggs on a regular basis.[69]

The other enterprise that many of the small rancher/farmers ventured into was the breeding of heavy workhorses. As settlers streamed into the West there was a demand for quality animals to plough and harvest, and many of the cattlemen produced the bigger animals along with the smaller saddle varieties.[70] This business too suffered from low standards when supply depended on stock that had originally been the progeny of the open range. One early pioneer recalled that the "the horse rancher was not very particular as to what kind of horse he had so long as they had four legs and the usual complement of eyes, ears and other organs."[71] In 1906 stallions across the province of Alberta were registered according to the Horse Breeders' Ordinance, to be made available at a fee for breeding privately owned mares. Of the 491 that were registered only 162, including eighty-one Clydes, thirty-five Percherons, ten Shires, ten Standardbreds and ten Thoroughbreds, were pure.[72]

Here too, change for the better came before World War I. Dealers began to import certified purebreds from the East and overseas. Small breeders bought up this stock, and as they took control of their pastures, they started producing a better commodity.[73] The settlers' shortage of cash and the impossibility of wiping out very quickly the after-effects of indiscriminant breeding on the frontier handicapped progress. Numbers marketed seem to have peaked after 1906 and then to have begun to decline prior to the war,[74] not only as a result of competition from steam but also from the fact that the period of rapid settlement had ended and the best lands were occupied.[75]

Thus the horse business tended to become one more of a number of mixed-farming approaches that supplemented the beef trade on the ranch/farms of southern Alberta and Saskatchewan in the early twentieth century. By World War I the agricultural industry had been almost completely transformed from what it had once been in those regions. The wheat farmers had taken over most of the plains, and ranchers become mixed farmers were now firmly established on the higher elevations. As noted previously, not all the great ranches had disappeared. Perhaps it is now possible to visualize a little more clearly what made the ones that survived different from the rest. In 1902 the Bar U had been taken over and held together as a unit by George Lane and the firm of Gordon, Ironsides and Fares. Lane was eventually to buy out his partners and he would continue in the business until his death in 1926. He also was far from just a rancher. In the last two to three decades of his life he experimented with all forms of agricultural activity from finished beef to grain, dairying, and hog production.[76] His outfit thus became what L.V. Kelly has called a "mixed farm ... conducted on a huge scale."[77] While this seems to have helped to sustain Lane for a considerably longer period than might otherwise have been the case, it did not entirely insulate him from the financial predicament in which so many very large western Canadian agri-businesses have eventually found themselves. At his death all his livestock and land were taken by the banks.

Another of the big operations to stay in business after the war, the McIntyre Ranch on the Milk River Ridge, held some 55,000 acres of deeded land which stayed in the hands of the family until 1947. The McIntyres kept pretty much to the cattle business, but at the same time they saw to the production not just of hay and greenfeed but also of grain to ensure the survival of their stock. After the 1906–07 winter they regularly contracted out large portions of their land to neighbouring farmers who then grew crops of oats and barley on a share basis.[78] This gave the ranch enough roughage, feed grain, and straw to keep all its cattle from starving during the fiercest of the winters. The family also enjoyed the luxury of financial backing from business interests in Idaho.

Most of the present-day great ranches that were founded in the pre-war period started small and built up slowly over the course of decades as family operated ranch/farms. The Copithornes west of Calgary established themselves first as squatters on the original Cochrane lease. From the beginning they fenced, put up feed, and milked cows. It was mostly after the Great War that they expanded their holdings as the need arose for new generations of the family. Each expansion signalled the emergence of a new unit, which was operated and handled like a family farm though, admittedly, a rather large one. Lachlin McKinnon settled in 1895 some seventy miles east of Calgary with sixty head of cattle. He trained both his sons in all the arts of farming through which the family was able to assemble the LK Ranch of later years. In the Milk River country south of Medicine Hat, Walter Ross started in 1885 with four hundred cattle. He and his sons expanded rapidly only to lose virtually everything in the winters of 1906–07 and 1920. Both times members of the family had the tenacity to start over. They used what experience had taught them to eventually reach great-ranch status in Montana as well as in southern Alberta and Saskatchewan.[79]

These ranchers fit the mould described here at least to the extent that they survived the frontier period on the basis of small-scale operation or lost heavily trying to be big. In most cases as well they took up a variety of mixed-farming techniques rather than sticking strictly to pure ranching. It is only their ability to operate on a grand scale that makes them exceptional. As exceptions, however, they help to demonstrate the rule. From the early 1890s on, it is primarily the modest family ranch/farm that has managed not just to survive but to forge a permanent place in western Canadian agricultural history. It initially had the manpower to make the cattle business work and then to refine it and pay attention to the details of undertaking a full slate of agricultural pursuits under trying environmental conditions. How fast the movement to mixed farming actually was completed is reflected in the Canadian census reports. They indicate that in all of Alberta and western Assiniboia in 1891 there were 15,511 milk cows, 7,792 hogs, 86,785 chickens and about 40,000 horses with over 200,000 head of beef cattle.[80] One decade later there were 50,741 milk cows, 48,984 hogs, 265,632 chickens and nearly 100,000 horses with just over 355,000 beef cattle.[81] In other words, while the number of beef cattle had less than doubled, all the other livestock had gone up by from two and a half to six times. To take a smaller area virtually all of which was part of the ranching frontier in earlier days, it is appropriate to concentrate just on the figures for western Assiniboia: in 1891 there were just under 10,000 horses, some 5,500 milk cows, 2,627 hogs and 32,114 chickens with 67,810 beef cattle. Ten years later there were over 25,000 horses, just under 9,500 milk cows, 4,820 hogs and 52,672 chickens with 72,720 beef cattle. While beef production had expanded only slightly, the other livestock had on average increased by close to 100 per cent.

The typical small rancher/farmer had begun working the 160-acre homestead and possibly a small lease, and then perhaps after starting a family, had doubled or even tripled his deeded holdings.[82] He ran thirty to fifty cows from which he raised calves, a dairy herd of about six to ten head, and ten to twenty hogs. He also kept around one hundred chickens and perhaps fifteen to twenty horses, some of which he used to work his own land and others that were bred and raised for the market.[83] He practised a full spectrum of plant husbandry to attain self-sufficiency in feed. Before the war the era not just of the great ranches but of what might be termed pure ranching in general had thus come and gone. Many of the men who continued thereafter to practise agriculture called themselves ranchers primarily out of habit and presumably as a reflection of the high esteem in which the cowboy had been held during the earliest frontier stage when his skills and methods were most admired. However, it was no longer a reflection of the predominant agricultural technique practised in most areas of southern Alberta and Saskatchewan. "In this district we should not complain of full harvests and the cowboy having to turn his lariat into a hay fork," a journalist from Pincher Creek proclaimed in 1904 – "that is what we want and what makes for genuine prosperity."[84]

7 Conclusion

The vision of the western Canadian ranching frontier presented in this work shows a land that was not nearly as Old World in culture, spirit, and agricultural form as many have believed.[1] Most aspects of life were moulded and manipulated by the frontier and natural environments with which the people from the East, overseas, and south were confronted. Unquestionably, one of the results was a considerable amount of lawlessness. Rustling in particular mushroomed at times virtually out of control, in part because a small police establishment found itself battling a monumental open range at a time when such tools as suitable jails, adequate laws, extensive fence networks, and support services for basic provisions including food and firewood were lacking.

As Frederick Jackson Turner pointed out a hundred years ago, the weakness of traditional Old World institutions is a standard predicament on frontiers.[2] This is one of the circumstances that gives frontiers special, if not unique, characteristics. One traditional institution in short supply on the Canadian as on the American ranching frontier was the family. Initially single young men ventured west in far greater numbers than either married couples or women. As a result the family itself was, relatively speaking, far less prominent than in more mature societies. This unquestionably helped to lower respect for the law in a general way. Men who live outside families behave in a much less "civilized" manner than those ensconced within that hallowed institution.[3] When part of a family, they are likely to be concerned with establishing a culture based on home, church, school, law enforcement, and domestic values. Far from taking up lives of crime they are inclined to work towards a social setting in which wives, sons, and daughters can be securely insulated from the basest aspects of the world around them.

Single men, on the other hand, when they are numerically preponderant in comparison to the family type in any society, are inclined to establish a culture devoted to the satisfaction of basic animal urges. They compete with each other on the most fundamental levels (often simply by making bizarre bets) and seek sexual satisfaction and unconstrained entertainment in various forms of night life.[4] Many are also not particularly reluctant to break the law and therefore get involved in a host of nefarious activities. One of these on the ranching frontier was rustling. The individual criminal had the mobility to move away from legal forces both before and after his crimes. He was no doubt unconcerned that he was contributing to the construction of a society that had little respect for authority.

Having said so much in general about lawlessness of varying types in western Canada, it would be wrong not to recognize that Canadians were somewhat less inclined towards one form of it than people in the ranching frontiers south of the border. As Breen has observed, range wars between "bona fide" cattlemen and squatters were largely avoided. In the Canadian West legislation providing for both the lease system and homesteading preceded settlement, as did land surveyors. This made it possible to identify boundaries between individual holdings and to describe exactly what piece or pieces of land belonged to what ranch or farm. The tendency therefore was for those who had possession of the land to feel more secure in it and somewhat less antagonistic towards anyone who strayed onto it. Moreover, when disputes did arise, there was some likelihood that the combatants would turn to the law and legal agents, including the Mounties. As a result there was only one major confrontation between ranchers and squatters that ended in violence. That was on the Walrond Ranch which, unlike some of the large lease operations, did not follow a live-and-let-live arrangement with squatters.[5]

A specific struggle between the Walrond and squatters is worth discussing in some detail as it helps to demonstrate both the extent and the limits of land disputes on the western frontier. Under the direction of its manager, Dr Duncan McEachran, the ranch routinely evicted squatters, normally with the assistance of the Mounties and after the proper legal processes had been utilized. In 1890, however, the usual procedures did not produce the desired result for the ranch, and violence occurred. In that year Robert Dunbar, originally a squatter, was informed by the Department of the Interior that his homestead patent on land that was part of the Walrond lease had been cancelled. He and his family were also instructed by McEachran that they were to stop working and making improvements on the land and leave. The land was first leased to a John Hollis. In 1888 the Hollis lease had been terminated as a consequence of a government effort to cut down on land speculation. The Walrond Ranch had agreed to take over the lease in exchange for 29,000 acres near Fort Macleod, which it was to give up for settlement.[6] The Hollis lease, having been taken out after 1884, had not been a closed lease. The

Department of the Interior's position, and that strenuously put forward by McEachran, was that since the Walrond had given up holdings that had been acquired under the original 1881 legislation in exchange for this land, it should be subject to the provisions of the earlier legislation. Therefore it was closed to settlement. However, when Dunbar received the notice he must have been shocked. He had been on the site southeast of Fort Macleod since 1882.[7] With the help of his two sons, who had joined him in 1883, Dunbar had built a home, plowed some land, and begun grazing cattle. A patent to the land had been granted him in 1888 and pre-emption rights given.[8] His sons had then built a house and settled near him.[9]

Dunbar refused to leave, and in late July 1890 cowboys from the Walrond Ranch rode out to the house of his sons and pulled it down. John Lamar, the foreman at the Walrond, wrote to McEachran a few days after the incident. "We met [one of the Dunbars] ... on our way over and we told him what we was going to do and he forbid us doing it but we went ahead and pulled it down just the same. The whole tribe of them are boiling over with wrath."[10] C.E.D. Wood, the editor of the *Macleod Gazette* and self-appointed champion of opposition to the federal government's lease legislation, took an avid interest in the affair and his newspaper covered it in detail. In 1891 twenty-five settlers in the Porcupine Hills petitioned the House of Commons to cancel the Walrond lease and change all the old leases to allow homesteading. In supporting the petition Liberal spokesmen in the house brought up the Dunbars' plight.

On 25 September 1891 several opposition MPs questioned Edgar Dewdney, then minister of the Interior, as to why settlers had been turned off land to which they had received homestead rights. Dewdney admitted that the Dunbar brothers had been on the land since the early 1880s and had been granted a patent, but this, he said, had been a mistake.[11] The conflict between the Dunbars and the Walrond was finally resolved when all the Dunbars were offered compensation by the government for their land and improvements.[12]

This was the most intense and widely publicized conflict between the ranchers and settlers, and it illustrates that recourse to legal authority emanating from Ottawa did in fact temper the tendency towards open conflict.[13] Would McEachran have been prepared to send out his own men to evict squatters by force had this problem arisen in the East? It could well be that because he knew that the police and other legal institutions were relatively weak under frontier conditions, he was more prepared to take matters into his own hands than he might otherwise have been. However, McEachran did this only after he had gone through the regular legal channels and, in the end, it was government intervention and action rather than the gun that settled the dispute.

Thus there is some substance to the argument that the Canadian West was more law-abiding than the American. The range wars between small ranchers and the hired guns of the big spreads in Montana, Wyoming, Arizona, Texas, New Mexico, and North Dakota were vicious and at times left the earth strewn with human bodies.[14] An occasional pulled-down house would have gone virtually unnoticed. Does this mean, then, that the Canadian frontier deserves the title "the tame West"? The answer, surely, is no. This study is not a comparison of the two frontiers on the basis of the per capita violence. On that basis, and with range wars counted, the Americans would almost certainly win hands down. The object here has been to argue that the first ranching society in western Canada was, like its counterpart to the south, deeply affected by its environment. This was expressed in thievery, prostitution, the whiskey trade, gunplay, and other forms of disorder.

With respect to the question of rustling, it might well be an injustice to the Americans to describe the Canadian West as tame. Inherent in this description is the message that Canadians were not like the society to the south with its wanton disregard for authority and flagrant abuse of civil standards. In fact the Americans might well have done a better job of fighting rangeland crime than the Canadians did. Vigilante groups organized at the grass-roots level to fill in where the regular peace officers were deficient seem to have been relatively effective.[15] Terry Jordan, cultural geographer and scholar of North American ranching frontiers, emphasizes that these vigilante groups were greatly feared by rustlers.[16] Their response to rangeland crime was fast, their convictions were achieved with little regard for due process, and their harsh punishment was meted out swiftly and efficiently. They probably dissuaded many from taking up the career of the outlaw.

In southern prairie Canada, by contrast, peace officers worked largely alone, bolstered only occasionally by a few ranchers or a stock detective appointed by one of the associations. Moreover, convictions were very hard to achieve. If given a choice, any rustler might well have picked the frontier north of the forty-ninth parallel to operate in. Some contemporaries considered this likely. In an article of 30 October 1884 entitled "Horse Stealing," the *Macleod Gazette* contended that it had become "too hot in Montana for horse thieves so may have headed north to Alberta."

The point is, however, that on almost any cattle frontier where the pastures were huge and unfenced and where the population was made up predominantly of single males, losses from theft were likely

Fort Macleod (ca. 1880s)

to be large. The existence of the Mounties and the determination with which they patrolled the open range does not necessarily point to a high success rate in enforcing laws emanating from Ottawa. Much has been said about the refined social behaviour of the ranching elite. However, it should not be forgotten that the New World constantly competed with the Old in setting cultural norms. A European-style ball at a North-West Mounted Police barracks in Fort Macleod might not have been the grand and gala event that would have been experienced near the turn of the century at Kensington Palace in London. Besides the effects of illicit whiskey and drunkenness there were the crude and hurriedly constructed barracks where the dance was held and the raw and unsightly appearance of the town itself. After one day in Macleod, a young lady who attended the ball in 1884 was "wild to get away." She estimated that the town was "one of the last places to live in all the world." It sat, she said, "on a bare flat spot high above the river, covered with small stones which the never ceasing wind drives hither and thither with little clouds of dust. The barracks lie south of the cluster of log huts called the town, and the whole effect is disheartening in the Extreme." It is not difficult to visualize her shaking her head as she ended her commentary with the words, "How the people live happily there I do not know."[17]

Image and reality obviously also diverge with respect to the practice of ranching itself. On close examination it is apparent that it was not nearly as profitable, particularly in the hands of the cattle barons, as some have tended to believe, and that it was deeply affected by the environment on virtually every level. The importance of the environment in shaping western Canadian ranching is, in the end, confirmed by the fact that the industry moved along a strikingly similar evolutionary path to that just to the south of the international border where conditions were more or less the same. In Idaho, Montana, and Wyoming not only did rustlers take cattle but severe winter weather following on the heels of poor grazing seasons devastated them, and wolves, fire, and disease reduced their numbers year after year. Moreover, the quality of the herds was diminished from the widespread mixing of breeds. As a result the ranchers there too climbed out of the saddle, built wire fences and wooden corrals, and put up hay and greenfeed. American cowboys of the later nineteenth century were "as likely to dig irrigation ditches, put up fences, or cut hay as ride herd."[18] The Americans as well imported better-quality stock from the East and practised selective breeding. Ultimately they too cut down their individual outfits to a practicable size. The winter of 1886–87 was the pivotal one for them. The rancher with a small herd of cattle tended to get through that horrendous season in relatively good shape: "He had hay enough to feed through storms and could gather his cattle around the ranch and partially shelter them." It was the "cattle barons" who "were the heaviest losers as they could not feed or shelter their immense herds."[19] When the storms subsided most of them cut their losses for good. In the words of a Montana rancher whose cattle numbers were reduced by half during the blizzards, "men who had large sums of money invested closed out the remnant of their herds and quit."[20] Consequently, by the 1890s the big companies from the East and Great Britain had faded and it was evident that "the future lay with … operations of two hundred head or less."[21]

The open range itself was one of the two most basic of all the environmental stimulants of change. It was only by responding to it that the ranchers achieved fundamental control over their livestock. It forced them to devise ways not just to begin to offer resistance to predators but to take steps to manage breed selection, to fight disease, and to get feed to their animals in the midst of the most severe winter storms. The other basic stimulant was unquestionably nature. Bad winter weather, prairie fires, and wolves were part of the landscape long before the entrance of the ranchers, and they certainly played a major part in persuading them to adjust their techniques.

This combination of frontier and natural circumstances that worked together to induce the earliest ranchers to change set off a sort of chain reaction. Once they had taken up fundamental mixed-farming practices, the ranchers found it relatively straightforward to go on to embrace one by one a number of techniques associated with that type of agricultural production. Many seem to have found the transition difficult only in the psychological sense. They saw themselves as ranchers in a society that loved the cowboy, and they instinctively feared a loss of status as they turned to farming. Ironically, this caused them to feel a certain amount of hostility towards some of the infrastructure they had to adopt to make the transition successful. Foremost amongst that infrastructure was the barbed wire fence.

Many cattlemen cursed the fences even as they set about the task of building them. These awful devices, they were heard insisting, were "driving out the rancher."[22] Cattle and horses that had formerly been free to wander, they complained, often ran into the wire, became entangled in it, and were severely cut by the dreadful barbs.[23] The wire was also responsible for augmenting death losses during winter storms as it prevented the cattle from drifting with the wind to new pastures. "This past winter was not so severe as the winter of '86," Howell Harris, the manager of the Circle Ranch asserted in the spring of 1907, "but these barb-wire fences that net the country now were not here then and they constitute a greater enemy to the rancher than a severe winter. In southern Alberta there is not enough snow to prevent cattle feeding, but a barb-wire fence will stop a tired herd drifting before a storm and cut them off from reaching a good feeding ground."[24]

Harris did not add that extensive networks of fences also enabled cattlemen to protect their herds from all the destructive forces of nature to an extent that had been impossible on the open range. This may be because the real reason for his animosity towards wire was that deep down inside he recognized it as a symbol of a new era in which his own profession would no longer be vital. "I shall never forget the first wire fence I ever saw," wrote a man recounting his ranching days in nineteenth century Texas.[25] "I saw a horse that had been cut across the knee, and we were told that the wire fence we had just passed was the cause. When I saw a … machine at work manufacturing it and was told that there were thousands of them at the same work, I went home and told the boys they might just as well … quit splitting rails and use barbed-wire instead." He realized then and there that eventually "wire would win." He also foresaw, ostensibly for the first time, that "the cow-boy's days were numbered."

What the men who disliked fences might have considered is that open range ranching was an expedient, a temporary solution for the frontier environment.[26] The open range was destined to be altered relatively quickly in Canada and elsewhere not as a consequence of wire or any other particular device but because it could not provide the close care and attention necessary to nurture livestock properly year round. It was because they were unable to abandon the ranching system completely enough that the big operations were doomed to follow their American counterparts into obscurity. And it was precisely because they managed to do so to a considerable degree that ordinary settlers were able to keep going and pass their holdings on to future generations. Through a process of adaptation settlers moved quickly beyond the initial frontier stage and established a reasonably sophisticated system of production for the era. Within approximately fifteen years a large percentage were operating family ranch/farms, and though their holdings were miniscule compared to the earlier great spreads, they were on average considerably larger than the bulk of those in Ontario and the East.[27]

In 1911 a guest speaker at an Oldtimer's Association meeting in the foothills remarked that there had been a "day when the newcomer" had been "looked upon with positive distrust and dislike" on the frontier. This situation, he said, had now changed as the newcomer – "the farmer and businessman" – had "won the confidence of the old ranchers" and demonstrated by his success that he was capable of introducing the country to a whole range of "new possibilities."[28] To agree with this speaker that the farming approach was proving to be the agricultural form of the future is not to suggest that the admiration Howell Harris, L.V. Kelly, and numerous of their contemporaries clearly felt for ranching was misplaced. In the final analysis it is largely to it – or frontiersmanship – that the western livestock industry owes its start. Ranching in its pure form was uneconomic, and it disappeared almost as suddenly as it started. However, it also provided the expertise for trailing the first herds to the frontier and helped the cattle industry endure long enough to gain a lasting foothold. Presumably, it is at least to some extent for those reasons that the cowboy has remained an icon in the parts of southern Alberta and Saskatchewan where beef production has continued to be prominent. One of the most obvious and best-known reflections of this fact is the Calgary Stampede.[29] When it was designed in 1912, the "big four" cattlemen, George Lane, A.E. Cross, Patrick Burns, and the Honourable A.J. Maclean, believed that the working cowboy was already only a "street curiousity," and they very much wanted to acknowledge his contribution. Therefore they planned a "reunion of old-timers to show what the country had come to and what from," by bringing together the "finest ropers and rough-riders of the North American continent in competition."[30] The survival of this celebrated affair along with a multitude of smaller stampedes and rodeos, and, as well, the persistence of western styles in rural communities, indicates that the imprint of the frontier may never completely be erased. This is a consequence of an image created by and for the men who rode the open range in a short but eminently important period of western Canadian agricultural development.

Notes

INTRODUCTION

1 See G.F.G. Stanley, "Western Canada and the Frontier Thesis," *Canadian Historical Association*, 1940, 111.

2 *Ranchers' Legacy: Alberta Essays by Lewis G. Thomas*, ed. P.A. Dunae, Edmonton: University of Alberta Press, 1986.

3 D.H. Breen, *The Canadian Prairie West and the Ranching Frontier, 1874–1924*, Toronto: University of Toronto Press, 1983, 21–2

4 Ibid.

5 "The Turner Thesis and the Canadian West: A Closer Look at the Ranching Frontier," *Essays in Western History*, ed. L.H. Thomas, Edmonton: University of Alberta Press, 1976, 154.

6 M. Laviolette, "The Tame West," *Calgary* (July 1988), 8–9, 21, 47.

7 Stanley, "Western Canada and the Frontier Thesis," 111.

8 Breen, *Canadian Prairie West*, 83–5.

9 For a brief overview of violence on the American frontier as well as an excellent select bibliography, see, R.M. Brown, "Violence," *The Oxford History of the American West*, ed. C.A. Milner et al., Oxford and New York: Oxford University Press, 1994, 393–425.

10 Breen, *Canadian Prairie West*, 85.

11 At the symposium on the cowboy at the Glenbow Institute in Calgary, 26–28 September 1997, Professor Simon Evans presented a very interesting paper on the numerous young British men who learned the tricks of the trade from the Americans and went on to provide a workforce for the ranchers and in some cases became successful ranchers themselves.

12 D. McEachran, "Impressions of Pioneers of Alberta as a Ranching Country," Ormstown, Quebec, n.d., 12, quoted in D.H. Breen, "The Cattle Compact: The Ranch Community in Southern Alberta, 1881–1896," unpublished Master's thesis, University of Calgary, 1968, 111.

13 Glenbow Archives, Mrs Charles Inderwick, Diary and Personal Letters from the North Fork Ranch, 1883–91, M376: letter of 13 May 1884, 8. For a printed copy of the letter and an explanation see

M.E. Inderwick, "A Lady and Her Ranch," *Alberta History* 15, no. 4 (autumn 1967), 1–9.

14 The newspaper used the British spelling "ranche." This form was used for many of the ranches with British or Canadian ownership. For consistency the North American spelling is used in this work.

15 "Time to Think," *Calgary Herald*, 26 August 1887, quoted in T. Thorner, "The Not So Peaceable Kingdom," unpublished Master's thesis, University of Calgary, 1977, 34.

16 Breen, *Canadian Prairie West*, 35, 43, 119–20, 140–3, 177, 179.

17 Ibid., 55.

18 S. Evans, "Spatial Aspects of the Cattle Kingdom," *Frontier Calgary, 1875–1914*, ed. A.W. Rasporich and H. Klassen, Calgary: University of Calgary Press, 1975, 50–2. See also W.M. Elofson, "Adapting to the Frontier Environment: Mixed and Dryland Farming near Pincher Creek, 1895–1914," *Prairie Forum* 11, no. 2 (fall 1986), 32–3.

19 See W.M. Elofson, "Not Just a Cowboy: The Practice of Ranching in Southern Alberta, 1881–1914," *Canadian Papers in Rural History* 10 (1996), 209, and "Mixed and Dryland Farming," 33.

20 M. Hopkins, *Letters from a Lady Rancher*, introduced by S. Jamison, Calgary: Glenbow-Alberta Institute, 1982; Claude Gardner, *Letters from an English Rancher*, ed. H. Dempsey, Calgary: Glenbow-Alberta Institute, 1988.

21 Inderwick, Diary and Letters: letter of 13 May 1884, 8.

CHAPTER ONE

1 This is the definition used throughout this study.

2 See F. Ings, "Tales of the Midway Ranch," *Canadian Cattlemen* 4, no. 1 (June 1941), 38. The entire book-length "Tales of the Midway Ranch" was originally published in successive issues of the *Canadian Cattlemen* magazine through 1941 and 1942.

3 "The West of Edward Maunsell," part 1, ed. H.A. Dempsey, *Alberta History* 34, no. 4 (autumn 1986), 5.

4 See L.V. Kelly, *The Range Men*, 75th anniversary edition, Calgary: Glenbow-Alberta Institute, 1988, 47–9.

5 Ibid., 57.

6 See chapter 4 below.

7 Kelly, *Range Men*, 57–62; Edward Brado, *Cattle Kingdom: Early Ranching in Alberta*, Vancouver: Douglas & McIntyre, 1984, 37–8.

8 H.F. Lawrence, "Early Days in the Chinook Belt," *Alberta Historical Review* 13, no. 1 (winter 1965), 11.

9 For Lynch, see ibid., and Kelly, *Range Men*, 69, 73, 126. For Emerson, see H.C. Klassen, "The Ranching Business in Alberta: Exploring the

Histories of the Rocking P and Bar S Ranches," a paper presented at the Canadian Cowboy Conference, New Perspectives on Ranching History, 26–28 September 1997, Glenbow Museum, Calgary, Alberta.

10 G. MacEwan, *John Ware's Cow Country*, Vancouver: Greystone Books, 1960, 78.

11 Kelly, *Range Men*, 61–2; Brado, *Cattle Kingdom*, 43–5.

12 Ings, "Tales of the Midway," *Canadian Cattlemen* 4, no. 1, 38; Kelly, *Range Men*, 62.

13 Ibid., 60–2.

14 "The West of Edward Maunsell," 4–7.

15 The Cochrane was putting up hay as early as 1883 (Kelly, *Range Men*, 76), but this could only have been a very small fraction of what the ranch needed to get all its cattle through severe winters (see below, pp. 76–8).

16 Breen, *Canadian Prairie West*, 111–28.

17 In the census of 1901, only six ranch hands were reported living on the Bar U helping Fred Stimson. At that stage the ranch had over ten thousand head of cattle and something like eight hundred horses. Maunsell Bros. who had about two thousand head at the time, had one "labourer" and one "ranch hand" (Provincial Archives of Alberta, Edmonton, T-6425). In 1883 when the Cochrane Ranch estimated it had four thousand cattle to move from the Big Hill to the Waterton area, only eight cowboys were available for the drive (Kelly, *Range Men*, 76). In 1902 the Cochrane had about fourteen thousand cattle and "ten or a dozen cowboys" (J.J. Young, "A Visit to the Cochrane Ranch," 26–30).

18 "Cowboys in Winter," *Macleod Gazette*, 1 February 1887; Provincial Archives of Alberta, 72, 27/SE, V.P. LaGrandeur, "Memoirs of a Cowboy's Wife," unpublished manuscript, n.d., 10–11.

19 See Elofson, "Mixed and Dryland Farming," 33; Alberta Department of Agriculture, *Annual Report*, 1906, 71.

20 Kelly, *Range Men*, 51, 60.

21 For the foothills regions see W.M. Elofson, "Mixed and Dryland Farming," 32, 33. For the Wood Mountain and Cypress Hills area see F.W. Anderson, *Sheriffs and Outlaws of Western Canada*, Calgary: Frontier, 1973, 53. S. Hanson, "Policing the International Border," *Saskatchewan History* 19, no. 1 (spring 1966), 70. The Milk River Ridge and Cypress Hills are not well treed in some areas. Shelter for the cattle comes primarily from river canyons and gulches.

22 Elofson, "Not Just a Cowboy," 206.

23 Inderwick, Diary and Letters: letter of 13 May 1884, 24.

24 Brado, *Cattle Kingdom*, 176–93; Breen, *Canadian Prairie West*, 121.

25 Brado, *Cattle Kingdom*, 105, 140–2; Breen, *Canadian Prairie West*, 11–12.

26 Ibid., 9–11.

27 Ibid., 63–74; Kelly, *Range Men*, 72–4.

28 A.W. Rasporich, "Utopian Ideals and Community Settlements in Western Canada: 1880–1914," *The Canadian West*, ed. H.C. Klassen, Calgary: University of Calgary Press, 1977, 37–62.

29 R.D. Francis, *Images of the West: Changing Perceptions of the Prairies, 1690–1960*, Saskatoon: Western Producer Prairie Books,1989, 37–153.

30 "Financing the Palliser Triangle, 1908–13," *Great Plains Quarterly* 18, no. 3 (summer 1998), 257–68.

31 Indeed only a very small percentage could have been this large. See R. Cole Harris and J.Warkentin, *Canada before Confederation: A Study in Historical Geography,* Ottawa: Carleton University Press, 1991, 93–7; J.I. Little, *Ethno-Cultural Transition and Regional Identity in the Eastern Townships of Quebec*, Canadian Historical Association, Ottawa 1989.

32 See Edward Brado, *The Cattle Kingdom*, 58–80; Breen, *Canadian Prairie West*, 11–19.

33 Ibid., 16; *The Dominion Annual Register and Review,* ed. H.J. Morgan, Montreal: Dawson Bros., 1880–81, 211.

34 Breen, *Canadian Prairie West*, 19.

35 S. Evans, *Prince Charming Goes West: The Story of the E.P. Ranch*, Calgary: University of Calgary Press, 1993, 45–6; L.V. Kelly, *The Range Men*, 83, 97. Cochrane's two companies were the Cochrane Ranch Company and the British American Ranch Company.

36 Breen, *Canadian Prairie West*, 64.

37 Kelly, *Range Men*, 69.

38 Breen, *Canadian Prairie West*, 19.

39 Brado, *Cattle Kingdom*, 74.

40 Ottawa, Public Archives of Canada, Department of Interior papers, RG15, B2a, box 1, f. 13, vol. 10, f. 142709, part 1: letter from M.H. Cochrane, 20 March 1883; ibid.: A.M. Burgess to D.L. Macpherson, 4 June 1883. Previously, federal officials had banned sheep from leases in the Canadian West as cattlemen believed that they killed the grass by chewing it off too low to the ground.

41 "Town Topics," *Calgary Herald*, 19 September 1888; "The Week's Local News," ibid., 26 September 1888. See also Lawrence, "Early Days in the Chinook Belt," 12.

42 He came out in July 1885 for a short stay (Glenbow Archives, M234, Cochrane Ranch Letter Book, 20, 21), and in 1888 to dispose of his sheep at the Big Hill ("Town Topics," *Calgary Herald*, 19 September 1988).

43 The other major shareholder was Duncan McEachran, who would run and eventually become a major shareholder in the Walrond Ranch. The Cochrane's business manager, John Milne Browning, and

its first operations manager, James Walker, were also small shareholders. Both were to leave the ranch before the end of its first decade (Brado, *Cattle Kingdom*, 64, 68, 69; C. Buchanan, "History of the Walrond Ranch Ltd.," *Canadian Cattlemen*, 3 March 1946, 171).

44 "All over the Range," *Macleod Gazette*, 6 December 1887; Brado, *Cattle Kingdom*, 75.

45 By this time the Cochranes had converted a considerable portion – some 63,000 acres – to deeded land (see Breen, *The Canadian Prairie West*, 149).

46 Ibid., 64. The holdings varied over time (ibid., 77).

47 S. Evans, "Spatial Aspects of the Cattle Kingdom," 50–2.

48 Evans, *Prince Charming Goes West*, 46; Brado, *The Cattle Kingdom*, 80–98.

49 Ibid., 81–104.

50 To see this problem from both sides it is necessary to read both J.R. Craig, *Ranching with Lords and Commons*, Toronto: William Biggs, 1903, and A. Staveley Hill, *From Home to Home: Autumn Wanderings in the North West*, London: Samson, Low, Marston, Searle & Rivington, 1887.

51 Brado, *The Cattle Kingdom*, 96.

52 Ibid., 94.

53 Ibid., 96.

54 Kelly, *Range Men*, 89.

55 Brado, *Cattle Kingdom*, 86.

56 J.R. Craig, *Ranching with Lords and Commons.*

57 Brado, *Cattle Kingdom*, 142–5.

58 Kelly, *Range Men*, 78.

59 A.B. McCullough, "Eastern Capital, Government Purchase and the Development of Canadian Ranching," *Prairie Forum* 22, no. 2 (fall 1997), 225.

60 Ibid., 220.

61 Brado, *The Cattle Kingdom*, 143–4.

62 Indeed, McEachran stated his regrets about having taken up ranching because of the problem of the mange alone. "The Mange," *Macleod Gazette*, 14 July 1899.

63 "Local Notes," ibid., 7 June 1895.

64 Breen, *Canadian Prairie West*, 149; Brado, *Cattle Kingdom*, 278.

65 Later the headquarters was moved west to Pekisko Creek.

66 Kelly, *Range Men*, 75.

67 Ibid., 72–4.

68 Breen, *Canadian Prairie West*, 64.

69 "Big Transaction," *Calgary Herald*, 5 February 1902; A.B. McCullough, "Winnipeg Ranchers: Gordon, Ironsides and Fares," Parks Canada, unpublished paper, 1994.

70 See G. MacEwan, *Pat Burns, Cattle King*, Saskatoon: Western Producer Prairie Books, 1979.

71 See LaGrandeur, "Memoirs of a Cowboy's Wife," 3–14; H.C. Klassen, "The Conrads in the Alberta Cattle Business, 1875–1911," *Agricultural History* 64 (summer 1990), 31–59.

72 See Breen, *Canadian Prairie West*, 44–7; see also S.M. Evans, "The Passing of a Frontier: Ranching in the Canadian West 1882–1912," unpublished PHD thesis, University of Calgary, 1976. For the Stair Ranch, see D.C. McGowan, *Grassland Settlers*, 4th ed., Victoria: Cactus Publications, 1975, 58–77.

73 Breen, *Canadian Prairie West*, 64–5; Kelly, *Range Men*, 83, 97.

74 See "Copithornes: Dynasty Lives On," *Calgary Herald*, 7 February 1998.

75 Brado, *Cattle Kingdom*, 136–8; see also below, p. 148.

76 For the prohibition era see below, pp. 115–17. For A.E. Cross see H.C. Klassen, "Entrepreneurship in the Canadian West: The Enterprises of A.E. Cross, 1886–1920," *Western Quarterly* 22, no. 3 (Aug. 1991), 313–33.

77 Ibid., 323.

78 *Prince Charming Goes West*, 47–8. See also Breen, *Canadian Prairie West*, 109–20.

79 This was more important than perhaps one might expect. As Breen states, "cattlemen retained their dominant position in the southwestern countryside after 1896 simply by transferring their operations to the largest deeded holdings in the North-West Territories through purchase of great blocks of their former leases from the new Calgary and Edmonton Railway at a dollar fifty per acre (*Canadian Prairie West*, 77).

80 Ibid., 90, 91, 113–15, 116–17.

81 McCullough, "Personnel and Personalities," 70, and Breen, *Canadian Prairie West*, 149. For Walter Skrine on the Rocking S and George Emerson on the Rocking P, see H.C. Klassen, "The Ranching Business in Alberta."

82 Professor Evans, while emphasizing the political factors, demonstrates that he clearly has grasped some of the major environmental ones (*Prince Charming Goes West*, 56–60).

83 Breen, *Canadian Prairie West*, 165.

84 P. Voisey, *Vulcan: The Making of a Prairie Community*, Toronto: University of Toronto Press, 1988, 77–127; Elofson, "Mixed and Dryland Farming," 42–6.

85 *"Prairie Grass to Mountain Pass:" History of the Pioneers of Pincher Creek and District*, Pincher Creek: Pincher Creek Historical Society, 1974, 7 – the recollections of Frank Austin and Myra (Austin) Harshman.

86 The figures for 1884, 1888, 1890, 1892, 1894, 1895, and 1896 are found in Canada, *Sessional Papers*, Department of Interior Annual Reports. After 1888 the decline was more or less continuous.

87 Ibid., 26:9 (1893), n15, 133–5: Annual Report for F Division, 1 December 1892.

88 Ibid., 27:11 (1894), n15, 90: Annual Report for K Division, 1893.

89 Elofson, "Mixed and Dryland Farming," 32–42.

90 Glenbow Archives, Cross papers, M1543, f. 445: W. Skrine to Cross, 14 June 1901.

91 See *Census of Prairie Provinces, 1916: Population and Agriculture*, Ottawa, 1918, 44–127.

92 In Alberta the average deeded holding was 288.6 acres in 1901 and 352.5 acres in 1921 (*Sixth Census*, 1921, 5:xv).

93 *Prairie Grass to Mountain Pass*, 7 – the recollections of Frank Austin and Myra (Austin) Harshman.

94 Figures for the various types and numbers of farms are available for 1916 for Macleod, Calgary, Medicine Hat, Lethbridge and Maple Creek; see *Census of Prairie Provinces, 1916: Population and Agriculture*, 305, 310–11. For further discussion see, Elofson, "Mixed and Dryland Farming, 35–45.

95 The census reports for these years do not give ages. However, we can assume that most men who were prepared to undergo the ordeal of pioneering were neither old nor married. See Voisey, *Vulcan: The Making of a Prairie Community*, 3–9, 18–20; J.H. Gray, *Red Lights on the Prairies*, Toronto: Macmillan, 1971, 1–5.

96 *Fourth Census of Canada*, 1901, 1:132–3.

97 Calgary and vicinity had 43,204 males and 37,214 females in 1916. In 1911 it had 39,657 males and 25,529 females. Macleod and vicinity had 19,379 males and 14,504 females in 1916. In 1911 it had 18,231 males and 12,548 females. Maple Creek and vicinity had 28,126 males and 19,424 females in 1916. In 1911 it had 12,322 males and 7,408 females (*Census of Prairie Provinces, 1916: Population and Agriculture*, 44–127).

98 Ibid., 35.

99 "Cochrane Ranch Purchased," *Pincher Creek Echo*, 28 March 1905. L.V. Kelly believed that the open range was gone by 1902 (*Range Men*, 171.)

100 "Town News," *Pincher Creek Echo*, 1 August 1905.

CHAPTER TWO

1 McEwan, *John Ware*, 86; Glenbow Archives, Hatfield papers, M494: Hatfield to the provincial librarian in Edmonton, 10 December 1908; "Local Notes," *Macleod Gazette*, 28 June 1895; "Macleod Hounds,"

ibid., 12 January 1894; "Local Notes," ibid., 28 June 1895; Cross papers, f. 457: polo circular, 17 May 1904.

2 Breen, "The Turner Thesis," 154.

3 For definitions of the frontier and the other general forces that mould behaviour in a new society see Voisey, *Vulcan*, 3–9.

4 See "Mixed and Dryland Farming," 32–7.

5 For Old World cultural influences, see Thomas, *Rancher's Legacy.*

6 J.J. Young, "A Visit to the Cochrane Ranch," *Alberta Historical Review* 22, no. 3 (1974), 227.

7 See Thomas, *Ranchers' Legacy*, 16–24.

8 Inderwick Diary and Letters: letter of 13 May 1884, 3.

9 Hopkins, *Letters from a Lady Rancher*, 59: letter of June 1910.

10 Ibid., 92: Letter of September 1910; see also Inderwick Diary and Letters: letter of 13 May 1884, 18.

11 Cross papers, f. 457: polo circular, 17 May 1904.

12 Kelly, *Range Men*, 99.

13 See, for instance, "The Wolves Must Go," *Macleod Gazette*, 10 November 1892. On 2 February 1886, the paper reported that a coyote was roped to be used later for a hunt ("War on Coyotes").

14 Hatfield papers.

15 Ibid., Hatfield to provincial librarian in Edmonton, 10 December 1908.

16 See picture, p. 27.

17 Another was the Military Colonization Company Ranch, backed by ex-police officers. It was started for the purpose of raising horses for the British army (S.S. Jameson, *Ranches, Cowboys and Characters: Birth of Alberta's Western Heritage*, Calgary, Glenbow-Alberta Institute, 1987, 31).

18 "Alberta Stock Raising," 20 September 1888.

19 Now Quorndon.

20 Ings, "Tales of the Midway," *Canadian Cattlemen* 6, no. 1 (June 1943), 15; Kelly, *Range Men*, 94, 109.

21 For a succinct description of horse ranching in southern Alberta, see Hopkins *Letters from a Lady Rancher*, 59: letter of June 1910.

22 The durability of the horse on the open range was noted after the 1906–07 winter when few succumbed, unlike so many of the cattle, to the bitter cold and endless blizzards (Kelly, *Range Men*, 193).

23 Ibid., 224–5.

24 Ibid., 224.

25 "Horses for South Africa," *Macleod Gazette*, 21 February 1902.

26 See Elofson, "Mixed and Dryland Farming," 41.

27 Alberta, Department of Agriculture, *Annual Report*, 1913, 136. Prior to the war the peak marketings for the Pincher Creek district were in 1906 when 683 sales were recorded (ibid., 1906, 77).

28 "Expert Cattle Feeders," *Calgary Herald*, 9 February 1903.

29 "Cattle Losses at Crane Lake," *Macleod Gazette*, 13 April 1904.
30 H.W. Riley, "Herbert William (Herb) Millar," *Canadian Cattlemen* 4, no. 4 (March 1942), 168.
31 See S. Evans, "Stocking the Canadian Range," *Alberta History* 26, no. 3 (summer 1978), 4; *Prince Charming Goes West*, 58.
32 Brado, *Cattle Kingdom*, 64.
33 "Unique Bunch of Cattle," *Calgary Herald*, 10 February 1903.
34 Glenbow Archives, Stair Ranch Letter Book, M2388, 235: W.F. Cochrane to D.H. Andrews, 6 October 1891.
35 Evans, "Stocking the Canadian Range," 4.
36 Cross papers, f. 480: A. McCallum to A.E. Cross, 22 May 1908; ibid., f. 472: Cross to J.G. Rutherford, 19 September 1907.
37 F.W. Godsol, "Old Times," *Alberta Historical Review*, 12:4 (autumn 1964), 23.
38 Ibid.
39 Canada, *Sessional Papers* 27, no. 11 (1894), n. 15, 11: Report of the Commissioner, 28 December 1893.
40 "Alberta Cattle," *Macleod Gazette*, 4 August 1893.
41 A.A. Lupton, "Cattle Ranching in Alberta, 1874–1910: Its Evolution and Migration," *Alberta Geographer* 2 (April 1968), 50.
42 Kelly, *Range Men*, 133, 136, 141; Breen, *The Canadian Prairie West*, 215.
43 LaGrandeur, "Memoirs of a Cowboy's Wife," 14.
44 Cross papers, f. 480: Clay, Robinson & Co. to A.E. Cross, 29 July 1907; "A Menace to the Live Stock Trade," *Macleod Gazette*, 18 July 1902; "Stock Growers Pass Resolution," ibid., 5 December 1902.
45 For the actual figures of live cattle shipments to Britain and the United States, see Breen, *Canadian Prairie West*, 66, 204.
46 Cross papers, f. 508: Cross to Clay, Robinson & Co., 5 August 1910.
47 S. Evans, "Spatial Aspects of the Cattle Kingdom," 50–2.
48 H. Frank Lawrence, "Early Days in the Chinook Belt," 12–13.
49 Breen, "The Cattle Compact," 24–5.
50 S. Evans, "Spatial Aspects of the Cattle Kingdom," 50; Kelly, *Range Men*, 97;
51 Ibid., 107.
52 Ibid.
53 The Matador Ranch located in this area in 1904 (McGowan, *Grassland Settlers*, 81, 87, 183).
54 S. Evans, "Spatial Aspects of the Cattle Kingdom," 50.
55 "Leases to Americans," *Macleod Gazette*, 27 July 1886; "All over the Range," ibid., 12 April 1887; "American Invasion of Canada," ibid., 13 January 1903; "Where They Come From," *Calgary Herald*, 18 August 1904; "70,000 Young Americans Crowd into Canada," ibid., 23 November 1904.

56 W. McIntyre Jr., *A Brief History of the McIntyre Ranch*, Lethbridge: s.n., 1947; W.M. Pearce, *The Matador Land and Cattle Company*, Norman: University of Oklahoma Press, 1964.
57 Two of the large American leaseholders who stayed for years were the Spencers' Ranch (Kelly, *Range Men*, 101, 171, 172) and the Conrads' Circle Ranch (Klassen, "The Conrads," 31–59).
58 *Census of Canada*, 1890–91, 1:362–3.
59 Ibid., 1901, 1:446–7.
60 Ibid., Population and Agriculture, 1916, 216–17.
61 "City of the Uplands," 11 September 1888.
62 "As Others See Us," ibid.
63 See for instance, "Iowa Journalist Writes of Canada," ibid., 20 September 1904. A Canadian official is quoted: "We like them [Americans], we want them to emigrate to Canada in great numbers, the more the better. They make the best class of settlers, and after they have been there five years they make the best kind of Canadians."
64 For a humorous story of high-handed and well-bred Englishmen who did not fit in socially, see Kelly, *Range Men*, 89. Kelly's admiration for frontier cowboys and dislike of certain types of Britons is clear throughout much of this work.
65 "Kind of Men Canada Needs," *Calgary Herald*, 1 February 1904.
66 Cross Papers, f. 458, May 1895.
67 "The Remittance Men," ibid., 26 November 1904.
68 "Came out to Be a Cowboy."
69 Kelly, *Range Men*, 121.
70 Inderwick Diary and Letters: letter of 13 May 1884, 16–17.
71 *Letters from a Lady Rancher*, 23–4: letter of October 1909.
72 Stair Ranch Letter Book, 196: Andrews to John Coy Jr, 11 May 1891.
73 25 April.
74 "Making Bad Men," *Macleod Gazette*, 16 May 1888.
75 Cross papers, f. 468: Cross to W.M. Bell Macdonald, 16 November 1906.
76 Ibid.
77 Ibid. f. 457.
78 *Rancher's Legacy*.
79 For a brief summary of their life, see *Letters from a Lady Rancher*. v–xv.
80 Kelly, *Range Men*, 60–2, 54.
81 McGowan, *Grassland Settlers*, 69.
82 Bob Newbolt, "Memories of the Bowchase Ranch," *Alberta History* 32, no. 4 (autumn 1984), 4–7.
83 Kelly, *Range Men*, 84.
84 Ibid., 75; J.R. Craig, *Ranching with Lords and Commons*, 243; C.E. Denny, *The Law Marches West*, Toronto: Dent, 1972, 187, 274.

85 For a good first-hand account of the cattle drive, see S.E. White, "The Drive," *The Complete Cowboy Reader: Remembering the Open Range*, ed. T. Stone, Red Deer: Red Deer College Press, 1997, 213–30.
86 I have been a rancher for years in western Canada. The description that follows is based on my own experiences. Kudos go out to the early cowboys, however, because the ranges that the cattle grazed in were much bigger and the periods of little human contact were greater. Therefore, the cattle were even more wild and difficult to control than those I have encountered.
87 T. Grant and A. Russell, *Men of the Saddle: Working Cowboys of Canada*, Toronto: Von Nostrand Reinhold, 1978, 38.
88 The early Cochrane disasters were well known, and common wisdom among the cowboys and ranchers asserted that the problem was the eastern management inexperience. See Lawrence, "Early Days in the Chinook Belt," 13–14.
89 The fact that there was not a stampede as far as we know in the beginning suggests that a cooling-off period must have been allowed.
90 Kelly, *Range Men*, 72.
91 The author has been on many cattle drives and has seen this happen numerous times.
92 Kelly, *Range Men*, 72.
93 Ibid., 72–4; W. Naftel, "The Cochrane Ranche," Canadian Historic Sites, no. 6, Ottawa: Parks Canada, 1997, 15; Brado, *Cattle Kingdom*, 72.
94 Kelly, *Range Men*, 74.
95 White stayed on as manager until January 1885 (Cochrane Ranch Letter Book: W.F. Cochrane to M. Cochrane, 14 January 1885).
96 These two episodes are recounted with noticeable emotion and literary flare in Kelly, *Range Men*, 72–4. Brado estimates the losses on the second drive at three thousand head (*Cattle Kingdom*, 72).
97 Kelly, *Range Men*, 74. Senator Cochrane himself estimated that three thousand were lost in this second winter (Naftel, "The Cochrane Ranche," 15).
98 Ibid. Kelly's figures agree with what one cowboy later said about the numbers that were trailed to Waterton; see Lawrence, "Early Days in the Chinook Belt," 13–14.
99 Ibid., 12–13.
100 Hatfield papers: Hatfield to provincial librarian in Edmonton, 10 December 1908.
101 Kelly, *Range Men*, 78.
102 Ibid.
103 Ibid.
104 Ibid., 88.

105 Ibid., 76. The Kerfoot family still ranches in the Cochrane area west of Calgary. Hamish Kerfoot has taken a keen interest in the history of ranching.
106 Stair Ranch Letter Book, 350: D.H. Andrews to A.M. Nanton, 29 October 1892.
107 Kelly, *Range Men*, 54, 91, 95, 107.
108 G. MacEwan, *John Ware's Cow Country*.
109 Ibid., 80–1.
110 After the Bar U, Sundance went into the tavern business in Calgary for a short time before returning to the United States and then moving on to South America to finish up a life of crime. See Donna B. Ernst, "The Sundance Kid in Alberta," *Alberta History* 42, no. 4 (autumn 1994), 10–15.
111 T.G. Jordan, *North American Cattle-Ranching Frontiers: Origins, Diffusion and Differentiation*, Albuquerque: University of New Mexico Press, 1993, 298–307.

CHAPTER THREE

1 See Jordan, *North American Cattle-Ranching Frontiers*, 123–267.
2 See Evans, "Spatial Aspects of the Cattle Kingdom," 53–4.
3 R.G. Mathews, "Ranching in the Canadian West," *Macleod Gazette*, 6 November 1903.
4 MacEwan, *John Ware's Cow Country*, 75.
5 Kelly, *Range Men*, 107.
6 Sometimes the rider would simply pull the horse's left eyelid down as he mounted so that the animal could not watch him (Will James, *Smoky the Cow Horse*, New York: Charles Scribner's Sons, 1929, 92).
7 Newbolt, "Memoirs of the Bowchase Ranch" 13–14.
8 Ibid., 4.
9 Kelly, *Range Men*, 88.
10 McEwan, *John Ware's Cow Country*, 75.
11 E. Hough, "The Cowboy," *The Complete Cowboy Reader*, 25.
12 Some ranchers preferred the more convenient, less bloody, and less effective method of stretching rubber bands over the testicles. These cut off the blood circulation and cause them to atrophy.
13 Theodore Roosevelt, "The Round-Up," *The Complete Cowboy Reader*, 206.
14 F. Ings, "Tales of the Midway," *Canadian Cattlemen* 6, no. 2 (September 1943), 15, 18.
15 Ibid.
16 Roosevelt, "The Round-Up," 206.
17 This happened to a rider from the Samson Ranch in 1887 ("Cowley Death," *Calgary Tribune*, 26 August 1887).

18 MacEwan, *John Ware's Cattle Country*, 186–7; *The Grass Roots of Dorothy*, ed. H.B. Roen, Dorothy, Alberta: Dorothy Community, 1971, 113–14.
19 Kelly, *Range Men*, 143.
20 Ibid., 116.
21 Canada, *Sessional Papers* 28, no. 9 (1895), n. 15, 21: Annual Report for Macleod District, 1894.
22 LaGrandeur, "Memoirs of a Cowboy's Wife," 10.
23 Ibid., 160.
24 "Contagious Sore Eyes in Cattle," *Macleod Gazette*, 27 June 1902.
25 "Vaccination of Cattle," *Calgary Herald*, 16 January 1903.
26 A disease that causes very large growths on the jaw bone; see Ings, "Tales of the Midway, *Canadian Cattlemen* 5, no. 4 (March 1943): 170.
27 "Foot and Mouth Disease," *Macleod Gazette*, 2 January 1903.
28 Canada, *Sessional Papers* 25, no. 10 (1892), n. 15, 94: Annual Report for A Division, 1 December 1891; ibid. 26, no. 9 (1893), n. 15, 5: Anual Report of the Commissioner, 19 December 1892; ibid. 27, no. 11 (1894), n. 15, 3: Annual Report of the Commissioner, 28 December 1893.
29 Kelly, *Range Men*, 160.
30 And sometimes tar and linseed oil ("Mange at Gleichen," *Calgary Herald*, 16 February 1904).
31 "Government Orders Dipping Tanks," *Macleod Gazette*, 22 June 1904. Later in 1904 the Territories were declared a mange area by the minister of Agriculture and ranchers were ordered to dip their herds ("Dominion of Canada, Order of the Minister of Agriculture," ibid., 19 August 1904).
32 Cross papers, f. 466: Cochrane to Cross, 12 June 1904; f. 454: Cochrane to Cross, 31 May 1904; ibid., 3 September 1904.
33 Kelly, *The Range Men*, 162.
34 Cross papers, f. 466: Cochrane to Cross, 21 October 1906.
35 Ibid.: W.F Cochrane to A.E. Cross, 12 June 1904.
36 H. "Dude" Lavington, *Nine Lives of a Cowboy*, Victoria: Sono Nis Press, 1982, 18–19. This episode took place in 1913 near Big Valley. At that time this area was also a ranching frontier about to become a mixed-farming frontier.
37 Cross papers, f. 470: Douglass to Cross, 20 Jan. 1907; ibid.: Douglass to Cross, 27 Jan. 1907; ibid., f. 471: Douglass to Cross, 16 Mar. 1907; ibid., Douglass to Cross, 24 April 1907.
38 "The Mange," 14 July 1899.
39 Kelly, *Range Men*, 181–2, 186.
40 Lavington, *Nine Lives of a Cowboy*, 18; Kelly, *Range Men*, 186.
41 "Range Notes," *Macleod Gazette*, 17 August 1894.

42 Kelly, *Range Men*, 115.
43 Emerson, "The Cowboy," 26.
44 Lawrence, "Early Days in the Chinook Belt," 3.
45 Roosevelt, "The Round-Up," 205.
46 H.A. McGusty, "An Englishman in Alberta," *Alberta Historical Reveiw* 14, no. 1 (winter 1966), 13–14.
47 Ings, "Tales of the Midway," *Canadian Cattlemen* 6, no. 4 (March 1944), 141. Some Canadian ranches chose to stay with European breeds that in time were trained for ranching (ibid., 6, no. 1, June 1943, 2).
48 Kelly, *Range Men*, 101.
49 See R.W. Slatta, *Cowboys of the Americas*, New Haven, CT: Yale University Press, 1990.
50 "Memoirs of an Itinerant Cowhand," *Canadian Cattlemen* 5, no. 3 (December 1942), 168. The use of this hat in the Canadian West is also verified by pictures in the Glenbow Archives.
51 Stair Ranch Letter Book, 350: D.H. Andrews to A.M. Nanton, 29 October 1892.
52 In the American Northwest as well as the Canadian prairie West; see Jordan, *North American Cattle Ranching Frontiers*, esp. 267–307.
53 Simon Evans at the symposium on the cowboy at the Glenbow Institute in Calgary, 26–28 September 1997.
54 See, for instance, "The Cow Business," *Macleod Gazette*, 14 November 1884. See also Elofson, "Adapting to the Frontier Environment," 315, 323–4.
55 Breen, *Canadian Prairie West*, 101–35; "Central Stock Association," *Macleod Gazette*, 18 May 1886.
56 Cross papers, f. 457: sec. tres. High River Stock Association to Cross, 3 October 1904; ibid., f. 468: R.G. Mathews to Cross, 25 June 1906.
57 "Central Stock Association Meeting," *Macleod Gazette*, 18 May 1886.
58 Cross papers, f. 457: sec. tres. High River Stock Association to Cross, 3 October 1904.
59 "All Over the Range," *Macleod Gazette*, 11 April 1885.
60 "The Stock Meeting," ibid., 1 June 1886.
61 See Breen, *Canadian Prairie West*, 101–35.
62 Kelly, *Range Men*, 157.
63 "Local and General," *Macleod Gazette*, 22 November 1901.
64 "Alberta Cow Country," *Macleod Gazette*, 30 November 1886.
65 For cowboy culture see Slatta, *Cowboys of the Americas*, and *Comparing Cowboys and Frontiers*, Norman: University of Oklahoma Press, 1997.
66 Kelly, *Range Men*, 2–3.
67 "It Is Wrong," *Macleod Gazette*, 6 June 1888.
68 Newbolt, "Memories of the Bowchase Ranch," 7.
69 Hopkins, *Letters from a Lady Rancher*, 21: letter of October 1909.

70 LaGrandeur, "Memoirs of a Cowboy's Wife," 6.
71 Ibid., 11.

CHAPTER FOUR

1 Inderwick, Diary and Letters: letter of 13 May 1884, 1, 26.
2 This is dividing the acreages of the great ranches by the number of cowboys. As we have seen, the first leases of the Cochrane, the Walrond, and Oxley were considerably larger than 200,000 acres and their ranch hands tended to number about ten.
3 MacEwan, *John Ware's Cow Country*, 37–41.
4 See Elofson, "Not Just a Cowboy," 212.
5 Glenbow Archives, William Brown papers, M2375, 785: Brown to Lindsay Howe and Co., 9 January 1893.
6 Ibid., 831–2: Brown to Lindsay Howe and Co., 5 July 1893.
7 Ibid., 835: Brown to W. Middleton, 10 August 1893.
8 Ibid., 855–6: Brown to Middleton, 11 May 1894.
9 E.W. Moss, doctor of veterinary medicine, Bassano, Alberta, 10 March 1991.
10 Brown papers, 858–60: Brown to Middleton, 31 May 1894.
11 Ibid.
12 Ibid., 861–2: Brown to Fuller, 2 June 1904.
13 Inderwick, Diary and Letters: letter of 13 May 1884, 24; LaGrandeur, "Memoirs of a Cowboy's Wife," 6. The Cochrane was putting up hay at Waterton even before the cattle were moved there (Kelly, *Range Men*, 76).
14 Ibid.
15 Perhaps as low as a hundreth of what it needed.
16 "Local and General" *Macleod Gazette*, 20 March 1903.
17 LaGrandeur, "Memoirs of a Cowboy's Wife," 6.
18 Canada, *Sessional Papers* 22, no. 13 (1889), n. 17, 20: Annual Report of the Commissioner, 13 December 1888.
19 Over the spring, summer, and early fall of 1938 my own father, working principally with one hired man, a hand post mall, and a hand post hole digger, built four miles of four-strand barbed wire fences on his farm west of Ponoka, Alberta. He and my grandfather ran a mixed farm in those days that required a great deal of other work as well, including seeding, haying, calving, harvesting, and field cultivation. My father helped with all of that too.
20 Kelly, *Range Men*, 87.
21 Ibid., 171.
22 Young, "A Visit to the Cochrane Ranch," 29.

23 Most recently, Hugh Dempsey has done an admirable and accurate job of depicting the horrors of this winter (*The Golden Age of the Cowboy,* Saskatoon and Calgary: Fifth House, 1995, 144–50).

24 The Cochrane was able to access large supplies of feed by contracting the Blood Indians to put up its own hay and by harvesting oats (J.J. Young, "A Visit to the Cochrane Ranch," 29; Evans, *Prince Goes West*, 58). It seems highly doubtful, however, that the ranch ever reached the point where it could feed all its cattle through a long, cold winter.

25 "All Over the Range," 22 February 1887.

26 Ings, "Tales of the Midway Ranch," *Canadian Cattlemen* 5, no. 4 (March 1943), 163.

27 Kelly, *Range Men*, 100.

28 Ibid., 101.

29 "The Roundup of 1887," *Alberta Historical Review* 13, no. 2, (spring 1965), 23.

30 Kelly, *Range Men*, 100.

31 Ibid.

32 Canada, *Sessional Papers* 22, no. 13 (1889), n. 17, 20: Annual Report of the Commissioner, 13 December 1888.

33 Kelly, *Range Men*, 132.

34 Canada, *Sessional Papers* 26, no. 9 (1893), n. 15, 83: Annual Report for K Division, 1 December 1892.

35 Kelly, *Range Men*, 132.

36 Ibid., 137.

37 Canada, *Sessional Papers* 26, no. 9 (1893), n. 15, 83: Annual Report for K Division, 1 December 1892.

38 Stair Ranch Letter Book, 416–17: to C. Akers, 15 March 1893.

39 Ibid. The Stair Ranch inventory dropped from around 5,700 to 3,553, but the estimate did not adequately reflect numbers in the Cypress Hills where the majority were located (ibid., 412–15). On 5 June Andrews estimated Cypress Hills cattle at 2,300 (down 500 from 15 March) but the cowboys could find only 2,100. "This leaves us about 200 short of my estimated tally but I hear a number of our cattle are on the American side of the line, & we are going over to gather them as soon as they commence their beef roundups there (ibid., 461–5: to Akers, 5 June 1893).

40 Canada, *Sessional Papers* 32, no. 12 (1898) n. 15, 15: Annual Report of the Commissioner, 17 December 1897.

41 Ibid. 33, no. 12 (1899), n. 15, 34: Annual Report for D Division, 30 November 1898.

42 Kelly, *Range Men*, 22–3.

43 Cross papers, f. 450: Selkirk to A.E. Cross, 5 June 1903.

44 Canada, *Sessional Papers* 28, no. 11 (1904), n. 28, 14: Annual Report for A Division, 30 November 1903.
45 "Losses at Crane Lake," *Macleod Gazette*, 13 April 1904.
46 See above, p. 82, and n. 39.
47 W. Stegner, *Wolf Willow* (New York, 1955), 137, tells us that "the net effect of the winter of 1906–07 was to make stock farmers out of ranchers. Almost as suddenly as the disappearance of the buffalo, it changed the way of life of the region."
48 Kelly, *Range Men*, 191.
49 Ibid.
50 Ibid.; McIntyre, *A Brief History of the McIntyre Ranch*, 25.
51 The McIntyre Ranch, for example, had only three hundred to four hundred tons of hay for some nine thousand head (ibid.).
52 *Fort Macleod, Our Colorful Past*, Macleod: Fort Macleod History Book Committee, 1977, quoted in Dempsey, *The Golden Age of the Canadian Cowboy*,145.
53 Ibid.
54 Kelly, *The Range Men*, 191–2. Kelly's description is used in Dempsey, *The Golden Age of the Cowboy*, 148.
55 M.V. Watt, "McCord's Ranch – A Character of Sounding Lake," *Canadian Cattlemen* 16, no. 1 (January 1953), 38.
56 Kelly, *Range Men*, 191; Canada, *Sessional Papers* 42, no. 14 (1907–08), n. 28, 56: Annual Report for D Division, 1 November 1907.
57 M. Terrill, "'Uncle' Tony Day and the 'Turkey Track,'" *Canadian Cattlemen* 6, no. 1 (June 1943), 13.
58 LaGrandeur, "Memoirs of a Cowboy's Wife," 5.
59 Cross papers, f. 467: Cross to Douglass, 3 October 1906.
60 Ibid.: Cross to Douglass, 21 July 1906.
61 Ibid., f. 475: Douglass to Cross, 23 May 1907.
62 Ibid., f. 472: McCallum to Cross, 6 February 1907.
63 Ibid., f. 470: Cross to McKinnon, 23 January 1908.
64 By the agreement Douglass was to be responsible for the animals starting in the fall (ibid., f. 467, Douglass to Cross, 13 September 1906).
65 Ibid.
66 Ibid., f. 466: Cochrane to Cross, 21 October 1906.
67 Ibid., f. 469: H. Scott to Cross, 11 October 1906; ibid.: Cross to Scott, 23 October 1906.
68 Loose management practices near Bassano are confirmed in other correspondence. In a letter of 26 January 1908, a full year after the winter of concern, James Russell, the manager of the Lynn Cross Ranch at Rosebud, told Cross that "about a couple of weeks ago I saw another steer with your brand, he will be a four year old, will

weigh about 1400, & also I heard of another out by the Hand Hills, & at the same time I was told there were a few more with your brand went through the dip at the Hand Hills Tank. I suppose they will be all on this Range in this neighborhood. I heard it said that some person further down the Red Deer River had some cattle keeping for you (f. 475)."

Cross had given up the Bassano lease because of his horrendous losses the year before. It seems that his livestock had become dispersed over an incredibly large area during that catastrophe and that getting them all back again was turning out to be a real stretch. In the same letter Russell offered to have the stock association watch for the A7 brand at the stockyards. To this Cross agreed (ibid., f. 475, Cross to Russell: 10 March 1908). The fact that he was still looking for strays a year later tells us that there simply was no way in which he could have been tending to their needs effectively. When one considers that this particular animal weighed around 1,400 pounds, one is convinced Cross could not have done an efficient job of marketing his stock. At that heavy weight the steer must have been very close to ready for slaughter and yet it was ambling about the country miles away from its owner's grasp (ibid.).

69 *The Grass Roots of Dorothy*, 105.

70 See letters between Cross and Douglass through January, February, and March 1907 (Cross papers, f. 471).

71 *The Grass Roots of Dorothy*, 105.

72 Cross papers, f. 470: Douglass to Cross, 20 January 1907.

73 Ibid.: Douglass to Cross, 27 January 1907.

74 Ibid., f. 471: Douglass to Cross, 16 March 1907.

75 Ibid.: J.S. Dennis, asst. to 2nd vice president of the CPR to Cross, 15 May 1907.

76 Ibid.: Cross to Dennis, 18 May 1907

77 Ibid., f. 473: Cross to Carl Wieting, 10 June 1907.

78 Canada, *Sessional Papers* 42, no. 14 (1907–08), n. 28, 56: Annual Report for D Division, 1 November 1907.

79 Ibid., 16: Annual Report for E Division, 1 November 1907, ibid., 75: Annual Report for K Division, 31 October 1907; Dempsey, *The Golden Age*, 149.

80 Breen, *Canadian Prairie West*, 147.

81 Kelly, *Range Men*, 192; Brado, *Cattle Kingdom*, 123. Dempsey, *The Golden Age*, 149, says 15,000 Bar U cattle were lost.

82 Ibid., 145; Breen, *Canadian Prairie West*, 147.

83 Ibid.

84 Kelly, *Range Men*, 192.

85 Dempsey, *The Golden Age*, 149.

86 See following chapter.
87 *The Grass Roots of Dorothy*, 122.
88 Stair Ranch Letter Book, 38: Andrews to Thomas Clary, 23 June 1890.
89 Ibid., 86: 29 September 1890.
90 Five rather than four because of the year the cow had been on the open range before the steer was born.
91 D.C. McGowan, *Grassland Settlers*, 76–7.
92 LaGrandeur, "Memoirs of a Cowboy's Wife," 13.
93 Kelly reports that "the winter of 1884–5 was the best, from a stockman's point of view, that had ever been experienced. Throughout the entire ranching country the cattle and even sheep rustled on frozen grasses, all cattle going through without a spear of hay being given them, and sheep rustling until nearly February (*Range Men*, 86).
94 Cochrane Ranch Letter Book. A diary with the letter book covers the period from 1 January 1885 to 17 December 1885.
95 See Elofson, "Adapting to the Frontier Environment," 319.
96 Coyotes were also suspected of taking their share. However, ranchers now recognize that because of their smaller physical stature, coyotes kill very few healthy animals. They may on occasions take a small calf that they find off by itself. Their method is to get between it and its mother, chase it off into the wilderness and trail it until it succumbs to hunger and exhaustion.
97 For instance, Stair Ranch Letter Book, 111: Andrews to Ross, 24 November 1890; ibid., 119: Andrews to Clinton, 4 December 1890; Cochrane Ranch Letter Book, 76–7: Cochrane to J.M. Browning, 21 February 1885; ibid., 14: weekly ranch report, 27 December 1884.
98 "The Wolves Must Go," *Macleod Gazette*, 10 November 1892.
99 "A Monstrous Wolfe," 2 February 1894.
100 "Big Timber Wolf," 26 January 1894.
101 Kelly, *Range Men*, 189.
102 Canada, *Sessional Papers* 25, no. 10 (1892), n. 15, 9–10: Report of the Commissioner, 31 December 1891.
103 Stair Ranch Letter Book: Andrews to N. Jensen, 8 September 1890.
104 "Range Notes," *Macleod Gazette*, 17 August 1894.
105 Ibid., 7 September 1894.
106 *Macleod Gazette*, 22 November 1901.
107 "Range Notes," ibid., 7 September 1894.
108 "Local Notes," ibid., 16 August 1895; for further discussion see Elofson, "Adapting to the Frontier Environment," 319.
109 Hay supplies were destroyed over and over again. Besides the examples given in text, the reader might consult Canada, *Sessional Papers* 42, no. 14 (1907–8), n. 28, 72: Annual Report for A Division, 31 October 1907 for destruction near Maple Creek in 1907: "There has been an

unusual number of prairie fires recently and a correspondingly large extent of country burnt and winter feed destroyed." See also S. Raby, "Prairie Fires in the North-West," *Saskatchewan History* 19, no. 3 (spring 1966), 81–99.

110 "Prairie Fire Aftermath," *Calgary Herald*, 29 March 1998.

111 Also the threat of starting fires over such a vast country where settlement was so sparse, detection so difficult. The yearly reports of the NWMP indicate that many of those who started prairie fires were caught, but as many surely escaped (Canada, *Sessional Papers*, 27, no. 11 (1894) n. 15, 28–9: Annual Report for Macleod District, 30 November 1893).

112 Ibid., 86: Annual Report for K Division, 1 December 1893.

113 Kelly, *Range Men*, 273. The bones for fertilizer were often the first crop taken off the virgin lands.

114 Cochrane Ranch Letter Book 29, December 1885.

115 Ibid., 7–9: Cochrane to James Cochrane, 19 December 1884. Even worse, in the Lethbridge area fire threatened to wipe out ranching altogether. See Canada, *Sessional Papers* 26, no. 9 (1893), n. 15, 88–9: Annual Report for K Division, 30 November 1892; ibid., 132: Annual Report for E Division, 1 December 1892.

116 Cochrane Ranch Letter Book, 20–2: Cochrane to M.H. Cochrane, 4 January 1885.

117 Cochrane noted in his diary for 13 April 1885 (26) that, "Fire started out from below agency and burned towards Whoop Up and then St. Mary's." On 15 April it was finally "put out by rain" (26). The following fall and winter seem to have been equally difficult. In his diary for 14 August 1885 (27), Cochrane wrote, "fires in the mountains I think. Can scarcely see on the prairies." On 17 October (27) he noted that he had seen "fire in the north, think it is beyond Old Man's." And on 1 November (28) he "saw fire over by Dry Fork."

118 Ibid., 27, 15 October 1885.

119 John Harris papers, Lethbridge: Howell Harris to John Harris, 5 July 1889, quoted in Klassen, "The Conrads in the Alberta Cattle Business, 1875–1911, 47.

120 Canada, *Sessional Papers* 25, no. 10 (1892), n. 15, 24: Annual Report for E Division, December 1891.

121 Ibid. 26, no. 9 (1893), n. 15, 88–9: Annual Report for K Division, 1 December 1892; ibid., 132: Annual Report for E Division, 1 December 1892. According to L.V. Kelly (*Range Men*, 137), 1892 was a bad season for fires: "some were set out by bone-pickers."

122 Canada, *Sessional Papers* 27, no. 11 (1894), n. 15, 86: Annual Report for K Division, 1 December 1893.

123 Ibid., 9: Annual Report of the Commissioner, 28 December 1893.

124 Ibid., 24: Annual Report for Macleod District, 30 November 1893.

125 For the Maple Creek area 1895 was also a fairly bad year (ibid., 29, no. 11 (1896) n. 15, 26: Annual Report for A Division, 30 November 1895), and 1898 was for the Macleod area (ibid., 33, no. 12 (1899), n. 15, 34–5: Annual Report for D Division, 30 November 1898).

126 Kelly, *Range Men*, 168.

127 Ibid.

128 E.S. Warren, "The Worst Fire I Ever Saw," *Canadian Cattlemen* 13, no. 7 (July 1950), 38.

129 Cross papers, f. 467, Douglass to Cross, 13 September 1906.

130 The Walrond account book for the years 1883–95 is in the Glenbow Archives in Calgary (Ralph C. and Kenneth R. Coppock papers, M264). D.H. Andrews kept accounts of the Stair Ranch livestock numbers (see Stair Ranch Letter Book, 35, 140–1, 170–2, 220–3, 279–84, 326–31, 374–7, 412–15, 461–4, 487–90). He also recorded the deaths that he knew about. However, he did not give reasons for the deaths. He obviously did not record the deaths he was unaware of among the cattle he had on the open range.

131 Raby, "Prairie Fires in the North-West," 82.

132 "All over the Range," *Macleod Gazette*, 9 November 1886.

133 Kelly, *Range Men*, 104.

134 "Death of Mr. J.C. Dunlap," *Macleod Gazette*, 15 November 1885.

135 "Frozen to Death," *Macleod Gazette*, 26 Nov. 1891.

136 H. Dempsey, *Golden Age of the Canadian Cowboy*, 147–8.

137 Ibid., 148.

138 Kelly, *Range Men*, 130–1.

CHAPTER FIVE

1 P. Sharp, *Whoop-Up Country: The Canadian-American West, 1865–1885*, 2nd. ed., Helena: Historical Society of Montana, 1960; C.E. Denny, *The Law Marches West*, Toronto: Dent, 1972, 1–229; J. Jennings, "The Plains Indians and the Law," *Men in Scarlet*, ed. H.A. Dempsey, Calgary, 1974, 50–65; and "Policemen and Poachers – Indian Relations on the Ranching Frontier," *Frontier Calgary*, ed. A.W. Rasporich and H. Klassen, Calgary: University of Calgary Press, 1975, 87–99; D.H. Breen, *Canadian Prairie West*; "The Mounted Police and the Ranching Frontier," *Men in Scarlet*, 115–37; "Plain Talk from Plain Western Men," *Alberta Historical Review* 17, no. 3 (summer 1970), 8–14; and "The Canadian Prairie West and the Harmonious Settlement Interpretation," *Agricultural History* 47 (Jan. 1973), 63–75; R.C. Macleod, *The NWMP and Law Enforcement, 1873–1905*, Toronto: University of Toronto Press, 1976.

2 Breen, *Canadian Prairie West*, 82.
3 Canada, *Sessional Papers* 28, no. 9 (1895), n. 15,18: Annual Report for Macleod District, 30 November 1894.
4 Ibid., 24, no. 19 (1891), n. 19, 62: Annual Report for D Division, 20 November 1890.
5 Ibid., 28, no. 9 (1895), n. 15, 25: Annual Report for Macleod District, 30 November 1894.
6 "Policing the International Boundary Area in Saskatchewan," *Saskatchewan History* 19, no. 2 (spring 1996), 61–73.
7 "The Incidence of Crime in Southern Alberta, 1878–1905," *Law and Society in Canada: A Historical Perspective*, ed. D.J. Bercuson and L.A. Knafla, Calgary: University of Calgary Press, 1979.
8 "The Not So Peaceable Kingdom: Crime and Criminal Justice in Frontier Calgary," *Frontier Calgary*, 100–13.
9 "Violence on the Western Canadian Frontier: A Historical Perspective," *Violence in Canada: Sociopolitical Perspectives*, ed. J.I. Ross, Oxford: Oxford University Press, 1995, 10–39.
10 *The Golden Age of the Canadian Cowboy*, 104.
11 W. Beahen and S. Horrall, *Red Coats on the Prairies: The North-West Mounted Police, 1886–1900*, Regina: Centax Books, 1998. The authors set out to demonstrate how, albeit with difficulty, the Mounties transformed the West and helped to turn it into a secure and stable society.
12 Canada, *Sessional Papers* 36, no. 12 (1902), n. 28, 1–2. Numbers are also given for each division for 1901 (ibid., pt. 2, 3–4). The numbers were Maple Creek, 47; Macleod and Lethbridge, 131; Calgary, 51.
13 Ibid., 1–2.
14 Beahen and Horrall, *Red Coats on the Prairies*, 14.
15 PAC, RG18, Commissioner's Office Letter Book (B-3), vol. 48, 342–5, cited in Macleod, *The NWMP and Law Enforcement*, 22.
16 Ibid., 22 ff.
17 Ibid; Canada, *Sessional Papers* 25, no. 10 (1892) n. 15, 68: Annual Report for K Division, 1 December 1891.
18 14 March 1883. This detachment was actually at Regina but stands as an example of the kinds of things that could happen in any of them.
19 S. Evans, "American Cattlemen on the Canadian Range," *Prairie Forum* 4, no. 1, 1979, 121–35.
20 "Local Notes," *Macleod Gazette*, 6 November 1896.
21 See T. Thorner, "The Not So Peacable Kingdom" (Master's thesis).
22 Beahen and Horrall, *Red Coats on the Prairies*, 154–80. Until 1890 almost all the recruits were from the East – principally Ontario but also New Brunswick, Nova Scotia, and, after 1888, Quebec (ibid., 174). From 1890 enough men entered the force in Winnipeg and

Regina that recruitment in the East was no longer necessary. Presumably an increasing percentage of the men who joined after 1890 were westerners.

23 For which see ibid., 233–42.

24 For instance, an article entitled "Deserted" (*Macleod Gazette*, 31 May 1887) reported that "some of the men on the Milk river detachment deserted last week, taking their horses arms etc." See also next footnote.

25 "Items of Interest," ibid., 4 June 1883.

26 See, for instance, "Sad Death, "*Macleod Gazette*, 12 July 1887; "Constable Harrison," ibid., 13 September 1887; "Dr. Miller's Suicide," *Macleod Gazette*, 28 September 1887; "Lost on the Plains," ibid., 7 March 1891; "Corporal McNair of Wardner Shoots Himself," ibid., 29 April 1898; "Suicide," ibid., 17 November 1899.

27 Dr Louis A. Knafla at the University of Calgary on 11 December 1998.

28 G. Shepherd, "Tom Whitney of Maple Creek," *Canadian Cattlemen* 4, no. 4 (March 1942), 156.

29 F.W. Godsol, "Old Times," *Alberta Historical Review* 12, no. 4 (autumn 1964), 19.

30 "All over the Range," *Macleod Gazette*, 9 November 1886.

31 Kelly, *Range Men*, 78, 89, 108, 194.

32 Ewing, *The Range*, Missoula: Mountain Press, 1990, 34.

33 Cochrane Ranch Letter Book, diary, 16: 19 May 1885: "My six shooter was stolen from my chaps at Slaters"; 22 May, "I lent Davy my six shooter and gave him a box of ctgs."

34 Lawrence, "Early Days in the Chinook Belt," 13.

35 Newbolt, "Memoirs of the Bowchase Ranch," 1–10.

36 H. Maguire, "Shaunavon Tales," *Canadian Cattlemen* 13, no. 2 (February 1950) 47.

37 J.G. Donkin, *Trooper and Redskin in the Far Northwest: Recollections of Life in the North-West Mounted Police, Canada, 1884–1888*, Toronto: Coles Publishing, 1973, 222.

38 "Cowboy Runs Amuck," *Macleod Gazette*, 15 July 1904.

39 "Cowboy Defies Mounted Police and Is Shot," *Calgary Herald*, 13 July 1904.

40 T. Thorner, "The Not So Peaceable Kingdom" (Master's thesis), 65. The Prince Albert stage was also held up that summer (Donkin, *Trooper and Redskin*, 229–30).

41 Lawrence, "Early Days in the Chinook Belt," 17.

42 "A Fatal Quarrel," *Macleod Gazette*, 15 July 1885.

43 Canada, *Sessional Papers* 25, no. 10 (1892), n. 15: Annual Report for C Division, 30 November 1891; Anderson, *Sheriffs and Outlaws*, 65–6.

44 Canada, *Sessional Papers* 29, no. 11 (1896), n. 15, 41: Annual Report for Macleod District, 30 November 1895.
45 Ibid., 33, no. 11 (1897), n. 15, 136: Annual Report for E Division, 1 December 1896.
46 "Dave Akers, Life of the Pioneer Who Was Killed by Purcel," *Macleod Gazette*, 2 March 1894.
47 See pp. 234–49, 250–6, 256–61.
48 Kelly, *Range Men*, 162; see also "Murder," *Macleod Gazette*, 12 February 1891.
49 Canada, *Sessional Papers* 29, no. 11 (1896), n. 15, p 93: Annual Report for K Division, 1 December 1895; Kelly, *Range Men*, 149.
50 "Train Robbery," *Macleod Gazette*, 26 October 1886; "A Lively Chase," *Macleod Gazette*, 11 October 1901; "Road Agents Dynamite and Loot C.P.R. Limited," *Calgary Herald*, 12 September 1904; "Trainmen Tell Story of Hold Up on CPR," *Calgary Herald*, 13 September 1904; "Chasing Railroad Bandits Who Held Up Limited," *Calgary Herald*, 14 September 1904; "How Road Agents Robbed an Express," *Calgary Herald*, 4 August 1904.
51 *Range Men*, 3.
52 Ibid., 134.
53 Donna B. Ernst, "The Sundance Kid in Alberta," 14.
54 Newbolt, "Memories of Bowchase Ranch," 4.
55 G. Shepherd, "Tom Whitney of Maple Creek," *Canadian Cattlemen* 4, no. 4 (March 1942), 156.
56 "A Big Drunk," *Macleod Gazette*, 16 February 1886. For other reports of this nature see "Rioting and Drunkeness," 19 September 1884; "Macleod," *Calgary Tribune*, 11 November 1885; "Police News," *Calgary Herald*, 21 October 1902; and following footnote.
57 "The Six Shooter Again Is Called in to Settle a Dispute," 21 July 1885, cited in T. Thorner, "The Incidence of Crime in Southern Alberta." Unfortunately, to this stage Thorner's published work has been limited primarily to two articles. Hopefully some of his findings will be confirmed in a future major study.
58 "Veteran Mountie Tells of Adventures in West," *Albertan*, 23 April 1942, cited in Thorner, "The Incidence of Crime," 67.
59 "Accidental Shooting," *Medicine Hat Weekly News*, 19 December 1895.
60 "The Incidence of Crime in Southern Alberta," 56–7.
61 Calgary, 1973.
62 Another work written in a similar vein though mostly about outlaws from British Columbia is T.W. Paterson, *Outlaws of Western Canada*, Langley, B.C.: Mister Paperback, 1977. Some of the newspaper-recorded gunplay not cited previously is: "Accidental Shooting,"

Medicine Hat Weekly News, 19 December 1895; "Shooting Affray," *Calgary Tribune*, 27 February 1886; "The Deadly Revolver," *Macleod Gazette*, 6 December 1895.

63 Besides note above, see Cochrane Letter Book, diary entries for 6 and 21 February, 26, 28, and 31 March 1885; Ings, "Tales of the Midway," 1, 38; Kelly, *Range Men*, 60–2.

64 Jennings, "The Plains Indians and the Law," 50–65; "Policemen and Poachers: Indian Relations on the Ranching Frontier," 87–99.

65 Thefts by Indians were often recorded by the Mounties. See for instance Canada. *Sessional Papers* 25, no. 10 (1892), n. 15, 70–1: Annual Report for K Division, 1 December 1891; see also T.L. Chapman, "Crime and Justice in Medicine Hat, 1883–1905," *Alberta History* 39, no. 2 (spring 1991), 17–24.

66 Thorner, "The Not So Peaceable Kingdom" (Master's thesis), 61.

67 "Indians Shot," 30 August 1887.

68 This might be compared with concern expressed in the papers about the white men killed in gunfights; see for instance "A Fatal Quarrel," *Macleod Gazette*, 15 July 1885; "Dave Akers, Life of the Pioneer Who Was Killed by Purcel," ibid., 2 March 1894; "Cowboy Defies Mounted Police and Is Shot," *Calgary Herald*, 13 July 1904; "Accidental Shooting," *Medicine Hat Weekly News*, 19 December 1895.

69 "Bullets Flew Near Cardston," *Macleod Gazette*, 23 October 1903.

70 See, for instance, "Shot Him," *Macleod Gazette*, 11 January 1888; "Shot and Knifed," *Macleod Gazette*, 10 March 1893.

71 S.B. Steele, *Forty Years in Canada*, Toronto: Prospero, 2000, 225-6.

72 See, for instance, "Charcoal," *Macleod Gazette*, 30 October 1896; "Charcoal Adds Another Victim to His List," ibid., 13 November 1896; "Charcoal on Trial for Murder," ibid., 15 January 1897; "Charcoal on the Gallows," ibid., 19 March 1897; Anderson, *Sheriffs and Outlaws*, 49–51.

73 "Local Notes," *Macleod Gazette*, 22 November 1895; "Trouble in the North," ibid., 4 June 1897.

74 W. Hildebrandt, *Views from Fort Battleford: Constructed Visions of an Anglo-Canadian West*, Regina: Canadian Plains Research Centre, 1994, 100–2.

75 "Foul Murder of Land-Seeker," *Calgary Herald*, 4 September 1903.

76 Besides the above several notes see "In Town and Out," *Macleod Gazette*, 24 August 1882; "The South Peigan Indians are on the Rampage…," ibid., 4 October 1882; "Attacked by Indians," ibid., 4 August 1885; "The Lieutenant-Governor's Speech," ibid., 26 October 1886; "The Skeena Scare," ibid., 25 July 1888.

77 Inderwick, Diary and Letters: letter of 13 May 1884, 10–11.

78 Macleod, *The NWMP*, 136.

79 Kelly, *Range Men*, 111–12; "In Town and Out," *Macleod Gazette*, 4 September 1882; "The Whiskey Traffic," ibid., 7 December 1886; "Seized Forty Gallons," ibid., 20 August 1891.

80 Canada, *Sessional Papers* 22, no. 13 (1889), n. 17, 10–11: Annual Report of the Commissioner, 31 December 1888.

81 Gray, *Booze: When Whiskey Ruled the West*, Saskatoon: Fifth House, 1972. See also Voisey, *Vulcan*, 162–3.

82 *Range Men*, 111.

83 Canada, *Sessional Papers* 22, no. 13 (1889), n. 17, 46: Annual Report of the Commissioner, 10 December 1896. "There is no doubt that the time has arrived for some changes in the liquor laws. At present time the existing law is not obeyed or respected by the mass of the inhabitants of this part of the North-west."

84 Ibid., 22:13 (1889), n. 17, 16: Annual Report of the Commissioner, 10 December 1888.

85 R.C. Macleod, *The NWMP*, 134–6; Beahen and Horrall, *Red Coats on the Prairies*, 259–60. "The West of Edward Maunsell," pt. 1, 2–4; "Sent Down," *Macleod Gazette*, 12 April 1887; "Three Mounted Police Receive Stiff Sentences," *Calgary Herald*, 4 January 1904.

86 "The West of Edward Maunsell," pt. 1, 2–4.

87 Inderwick, Diary and Letters: letter of 13 May 1884, 12–13. See also "The West of Edward Maunsell," pt. 1, 4–7.

88 The Calgary Brewing and Malting Co. papers are in the Glenbow Archives in Calgary. They are a very extensive collection (M289, M339, M1543, M1548, M2601, M3358).

89 Thomas Thorner sums up the situation in "The Not So Peaceable Kingdom" (Master's thesis), 85: "According to the cases before the Justices of the Peace, these offences followed the general pattern of most crimes, increasing sharply in the late 1890s. Charges of possessing or selling liquor were limited to the period 1874–1891 when prohibition prevailed. Violations for possession first appeared in 1879 when eight persons were tried, and then fell off until only 1 case was recorded in 1881. Later in 1886 the number of these offences peaked at 65, then declined until 1891 when 12 cases were tried. However, the number of cases tried before the Justices of the Peace bore no relationship to the incidence of these offences. The bulk of the population feeling that prohibition was not justified, continued to ignore the ordinance to such an extent that enforcement of the law was often impossible. A member of the N.W.M.P. later noted that 'drinking seemed to be the chief pastime. Small dives were frequently searched by the police for illicit whisky and seizure and punishment of offenders were almost daily occurrences in Calgary.'"

90 Canada, *Sessional Papers* 26, no. 9 (1893), n. 15, 2: Report of the Commissioner, 19 December 1892.
91 Thorner, "The Not So Peaceable Kingdom" (Master's thesis), 85.
92 Ibid.
93 *Red Lights on the Prairies*; see also Voisey, *Vulcan*, 162–3.
94 Anderson, *Sheriffs and Outlaws*, 41–2, 48; S.W. Horrall, "The (Royal) North-West Mounted Police and Prostitution on the Canadian Prairies," *The Mounted Police and Prairie Society, 1873–1919*, ed. W.M. Baker, Regina: Canadian Plains Research Centre, 1998, 173–92.
95 Anderson, *Sheriffs and Outlaws*, 41–2.
96 See S.W. Horrall, "(Royal) North-West Mounted Police and Prostitution," 173–91.
97 Canada, *Sessional Papers* 25, no. 10 (1892), n. 15, 17: Annual Report for E Division, December 1891.
98 Ibid. 32, no. 12 (1898), n. 15, 39: Annual Report for D Division, 30 November 1897.
99 *Census of the Prairie Provinces, 1916: Population and Agriculture*, 104.
100 J.B. Bedford, "Prostitution in Calgary, 1905–1914," *Alberta History* 29, no. 2 (spring 1981), 2.
101 Ibid., 4.
102 *Census of the Provinces, 1916: Population and Agriculture*, 51.
103 Canada, *Sessional Papers* 32, no. 12 (1898), n. 15, 39: Annual Report for D Division, 30 November 1897.
104 Ibid. 41, no. 11 (1906–7), n. 28, 86: Annual Report for A Division, 31 October 1906.
105 Thorner, "The Not So Peaceable Kingdom" (Master's thesis), 89.
106 *Range Men*, 168, 183, 186–7, 188–9.
107 Cross papers, f. 485: James Russell to Cross, 23 October 1908.
108 "Stolen Horses Recaptured," *Macleod Gazette*, 1 July 1882; "In Town and Out," ibid., 15 July 82; "Horse Stealing," ibid., 14 July 1883; "Here and Here Abouts," ibid., 4 August 1883; "Horse Stealing," ibid., 3 October 1884; "Horse Thief Captured," ibid., 25 May 1886; "Increase the Force," ibid., 19 November 1897; "The Cattle Case," ibid., 24 December 1897; "Pocha Sentenced," ibid., 30 November 1900; "A Syndicate of Horse Thieves," ibid., 4 April 1904; "Arrested for Cattle Stealing," *Calgary Herald*, 9 April 1904; "Another Horse Case," ibid., 20 May 1904; "McLaughlin Sentenced to Seven Years," ibid., 23 May 1904; "Horse Stealing Case," ibid., 17 June 1904. Note further quotations on rustling below taken from the *Annual Reports* of the North-West Mounted Police.
109 *John Ware's Cow Country*, 82–3.
110 *Mounted Police Life in Canada; A Record of Thirty-one Years' Service*, London, New York, Toronto and Melbourne: Cassell and Company, 1916, 51–2.

111 "Atrocities of Outlaw Band in Assiniboia," *Calgary Herald*, 8 August 1904; "Atrocities of Outlaw Band in Southern Assiniboia," *Macleod Gazette*, 12 August 1904. See also Ernst, "The Sundance Kid in Alberta," 14; F. Anderson, *Sheriffs and Outlaws*, 53–6.

112 On 22 June 1900 the *Macleod Gazette* reported that "Jones and Nelson … have stolen over 300 head of horses and thousands of cattle from the northern ranges, all of which were driven into Canada and disposed of ("Stock Notes").

113 Anderson, *Sheriffs and Outlaws*, 53.

114 See S. Hanson, "Policing the International Border," *Saskatchewan History* 19, no. 1 (spring 1966), 70.

115 "Lynched in Montana," *Macleod Gazette*, 11 April 1885. For other such lynchings south of the border, see "Lynched in Helena," ibid., 21 February 1885; Kelly, *Range Men*, 75–6.

116 Ibid., 176; Canada, *Sessional Papers* 37, no. 11 (1904), n. 28, 58: Annual Report for E Division, 30 November 1903.

117 Kelly, *Range Men*, 72–3.

118 Ibid.

119 Ibid., 73.

120 Canada, *Sessional Papers* 31, no. 11 (1897), n. 15, 160: Annual Report for E Division, 1 December 1896.

121 M. Terrill, "Medicine Hat Pioneer, William Mitchell, 1878–1946," *Canadian Cattlemen* 9, no. 3 (December 1946), 150.

122 Kelly, *Range Men*, 176; Breen, *Canadian Prairie West*, 111.

123 "The Maverick Case," *Calgary Herald*, 7 January 1904.

124 Kelly, *Range Men*, 176.

125 That is, the brand had been remade with a "running" or "round iron," to look like his neighbour's brand. For the running iron see p. 125.

126 Stair Ranch Letter Book, 338; Andrews to Glengary Ranch Co., 10 September 1892. Patrick Burns was of course the well-known cattle merchant, meat packer and retailer, and founder of Burns Foods Ltd.; see G. MacEwan, *Pat Burns, Cattle King*.

127 *The Western Law Reporter* 12 (1910), 562. See also L.A. Knafla, "Violence on the Western Canadian Frontier," 22.

128 Provincial Archives of Alberta, files of the Justices of the Peace, 66.166, file no. 979. I am indebted to Dr Louis A. Knafla for this information.

129 Terrill, "Medicine Hat Pioneer, William Mitchell," 150.

130 Breen, *The Canadian Prairie West*, 52.

131 "On Conviction," 7 July 1893.

132 H. Maguire, "Cowboy Tales of 1896," *Canadian Cattlemen* 15, no. 8 (August 1952), 39. It is possible that this story is merely a yarn. Even

so, it demonstrates that contemporaries saw rustling as a way of life on the open range. A man who had ranched between the Cypress Hills and the international border once recalled that "cattle rustling, brand 'working,' and butchering ... was counted at as a form of free enterprise and legal tender for poaching when confined" to the stock that wandered across the border from American ranches (Terrill, "Medicine Hat Pioneer, William Mitchell," 150). Distinguishing between American and Canadian cattle has to have been difficult, particularly given the potential for subjectivity in the case of the man interested in increasing his herd.

133 Kelly, *Range Men*, 4.

134 Canada, *Sessional Papers* 41, no. 11 (1906, 07), n. 28, 62: Annual Report for K Division, 1 October 1906.

135 Ibid.

136 Breen, *Canadian Prairie West*, 108.

137 Canada, *Sessional Papers* 29, no. 11 (1896) n. 15, 3: Annual Report of the Commissioner, 10 December 1895.

138 Ibid.

139 Deane, *Mounted Police Life*, 166.

140 Ibid.

141 Ibid., 93, 154ff; Public Archives of Canada RG18 A1, N.W.M.P. papers, box 2, file 60, v. 242, f. 25, pt. 1; file 61, v. 243, f. 25, pt. 2; file 62, v. 261, f. 823; "American Cattle," *Medicine Hat Weekly News*, 3 December 1896; "Stray American Cattle," *Lethbridge News*, 7 September 1887.

142 Klassen, "The Conrads in the Alberta Cattle Business," 46, 47.

143 Canada, *Sessional Papers* 33, no. 12 (1899), n. 15, 3; Annual Report of the Commissioner, 20 December 1898.

144 Ibid.

145 Besides those cited in note 58 above, see "Range Horses," *Macleod Gazette*, 23 March 1886; "Horse Thief Captured," ibid., 25 May 1886; "A Syndicate of Horse Thieves," *Macleod Gazette*, 4 April 1902.

146 *Mounted Police Life*, 292

147 Canada, *Sessional Papers* 31, no. 11 (1897) n. 15, 9: Annual Report of the Commissioner, 10 December 1896.

148 Ibid. 32, no. 12 (1898), n. 15, 2: Annual Report of the Commissioner, 17 December 1897.

149 Ibid. 38, no. 11 (1904), n. 28, 59: Annual Report for E Division, 30 November 1903.

150 Ibid. 32, no. 12 (1898), n. 15, 4: Annual Report of the Commissioner, 17 December 1897.

151 Ibid. 38, no. 11 (1904), n. 28, 6–7: Annual Report of the Commissioner, 25 January 1904.

152 Ibid. 29, no. 11 (1896), n. 15, 3: Annual Report of the Commissioner, 18 December 1895.
153 Ibid. 38, no. 11 (1904), n. 28, 59: Annual Report for E Division, 30 November 1903.
154 Anderson, *Sheriffs and Outlaws*, 54.
155 Knafla, "Violence on the Western Canadian Frontier," 10–39. See in particular 22.
156 Canada, *Sessional Papers* 31, no. 11 (1897) n. 15, 9: Annual Report of the Commissioner, 10 December 1896.
157 Ibid. 29, no. 11 (1896), n. 15, 3–4: Annual Report of the Commissioner, 18 December 1895.
158 Herchmer mused that "the system of granting bail to horse and cattle thieves (while I believe it is almost imperative on the part of the judges to grant) is really a premium on this class of stealing. The country is so immense, and it is so hard to trace a man's property and horses and cattle, that this evasion of justice is quite easy. If it is impossible in these cases to refuse bail, a speedy trial would greatly reduce the chance of escape without trial." He took heart, though, that "some convictions have been obtained against cattle thieves, and, at present time, several are committed for trial one at least being a well-off rancher" (ibid.).
159 Ibid.
160 Ibid. 32, no. 12 (1898), n. 15, 59 60: Annual Report for K Division, 1 December 1897.
161 Ibid.
162 Ibid., 33, no. 12 (1899), n. 15, Annual Report of the Commissioner, 20 December 1898.
163 Breen, *Canadian Prairie West*, 108. Canada, *Sessional Papers* 33, no. 12 (1899), n. 15, 3: Annual Report of the Commissioner, 20 December 1898; ibid., 57: Annual Report for A Division, 1 December 1898.
164 Breen, *Canadian Prairie West*, 109.
165 Canada, *Sessional Papers* 33, no. 12 (1899), n. 15, 57; Annual Report for A Division, 1 December 1898.
166 Breen, *The Canadian Prairie West*, 109.
167 Canada, *Sessional Papers* 33, no. 12 (1899) 57: Annual Report for A Division, 1 December 1898
168 Ibid.
169 Ibid., 32, no. 12 (1898), n. 15, 59, Annual Report for K Division 1 December 1897.
170 Ibid. 33, no. 12 (1899) 57: Annual Report for A Division, 1 December 1898: "the territiorial Department of agriculture has taken over the issuing of brands under the new Brands Ordinance, and the office of Recorder at Macleod has been abolished. The new system is more

appreciated since it is better understood than at first and should do away with all possibility of brands on animals being altered from one to another character.

"To make the new system more effective, I would suggest the advisability of an official publication of the recorded brands both old and new by the department controlling them."

171 The early brand books are in the Glenbow Archives; see *Henderson's Northwest Ranchers' Directory and Brand Book*, Winnipeg, 1888.

172 Breen, *The Canadian Prairie West*, 108.

173 *Alberta Rancher's Directory and Brand Book*, Edmonton, 1907.

174 T. Thorner has made a start; see "The Not So Peaceable Kingdom: Crime and Criminal Justice in Frontier Calgary," and "The Incidence of Crime in Southern Alberta,"; Thorner and H. Watson, "Patterns of Prairie Crime: Calgary, 1875–1939," *Crime and Criminal Justice in Europe and Canada*, ed. Louis A. Knafla, Waterloo: Wilfrid Laurier Press, 1985. See also Knafla, "Violence on the Western Frontier," for a discussion of issues and the more important literature.

175 MacEwan, *John Ware's Cow Country*, 75.

176 Stair Ranch Letter Book, 86, 29 September 1890. In September 1890 D.H. Andrews acknowledged receipt of a cheque for $440 for the sale of seventeen steers from a rancher in Montana named Thomas Clary. He offered thanks and help for Clary on the Canadian side of the border.

177 "Range Horses," *Macleod Gazette*, 23 March 1886; "Horse Thief Captured," ibid., 25 May 1886; "A Syndicate of Horse Thieves," *Macleod Gazette*, 4 April 1902.

178 *Range Men*, 22.

179 *Cattle Kingdom*, 86.

180 I recently mentioned the one-in-three ratio to Sherm Ewing, noted longtime rancher and historian from Alberta and Montana. He informed me that it would have been about right. Indeed, he said that in the 1930s many of the operations that were practising widespread grazing south of the American border were still commonly achieving returns of around only 60 per cent. And through decades of fencing and upgrading of feeding and handling systems, they had improved their operations significantly over those of their frontier predecessors. Ewing is author of *The Range*, and *The Ranch: A Modern History of the North American Cattle Industry*, Missoula: Mountain Press, 1996.

181 H. "Dude" Lavington, *The Nine Lives of a Cowboy*, 97–8.

182 Ibid., 98.

CHAPTER SIX

1 *Prairie Grass to Mountain Pass*, 128
2 Canada, *Sessional Papers* 22, no. 13 (1889), n. 17, 20: Annual Report of the Commissioner, 13 December 1888.
3 "Range Notes," *Macleod Gazette*, 16 February 1886. Article argues against fencing the range for the sake of controlling livestock more closely. For further discussion see Elofson, "Not Just a Cowboy," 206.
4 Inderwick, Diary and Letters: letter of 13 May 1884, 24.
5 "All over the Range," *Macleod Gazette*, 4 August 1885.
6 Dr J. Rutherford, *The Cattle Trade of Western Canada*, Ottawa: Department of Agriculture, 1909, quoted in Kelly, *Range Men*, 200.
7 Canada, *Sessional Papers* 25, no. 10 (1892), n. 15, 93: Annual Report for A Division, 1 December 1891.
8 For irrigation in southern Alberta see A.A. den Otter, *Civilizing the West: The Galts and the Development of Western Canada*, Lincoln: University of Nebraska Press, 1982.
9 For local studies see Voisey, *Vulcan*; Elofson, "Mixed and Dryland Farming," 42–6. For a more general and more dramatic approach see D.C. Jones, *Empire of Dust: Settling and Abandoning the Prairie Dry Belt*, Edmonton: University of Alberta Press, 1987.
10 Elofson, "Not Just a Cowboy," 206–7.
11 "The Cochrane Ranch," *Macleod Gazette*, 3 October 1884; Cross papers, f. 471; Douglass to A.E. Cross, 11 March 1907, and other letters in the same file.
12 The Cochrane was putting up both hay and oats as early as 1885 (Cochrane Ranch Letter Book, diary, 21–7); Cross had enough hay at Nanton to feed all the cattle there through the 1906–07 winter (above, pp. 89–90); the Stair Ranch also was careful to lay in supplies of roughage, Letter Book, 399: Andrews to J.M. Richardson, 15 February 1893; ibid., 488: Andrews to Chas. Askers, 7 August 1893; Kelly paints the movement to feeding in general (*Range Men*, 22).
13 *Prairie Grass to Mountain Pass*, 7, the recollections of Frank Austin and Myra (Austin) Harshman.
14 McIntyre, *A Brief History of the McIntyre Ranch*, 25; LaGrandeur, "Memoirs of a Cowboy's Wife," 6.
15 Kelly, *Range Men*, 107.
16 Cross papers, f. 470: Cross to F.H. Berry, 1 September 1901.
17 "Local and General," *Pincher Creek Echo*, 10 May 1904.
18 "Mange," ibid., 24 May 1904.
19 Above, p. 91.

20 This is why for, instance, in 1906 Cross did not have a recurrence of the disease in his cattle at Nanton that, along with the forthcoming horrendous winter, was to so devastate his animals at Bassano (f. 480: McCallum to Cross, 3 September 1906). Cross's men had treated the herd for mange that spring and by keeping it separate from other herds were able pretty much to ensure that it did not come back. As a consequence there was no mention of it at Nanton in the fall and winter of 1906–07.

21 See S. Evans, "Stocking the Canadian Range," *Alberta History* 26, no. 3 (summer 1978), 1–8.

22 H.W. Riley, "Herbert William (Herb) Millar," *Canadian Cattlemen* 4, no. 4 (March 1942), 168.

23 Alberta, Department of Agriculture, *Annual Report*, 1908, 153.

24 Canada, *Sessional Papers* 28, no. 9 (1895), n. 13, 26. The pattern of breed quality development was very much the same with respect to horses.

25 Canada, *Sessional Papers* 33, no. 12 (1899), n. 15, 19: Report of the Commissioner, 20 December 1898.

26 Elofson, "Mixed and Dryland Farming," 209–14.

27 Canada, *Sessional Papers* 33, no. 12 (1899), n. 15, 19: Report of the Commissioner, 20 December 1898.

28 S. Evans ("Spatial Aspects of the Cattle Kingdom," 53–4) writes that "technological changes also encouraged small-scale more intensive operations. The winter of 1886–87 demonstrated the wastefulness of the open range system. The influx of more and more small herds served by scrub bulls frustrated every attempt to maintain or to improve the quality of stock. In succeeding years greater amounts of hay were put up, the time of calving was carefully regulated, and calves were weaned before the onset of winter. These innovations meant increased labour costs, and the optimum size of production units declined. The rancher-farmer could close herd his stock during the winter and feed them both natural hay and pasture crops. At the same time he could do something to protect his she-stock from the attentions of lower-class swains. He was rewarded by consistently higher rates of natural increase, and improved herd quality."

29 Gestation period for cows is nine months. F.W. Godsol was trying to time his breeding in the early 1880s ("Old Times," 23).

30 D.H. Andrews of the Stair Ranch scolded one of his workers in 1891 for allowing bulls to run with the cows in May and early June as this "only means dead cows and calves next Spring" (Letter Book, 209: Andrews to G. Anderson, 18 June 1891).

31 The Cochrane diary for the year 1885 illustrates the importance of this kind of regulation. One need only recall Billie Cochrane's

mention of death loss among cows that were trying to give birth outdoors in bad weather and among calves, many of them too immature to be attempting to manage on their own at the worst time of year.

32 See photograph, p. 141.

33 A.E. Cross, who as we have seen operated on his place at Nanton in much the same intensive manner as many of the smaller ranchers, seems to have done a relatively thorough job of spaying (Cross papers, f. 454: Cochrane to Cross, 31 May 1904).

34 K. Hughes "The Last Great Roundup," *Alberta Historical Review* 11, no. 2 (spring 1963), 1–2.

35 *Range Men*, 186.

36 "The Cow Business," *Macleod Gazette*, 14 November 1884. Also see McIntyre, *A Brief History of the McIntyre Ranch*, 25.

37 Cross papers, f. 480: McCallum to Cross, 5 May 1908; Stair Ranch Letter Book, 400: Andrews to Richardson, 15 February 1893: ibid., 488: Andrews to Chas. Akers, 7 August 1893. In 1904 the Walrond had two hundred acres in crops; "Local and General," *Macleod Gazette*, 10 June 1904; McIntyre, *Brief History of the McIntyre Ranch*, 25.

38 In 1904 the *Calgary Herald* ("Winter Feeding of Cattle," 22 November) reported that "winter feed is put up during the summer season, and in the winter the cowboys not only corral and feed the calves and weaker stock, but keep the entire herd supplied with food. Last winter they also found it necessary to feed the stronger cattle in the colder weather to keep them moving so that they should not become chilled and yield to their natural desire to sink down into a sleep that might know no up-rising."

39 Rutherford, *Cattle Trade in Western Canada*, quoted in Kelly, *Range Men*, 209.

40 Ibid., 200.

41 Ibid., 201.

42 "Winter Feeding of Cattle," *Macleod Gazette*, 22 November 1904.

43 Ibid.

44 Kelly, *Range Men*, 193–4.

45 "Expert Cattle Feeders," *Calgary Herald*, 9 February 1903; Alberta, Department of Agriculture, *Annual Report*, 1908, 151.

46 Ibid., 1914, 38.

47 Ibid., 4 April 1905, 2. See also Elofson, "Mixed and Dryland Farming," 35.

48 Hopkins, *Letters from a Lady Rancher*, 52, 57, 59, 98.

49 *Letters from an English Rancher*, v–xii, 41–52.

50 They maintained fences, cultivated the land, and put up greenfeed and hay. The Hopkins also managed a big garden, and Gardiner harvested oats, barley, and wheat.

51 There were exceptions of course. Gardiner, for instance, appears to have stayed with beef cattle and did not get into pursuits such as dairy or pork.
52 See, for instance, "Feed and Milk," *Pincher Creek Echo*, 24 May 1904.
53 *Prairie Grass to Mountain Pass*, 7: recollections of Frank Austin and Myra (Austin) Harshman.
54 "The Creamery," *Pincher Creek Echo*, 15 April 1909.
55 By 1903 the newspapers were regularly advertising cream separators.
56 Some operations themselves diversified into cheese production for the local market ("The Cheesemaker," *Pincher Creek Echo*, 20 September 1904).
57 See Elofson, "Mixed and Dryland Farming," 39.
58 Alberta, Department of Agriculture, *Annual Report*, 1913, 6.
59 Ibid., 1907, 8.
60 See Elofson, "Mixed and Dryland Farming," 38.
61 Northwest Territories, Department of Agriculture, *Annual Report*, 1899, 69.
62 See H.V. Lawrence, "Pigs," *Alberta Historical Review* 24 (1976), 9–13.
63 "Prospectus of Proposed Pork Packing Company," *Pincher Creek Echo*, 15 March 1904.
64 Northwest Territories, Department of Agriculture, *Annual Report*, 1900, 68–72.
65 Ibid., 1903, 193.
66 Ibid., 7.
67 Some also ran turkeys; see Canada, *Sixth Census*, 1921, 5, 725.
68 Alberta, Department of Agriculture, *Annual Report*, 1908, 128.
69 *Prairie Grass to Mountain Pass*, 7.
70 For further discussion of the horse business in general, see above, p. 28–9.
71 "Horse Breeders Meet," *Pincher Creek Echo*, 7 June 1904.
72 Alberta, Department of Agriculture, *Annual Report*, 1906, 72–3.
73 Elofson, "Mixed and Dryland Farming," 61.
74 Alberta, Department of Agriculture, *Annual Report*, 1905, 70; 1906, 77; 1908, 7; 1913, 137.
75 Elofson, "Mixed and Dryland Farming," 41.
76 C.I. Rithchie, "George Lane – One of the 'Big Four,'" *Canadian Cattlemen* 3, no. 2 (September 1940). Lane at one point fed, fattened, and slaughtered hogs and had a substantial dairy operation as well. Buildings presently preserved at the original Bar U headquarters near Longview help to demonstrate this.
77 *Range Men*, 193.
78 McIntyre, *Brief History of the McIntyre Ranch*, 25.

79 Much of the information contained in these descriptions comes from the author's personal knowledge of the ranching community in southern Alberta.
80 Kelly, *Range Men*, 143.
81 Canada, *Third Census*, 1891, 5, 220–1; *Fourth Census*, 1901, 2, 52–3.
82 The average size of the family farm in Alberta rose from 288.6 deeded acres in 1901 to 352.5 deeded acres in 1921 (*Sixth Census*, 1921, 5, xv).
83 Figures for the various species and farm numbers are available for 1916 for Macleod, Calgary, Medicine Hat, Lethbridge, and Maple Creek; see *Census of Prairie Provinces, 1916: Population and Agriculture*, 305, 310–11.
84 *Pincher Creek Echo*, 12 July 1904, 2.

CHAPTER SEVEN

1 At the Symposium on the Cowboy at the Glenbow Institute in Calgary, 26–28 September 1997, the guide to the exhibit explained that the Canadian West "was very law-abiding."
2 *The Frontier in American History*, New York, 1920; a summary of Turner's thesis is given on pages 1–38.
3 J.H. Gray, *Red Lights on the Prairies*, and *Booze*; P. Voisey, *Vulcan*, 26, 162, 163.
4 Besides the above, see, P. Berton, *The Klondike: The Last Great Gold Rush, 1896–1899*, Toronto: McClelland and Stewart, rev. ed. 1974, 352–416.
5 "A Hard Case," and "The Walrond Ranch Again," *Macleod Gazette*, 27 August 1891; "The Walrond Ranch's War on Settlers," ibid., 3 September 1891: "An Enemy to Southern Alberta," ibid., 24 November 1892. C.E.D. Wood, the *Gazette*'s editor, considered the Walrond to be the only lease land in which major conflict developed between ranchers and squatters.
6 Canada, *Official Reports of the Debates of the House of Commons*, 4th session, 6th Parliament, 29, 6155.
7 "An Enemy to Southern Alberta," *Macleod Gazette*, 29 August 1891.
8 *Debates of the House of Commons* 29, 6155.
9 Ibid. The eviction notice might have appeared to Dunbar as a mistake had he not been warned several months before by the land office in Lethbridge, the same office that had granted his patent.
10 Glenbow Archives, Dewdney papers, M320: J. Lamar to McEachran, 4 August 1891.
11 The Secretary of the Department of the Interior attempted to explain this in January 1891: "The agent of the department had specific

orders not to grant any homestead entries for lands in this Township 9. Unfortunately, that officer had overlooked those instructions and the provisions of the lease, and on 31 July, 1889, granted William and Samuel Dunbar the entries which it has been found necessary to disallow" (*Debates of the House of Commons* 29, 6156).

12 Strangely, while Dewdney argued that the sons were not bona fide settlers, he was willing to offer them compensation if they agreed to move (ibid.). See also "An Enemy to Southern Alberta," *Macleod Gazette*, 29 August 1891. Upon learning of this the *Gazette* wondered why, if they were not bona fide settlers, they should receive any compensation; and, as the fact of the willingness of the government to compensate seems to indicate, if the Dunbars were bona fide settters, why they must leave their homestead. In Dewdney's response to questioning in Parliament he made clear that the patent of the father, Robert Dunbar, was to be respected, while those of the two sons were not.

13 For some of the cases settled before the courts see "Squatters on the Leases," *Macleod Gazette*, 26 September 1884.

14 R.M. Brown, "Violence," *Oxford History of the American West*, 393–425.

15 For vigilantism in the United States see, for instance, R.R. Dykstra, *The Cattle Towns*, New York: Atheneum, 1973, 138–9, 146–7, 288–9, and Brown, "Violence."

16 Symposium on the Cowboy, Glenbow Museum, Calgary, 28 September 1997.

17 Inderwick, Diary and Letters: letter of 13 May 1884, 14.

18 R. White, "Animals and Enterprise," *Oxford History of the American West*, 267; to view this entire process in detail see Jordan, *North American Cattle Ranching Frontiers*, 267–307.

19 G. Stuart, "End of the Cattle Range," *Complete Cowboy Reader*, 242. See also Stuart's *Forty Years on the Frontier*, Glendale, California: Arthur H. Clark, 1967.

20 Ibid.

21 White, "Animals and Enterprise," 267. The same historical movement to smaller operations is clearly discernable on farms in Alberta; see Voisey, *Vulcan*, 138–9.

22 Hughes, "The Last Great Roundup," 1–2.

23 See W.S. James, "Style on the Ranch," *Complete Cowboy Reader*, 114–15.

24 Hughes, "The Last Great Roundup," 1–2. Wire was also accused of bringing an end to the cowboy's "glorious freedom" (*Pincher Creek Echo*, 19 January 1911, 4).

25 James, "Style on the Ranch," 116.

26 Similarly temporary and relatively unsophisticated solutions had to be found at one time or another on all agricultural frontiers in

Canadian history; see for instance R. C. Harris and J. Warkentin, *Canada before Confederation: A Study in Historical Geography*, New York: Oxford University Press, 1974, 49, 135–6.

27 In Alberta the average size of the family farm rose from 288.66 acres in 1901 to 352.5 acres in 1921 (*Sixth Census of Canada, 1921: Agriculture*, xv). The average farm in Ontario had 97.76 acres of land and that in Quebec had 97.77 acres (*Fifth Census of Canada, 1911: Agriculture*, xvi).

28 *Pincher Creek Echo*, 19 January 1911, 4.

29 For which see L. English, "The Calgary Exhibition and Stampedes: Culture, Context, and Controversy, 1884–1923," University of Calgary, Master's thesis, 1999.

30 Kelly, *Range Men*, 216.

Index